TRANS-AM RACING

1966-85

Detroit's battle for pony car supremacy

Albert R. Bochroch

Motorbooks International
Publishers & Wholesalers Inc
Osceola, Wisconsin 54020, USA ®

First published in 1986 by Motorbooks International
Publishers & Wholesalers Inc, PO Box 2, 729 Prospect
Avenue, Osceola, WI 54020 USA

Printed and bound in the United States of America

Library of Congress Cataloging-in-Publication Data
Bochroch, Albert R.
   Trans-Am racing, 1966-85.
   Includes index.
   1. Trans-Am Championship—History.   I. Title.
GV1034.05.T72B63   1986   070.4'497967'2   86-18232
ISBN 0-87938-229-5

All photographs furnished by Albert Bochroch unless
otherwise noted.

To John and Peggy Bishop

Contents

Acknowledgments

So many members of the racing world were kind enough to supply me with information and photographs that, in expressing my gratitude, I beg the forgiveness of anyone I may have overlooked.

Scott Bailey, Charles Betts, John Bishop, Tom Blattler, Helmut Brandt, Doc Bundy, Don Cox, Lee Dykstra, Steve Erlichman, Bert Everett, George Follmer, Dan Gurney, Fran Hernandez, Louis Helverson, Al Holbert, Bob Holbert, Deke Houlgate, Parnelli Jones, Dan Luginbuhl, Otis Meyer, Lloyd Northard, Bernard Mullins, Lowell Paddock, Tim Parker, Roger Penske, Richard Perry, Sam Posey, Paul Preuss, George Rappelyea, Bob Sharp, Robert J. Sinclair, Lew Spencer, Judy Stropus, John Timanus, Jonathan Thompson, Bob Tullius and Steven Yuhas.

Also, the Sports Car Club of America permitted reprinting of material from its *1986 SCCA Media Guide*.

Foreword by

Parnelli Jones
racing parts

20555 EARL STREET ● TORRANCE, CALIFORNIA 90503 ● TEL: (213) 371-7548

I was real pleased to hear that Al Bochroch was writing a history
of the Trans-Am.

For my money during those years that the factories were involved,
the Trans-Am series produced the best road racing that this
country has ever seen.

I realize that I'm best known as an oval track racer. That's
understandable, as I've won a lot more races on the ovals. But
I was also very comfortable on road courses. Road racing came
very natural to me, and I got a lot of personal enjoyment out of
running them. I didn't have to work as hard on a road course
as I did on the oval track.

But that wasn't always true of the Trans-Am. I don't think I
ever raced in a series that was any more competitive. If you
car wasn't 100 per cent, someone was sure to blow your doors off.
Another first for the Trans-Am was the fabulous preparation of
the Detroit teams. I think even Bud Moore learned things in
the Trans-Am that he took back to NASCAR.

The Trans-Am had more than super car preparation. I don't want
to sound big-headed, but I think the other drivers learned
from me too. As I told Al Bochroch, in my opinion I think that
guys like Mark Donohue and George Follmer learned to be better
race drivers against competition like Gurney and myself. Those
guys found that they had to drive harder than they ever had.

I know its a contradiction but I think that one of the things
that made the Trans-Am so great — that business of giving all the
points to the manufacturer — also was one of the big reasons for
its downfall. After all, what car maker wants to lay out that
kind of money and then take the flack when another manufacturer
wins the series? Giving points to the drivers, as well as to the
manufacturers, may have taken off some of the heat.

Having seen some of Al Bochroch's other racing histories I
certainly feel that he was the right man to do this book.

Parnell Jones

DISTINCTIVE RACING DECOR

Chapter I

That first race went unreported

Car and Driver ignored it. *Road & Track* buried it with a couple of lines within its report on the 12-Hours. Oddest of all, although it ran a picture caption story on the Sebring 12-Hours, *Sports Car* magazine, the official publication of the SCCA, didn't print a word about the club's first Trans-Am.

Among the monthly enthusiast publications, only the long-dormant, recently revived *Sports Car Graphic* covered The Four-Hour Governor's Cup Race For Sedans.

As Sebring was a fixture on the international calendar, it drew a large motoring press. By 1966 the Ferrari-Ford battle had reached Hatfield-McCoy intensity and the 1966 Sebring hosted more US and overseas publications than ever.

The 12-Hours was also on coast-to-coast radio via a 100-plus-station network put together by Triangle Broadcasting. A division of the Annenberg publishing empire that included *TV Guide, Seventeen, The Daily Racing Form* and *The Philadelphia Inquirer*, Triangle was one of the first to broadcast and film auto racing.

Triangle had covered Sebring before. The crew showed up in mid-week and taped dozens of driver and personality interviews for use during those long twelve hours. Les Keiter, whose specialty was boxing, Chris Economaki and I were the announcers. I also did a syndicated weekly radio show which originated in Triangle's headquarters station in Philadelphia. Come summer, it was my pleasure to phone back radio reports of Le Mans and several European GPs.

It was around this time that I quit my job so that I could write full time and cover more overseas racing. To help pay the freight, having been in advertising and public relations, I began working with a couple of former clients on their racing projects. Because I was unsure of my prospects, during the first couple of years I took on a bewildering array of writing, photography and PR assignments.

Motoring journalism wasn't new to me. I'd been moonlighting for *Motoring News* in America since shortly after the English weekly began in the late fifties. And, beginning with its first issue, I had pieces in *Car and Driver*. Before the sixties were over I was a contributing editor to several other publications including *Competition Press* and *Road & Track*.

Particularly interesting were the summers of 1966 and 1967 when the SCCA retained me to help out on CanAm (Canadian-American Challenge Cup) publicity. Until the summer of 1970, shortly before it went belly-up, I'd also been the Bridgehampton Race Circuit's press director.

But it was the PR work that brought me closest to the Trans-Am. DuPont, a client that went back to my agency days when I handled Roger Penske's Telar and Zerex Specials, now used me on the introduction of Nomex, as well as its racing programs with John Mecom and Lloyd Ruby for its line of No. 7 automotive products.

Castrol, another of my clients, enjoyed a tie-in with both the Cougar and Mustang Trans-Am teams. It was unusual for Ford to allow such tie-ins and if it hadn't been for Lincoln-Mercury PR man Monty Roberts, who took me to see Lincoln-Mercury President Leo Beebe, it may never have happened.

All of this put me in the catbird's seat. But there were days when I wondered if the writer and the PR man had seen the same race.

Ken Miles and Lloyd Ruby brought Ford's GT40 its first win in the 1965 Daytona 2000. But the 1965 Le Mans, the race that Henry Ford said he wanted to win above all others, escaped him in spite of an eleven-car entry of six prototypes and five Cobras.

Ferrari matched Ford's eleven-car entry and won its eighth, and possibly last, Le Mans. All Ferrari prototypes suffered serious problems, the win going to the North American Racing Team 250LM entered by Luigi Chinetti. Appropriately, it was Chinetti who brought Ferrari its first win at Le Mans in 1949.

Chinetti's drivers were the late Masten Gregory, who became the third American to win the 24-Hours, and, in his first major victory, the future world champion, Jochen Rindt.

Rindt was relatively unknown when Alfa brought him to Sebring. But the hawk-nosed young German would have been ignored if he had walked across Lake Sebring.

A. J. was there! Indy winner Foyt was in the neat white number 4 Mustang, and he was mobbed. No stranger to road racing, A. J. had won two Nassau features for John Mecom. And, with Dan Gurney in 1967, he would bring Ford an all-American win at Le Mans. How fitting, in view of the big names that were to rule the Trans-Am, for America's number-one hero-driver to run the first Trans-Am.

Sebring promoter, the late Alec Ulmann, repeatedly tried to swell the gate by holding preliminary events. But the Thursday or Friday curtain raisers usually saw more bodies in the pits than in the stands. Even though the Friday, March 25, 1966, Trans-Am (the Four-Hour Governor's Cup Race For Sedans) had a good forty-four-car entry, the crowd was small.

Typical of the early Trans-Ams was that only nine of the forty-four starters—one Dodge Dart, three Ford Mustangs, three Plymouth Barracudas, two Chevrolet Corvairs—were over-2 liters. Of the thirty-five under-2s, six were Autodelta-prepared works Alfa Romeo GTA 1600s; two were

Alan Mann factory-backed Ford Cortina Lotus.

Practice times over the flat, rough thirteen-turn, 5.2 mile course indicated that the Alfas and Cortinas would stay reasonably close to the big iron. The remainder of the field—eight Minis, five Saabs, a couple of Fiat Abarths, assorted BMWs, Volvos, Renault Gordinis, a stray Opel Kadett and a 600 cc Honda, known as the "shoe"—were spear carriers.

Making the David and Goliath bit plausible was the caliber of the small-car drivers. In addition to Rindt, Alfa used the European sedan champions and GP drivers, Andrea De Adamich and Theodoro Zeccoli, with strong local support from veterans Paul Richards, Gaston (Gus) Andrey, Howard Hanna and the transplanted Australian/Canadian/American, Horst Kwech.

Both Alan Mann Cortinas were contenders. Not only had they been tuned by Colin Chapman, their drivers were Sir John Whitmore and Peter Proctor. Given an outside chance was the works-entered 1275 cc Mini Cooper S of Paddy Hopkirk. A leading rallyist of the time, the Irishman also was a formidable racer, having earned class wins at Spa and Le Mans.

There were a number of rollovers during practice, Rindt's being the most conspicuous as no one bothered to hammer out the dents and he went on to win.

Rather than line up on the results of practice times, which would have placed the works Alfas and Hopkirk's Cooper near the front, the grid was based on displacement. The Mustangs, Barracudas, Tullius Dart and a pair of Corvairs were followed by five BMW 1800Tisas. However, starting positions were

---

ALFA ROMEO 1600GTA, 1966-69
Engine: dohc inline 4, 95 ci (1570 cc), 150 hp, dual 2-barrel Weber carb
Transmission: 5-speed
Brakes: front, disc; rear, drum
Suspension: front, unequal-length wishbones, coil springs, antisway bar; rear, live axle, coil springs, trailing links
Chassis: front engine, rear-wheel drive
Weight: 1900 lb
Notes: Street car had 1570 cc, 126 hp, 2000 lb.

relatively meaningless in a long race on an easy-to-pass circuit such as Sebring.

Foyt's Mustang and Charley Rainville's Barracuda ran side by side for the first two laps. Then A. J. got out front, followed by the Dart and Rindt's Alfa. Tullius took the lead when Foyt pitted on lap thirteen, only to be set back by a six-minute pit stop. The beginning of the third hour saw Rindt move out front and stay there.

Twenty-six of the forty-four starters finished. Except for the Corvairs, all the American sedans had been fast before suffering from excessive brake wear, tire failure and overheating. Both Ford Cortinas and the Hopkirk Cooper also retired. The Mustang of Dick Thompson (Washington DC dentist/driver) registered an 88.80 mph fastest race lap, but finished last, completing twenty-eight laps to the winner's sixty-seven. Except for the second-place Tullius Dart, Alfas filled the first five places. Worth noting is that the 6982 cc (427 cid) Ken Miles/Lloyd Ruby Ford Mark II prototype won the next day's Sebring 12-hours with a record 98.631

mph race average. Rindt's 1570 cc (97 cid) Alfa sedan averaged 87.17.

BMW 1800Tisa, 1966-68
Engine: sohc inline 4, 108 ci (1741 cc), 185 hp, dual 2-barrel Solex carb
Transmission: 4-speed
Suspension: front, struts, coil springs, antisway bar rear, independent semitrailing arm, coil springs, antisway bar
Chassis: front engine, rear-wheel drive
Weight: 2000 lb
Notes: Street car had 1741 cc, 124 hp, single 2-barrel, 2285 lb.

BMC Mini Cooper S
Engine: ohv inline 4, 68 ci (1275 cc), 105 hp, dual 1-barrel SU carb
Transmission: 4-speed
Brakes: front, disc; rear, drum
Suspension: front, upper and lower wishbone, Hydrolastic springs; rear, independent trailing arms, Hydrolastic springs
Chassis: front engine, front-wheel drive
Weight: 1250 lb
Notes: Street car had 1275 cc, 78 hp, 1415 lb.

Chapter 2

"The time for racing small sedans was just right"

"I don't believe that Detroit got out of the Trans-Am because it lacked popularity. That came later. It was a number of things.

"The manufacturers made changes in their marketing objectives. They may have gotten sick of beating each other's brains out every week. I think that the series may simply have run its course. There were the environment problems. Then too, the cost of running a Trans-Am factory team went out of sight."

John Bishop, the man making these remarks, joined the Sports Car Club of America (SCCA) staff in 1955 as its director of competition. He became the club's executive director in 1956 and ran the SCCA until the summer of 1969. When politics cost Bishop the backing of the SCCA board, he went on his own and founded the International Motor Sports Association (IMSA).

To no one's surprise, as he is a knowledgeable, clear-thinking, straight-arrow of a man, John Bishop's IMSA replaced the SCCA as the dominant force in American road racing.

"In the beginning almost all of us in Westport," Bishop continued, "were lukewarm about the Trans-Am. We thought it was getting too close to stock car racing. And I guess that some of us had our minds on the CanAm, which would be coming along later in 1966.

"Frankly, most of us were a little scornful about racing small sedans. We thought they were amusing. Sure, we knew that the Washington region had been holding sedan races at Marlboro. And we knew that there was an FIA/International small sedan championship. And, of course, we realized that drivers

such as Henry Taylor, Sir John Whitmore, Frank Gardner and Jackie Stewart had been driving Ford Cortinas over here at such places as Marlboro and Bridgehampton.

"Yes, I think we were aware of the coming popularity of the muscle cars too. But the mood of the early sixties was strongly anti-sedan racing. But we were dead wrong. The time for racing small sedans was just right."

What made the time "just right" were two seemingly unrelated events. One had taken place in 1961 when the Sports Car Club of America, following years of bitter, largely foolish arguments, finally shed its outdated, "amateurs only" racing policy.

The seven New England collectors who founded the SCCA in February of 1944 had little interest in racing. Their primary objective was to preserve classic American sports cars such as the Mercer, Duesenberg and Stutz.

The major influence in the SCCA's shift toward racing was returning veterans of World War II. Particularly important were Sam Collier, his brother Miles and George Rand. These men had led the prewar Automobile Racing Club of America (ARCA) during the thirties and early forties. But the ARCA disbanded the day following Pearl Harbor. It was inevitable that former ARCA members would inspire the fledgling SCCA.

Going "pro" turned the SCCA into a different organization. In place of "travel money" and corrupting under-the-table deals, those SCCA drivers who had the talent and the backing now could turn professional and race for cash. Contrary to SCCA doomsday followers, who had preached that the club's amateur racing program would vanish or be badly damaged, those who wished to retain their amateur status never had it so good.

Beginning at Riverside in 1964, the SCCA began holding its annual runoffs. A carnival of road racing that matches class winners from each of the club's 100-plus regions, the end-of-season American Road Race of Champions produces fierce racing and true national champions.

Going pro also gave the SCCA the chance to sanction a good professional road racing series that was already established. And it wasn't a moment too soon.

The once powerful United States Auto Club (USAC), which currently is down to a single major event (the Indianapolis 500), had long harbored the desire to run sports car races. Filling the vacuum created by the SCCA's old policy, from 1959 through 1961 USAC sponsored a world-class mini series of big-bore sports car races on the West Coast.

Timed to follow the US Grand Prix at Watkins Glen (the Canadian GP did not begin until 1967), the GP circus ran one or two sports car races in Canada before heading for Riverside, Laguna Seca and Seattle.

Not only did Europe's top Formula 1 teams appreciate the American purses, they also looked forward to these end-of-season junkets as holidays. The pool at Riverside's Mission Inn may not have rivaled Monte Carlo's yacht-filled harbor, but very few of the GP drivers, or their "exquisite birds," ever missed it.

The big names, big cars and good crowds they attracted also pleased West Coast promoters. This was the period that saw many Americans driving for European GP teams. For superstars such as Phil Hill, Dan Gurney, Ritchie Ginther, Carroll Shelby, Masten Gregory and Bob Bondurant, the West Coast races were a chance to shine before the hometown folks, and to tangle with such stateside-based lions as Walt Hansgen, Bob Holbert and Roger Penske.

Ironically, during the three years that USAC ran the West Coast sports car races, it was SCCA-trained corner workers and race stewards who did most of the work. John Bishop said that professional racing put a heavy load on the SCCA's headquarters staff. But he also said that the benefits to the club were enormous.

ACCUS (Automobile Competition Committee United States) is the American arm of the Paris-based FIA (Fédération Nationale de l'Automobile) which arranged international racing's rule-making, date-setting and track-safety regulations. It gave the SCCA's professional racing adolescence a big boost toward maturity by awarding the club the sanctioning rights to two events on the international calendar, the Daytona 3-Hours and Sebring.

By the end of 1963 the SCCA was putting on the US GP at Watkins Glen as well as having launched the United States Road Racing Championship, the first of its own major pro racing series. Pro rallying soon followed. Until the early seventies, the club seemed to have a magic touch.

The seemingly other "unrelated" event that made the Trans-Am so very appropriate is that Detroit made the right cars at the right time. Were someone so foolhardy as to try to pinpoint the precise time and place of the Trans-Am's birth, it may have taken place in the Ford pavillion at the New York World's Fair during the early afternoon of April 17, 1964.

My recollection is that those of us who were invited to this particular Ford press conference met in a basement garage on New York's East Side. Then, after Ford's Cal Beauregard had doubled us up, we drove one of the new Mustangs over the Queensboro Bridge and on to Flushing.

The speakers that pleasant spring day were Henry Ford II and Lee Iacocca. It was the only time I ever heard anyone from Detroit underestimate the potential volume of a new model.

One of the speakers, I believe it was Ford, said they were looking forward to first-year sales of 250,000. In fact, during its first twelve months Mustang sales reached 418,000 units.

The Ford Mustang was far from being Detroit's first small, under-5000 cc (303 cid) sedan with sporty pretensions. Ford's own 1960 Falcon, Chrysler's Valiant, Dodge's Dart and Chevrolet's much abused Corvair had all beaten Ford's pony car off the board.

Within days of the Mustang's debut, Chrysler filled a gap in its line when it introduced the Barracuda.

The SCCA's interest in saloon car racing had been a poorly kept secret. Waiting in the wings was a classy field of pedigreed imports. Led by handsome, sneaky-fast, factory-backed Alfa Romeo 1600 cc coupes and internationally race-bred Ford Cortina saloons that had been tweaked by Colin Chapman, these small-engined Europeans gave the big Detroit iron fits.

Porsche, as is its wont, managed to get the rules changed. Introduced in 1964, the Porsche 911 was, and still may be, one of the world's best sports cars. To think of the 911 as a sedan takes a good deal of imagination. However, Stuttgart had lots of clout. By the start of the 1967 Trans-Am season the 911 had been reclassified as a small, under-2000 cc (123 cid) sedan.

PORSCHE 911, 1966-69
Engine: sohc flat-6, 121 ci (1998 cc), 220-250 hp, dual 3-barrel Weber or Solex carb
Transmission: 5-speed
Brakes: 4-wheel disc
Suspension: front, longitudinal torsion bars, struts; rear, transverse torsion bars, trailing arms
Chassis: rear engine, rear-wheel drive
Weight: 1850 lb
Notes: Street car was 911S, 1998 cc, 181 hp, 6 single-barrel or 3 2-barrel Weber, 2000 lb. The 911 was outlawed as a "sedan" by the FIA for the 1970 season.

Big car specs called for SCCA/FIA homologated (approved) sedans with 116 inch wheelbase and 5000 cc (303 cid) engine displacement. Changes would come along. But for their first seven years, Trans-Am sedans were required to conform to FIA Groups 1 and 2, regulations that edged them closer to street machines than to all-out race cars.

Good things happened. After 1.4 million in sales and almost ten years of constant harassment, even the staunchest Corvair supporter was eager for a new, small sedan. Clean lined and looking somewhat like a Ferrari coupe, the 1967 Z-28 Camaro would turn the Trans-Am into an "only one shall survive" gladiator contest.

It is debatable whether race fans found the men or the machines more appealing. For starters the drivers included Indy winners, international rally stars, NASCAR (National Association for Stock Car Automobile Racing) champions, Grand Prix regulars, winners of Le Mans and the cream of American road racers.

What may have put the icing on the early Trans-Am cake was that the SCCA made it a manufacturers' championship. Unlike almost all other major series, in which points earned by drivers are the prime consideration, Trans-Am points went to the car.

Showing unprecedented enthusiasm, Detroit used the Trans-Am as the showcase for its new breed of automobile.

Chapter 3

The Trans-Am was looking good

The racing continued in that first year, but there was a two-and-a-half-month gap before the second race. Some teams had more time to plan and prepare, this time with experience. The result was different. Held on June 12 over the 2.86 mile Mid-America Raceway in Wentzville, Missouri, the second Trans-Am pulled twenty-seven entrants. Under-2-liter cars were again in the majority. Only this time the laurels went to Detroit.

Alfa Romeo left its GTAs in the hands of American veterans but the English Fords used their biggest guns, Belgian ace Jacky Ickx, German champion Hubert Hahne and Sir John Whitmore. Sam Posey, who became a Trans-Am regular, shared an Alfa with former Lime Rock owner Harry Theodoropopulous to finish fourth. Scott Harvey and Les Netherton brought their Barracuda home in fifth.

The Tullius/Tony Adamowicz Dart limped in fifteenth while the last runner, motoring journalist Brock Yates, was nineteenth.

The big news from Wentzville was that Bob Johnson and Tom Yeager gave Mustang its first win. Johnson, a Columbus, Ohio, caterer, had won several SCCA national titles and had driven a Cobra for Carroll Shelby in the 1965 Le Mans. The Gus Andrey/Horst Kwech Alfa finished on the same lap as the winning Mustang, with the third place Ickx/Hahne Cortina one lap down.

Louden, New Hampshire's tight, hilly 1.6 mile Bryar had, somewhat incongruously, once been on NASCAR's annual mid-summer northern tour. Bryar too had an under-

2 winner. This time it was Allan Moffat, the Canadian-born Detroiter who did much of his racing in Australia. Averaging 68.8 mph, Moffat brought the Ford Cortina its first trip to victory lane.

Sixteen of the twenty-four starters completed the 250 mile, 156 lap run with Bruce Jennings' Barracuda eighty-two seconds behind the Cortina. One lap down was the

Sebring, March 1966. The 1960s American racing scene was brightened by Linda Vaughn's big smile.

Kwech/Andrey Alfa, followed by the Johnson/Yeager Mustang. Australia's Frank Gardner brought a second Ford Cortina home in fifth, but Sir John's bad luck continued when, after running with the leaders, he retired on lap ninety-four.

In sixth place was the Skip Barber/Peter Lake Mustang. The Tullius Dart was seventh. Eighth and ninth were the Hanna and Taylor/Pratt Alfas, the Russ Norburn/Pete Feistman Mustang rounding out the first 10.

The Trans-Am was looking good. The cars were well matched. Only one second separated the first eight qualifiers at Bryar. Lead changes were frequent and spectators seemed to relate to the machinery.

PLYMOUTH BARRACUDA AND DODGE DART, 1966

Engine: ohv V-8, 273 ci (4403 cc), 300-330 hp, single 4-barrel carb
Transmission: 4-speed
Brakes: front, drum; rear, drum
Suspension: front, independent upper and lower A-arms, torsion bars, antisway bar; rear, live axle, leaf springs
Weight: 2750 lb
Notes: Street cars were the Formula S and Dart GT, 273 ci, 235 hp, 2940 lb.

Trans-Am number four, the VIR 400, was held July 31 over the rolling, 3.23 mile Virginia International Raceway near Danville,

Virginia. Pulling thirty-six cars, the under-2s again outnumbered the big cars, twenty-seven to nine.

Ford got its act together and took the first two places. Equally newsworthy was participation of four of stock car racing's brightest stars: the storied Curtis Turner, King Richard Petty, Wendell Scott (the first Black to really make it in big-time auto racing) and the future three-time NASCAR champion, David Pearson.

Making his first Trans-Am appearance was Team Lotus driver, Dickie Attwood, who shared a Cortina with Frank Gardner. Another new face was that of Craig Fisher, whose ride with Allan Moffat also was in a Cortina. (Fisher was to become best known for being the first to drive a Trans-Am Camaro.)

Certain retirements at VIR were as interesting as the race itself. David Pearson destroyed Brock Yates' Dodge in practice. And Richard Petty, who was to have shared Charlie Rainville's Barracuda, started well and was running a strong second until lap five when he went off course and got stuck in the infield mud.

After Petty dug himself out he was in twenty-first place. But he started to fly and by lap thirteen was up to tenth. Then he went even deeper off course and remained stuck.

Dick Thompson's Mustang was holding third when he handed it over to Wendell Scott on the forty-third lap. Scott made it halfway around the course before he went off in a big way. In finding his way back to the track the stock car driver became lost and tried to power his way through the infield, a tactic that was rejected by the Dart's suspension when Scott tried to jump a ditch.

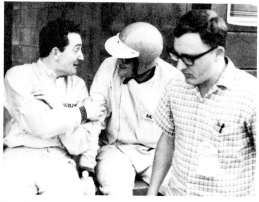

BMC drivers Paddy Hopkirk, left, and Andrew Hedges in pits as British Motor Corporation's racing manager, Stuart Turner, passes.

FORD CORTINA LOTUS

Engine: dohc inline 4 (Ford derived), 95 ci (1570 cc), 145 hp, dual 2-barrel Weber carb
Transmission: 4-speed
Brakes: front, disc; rear, drum
Suspension: front, struts, coil springs, antisway bar; rear, live axle, semifloating, leaf springs
Chassis: front engine, rear-wheel drive
Weight: 1750 lb
Notes: Street car had 1570 cc, 115 hp, 1820 lb.

The Johnson/Yeager Mustang nipped the Feistman/Norborn pony car by nine seconds to give Ford a one-point lead over Chrysler after four races. Alfas filled the next three places. Paul Newman finished sixteenth in a Saab 96 and none of the stock car drivers went the 400 miles.

In 1966 the American road course with the most small sedan experience was Marl-boro Raceway in the Maryland suburbs of Washington. Run by the SCCA's capable Washington region, the 1.9 mile circuit had seen Jackie Stewart bring Ford of Britain's Cortina the 1964 FIA Sedan Championship.

Staged on August 14, The Great Race, as the fifth Trans-Am was called, had a full field of thirty-six starters. But again, twenty-seven of them were under-2 liters.

A twelve-hour enduro, The Great Race was a great day for local favorite Bob Tullius,

A. J. Foyt's Mustang led for most of the first 13 laps in this first Trans-Am. Note dragging tail pipe.

Plymouth engineer Scott Harvey's Team Starfish Barracuda finished sixth in the Sebring Trans-Am inaugural.

who had begun his racing career at Marlboro in 1961. Aside from two Corvairs, the V-8s qualified near the top, except for the second and third fastest Whitmore/Gardner Cortina and Winkler/Van Der Vate Alfa.

Although the winning Tullius/Adamowicz Dart covered a record 689 miles with a 57.375 mph race average and finished four laps out front, it had been the Gardner/Whitmore Cortina that set the pace for over two hours. A Barracuda driven by Plymouth engineer, rallyist, house racer Scott Harvey and Charley Rainville was second. The Hal Keck/Charles Krueger Dart was fourth and the Posey/Theodoropopulous Alfa GTA fifth.

Two more Alfas followed the sixth-place Whitmore/Gardner's Cortina, with ninth going to Johnson/Sessler in the best-placed Mustang, as still another Alfa came in tenth. Prominent among the nine DNFs (did not finish) were Canada's Jacques Duval and the Cortina team of Ickx and Hahne.

Marlboro was fifth in what was to have been an eight-race series. But Las Vegas was first shifted to Willow Springs and then dropped. With two events to go, the standings were as listed below:

Over-2 liters

Ford	26
Chrysler/Plymouth	25
Dodge	14
Chevrolet	3

Under-2 liters

Alfa Romeo	23
Ford of Britain	15
BMW	4
Volvo	2

Second-place finisher Bob Tullius' Dodge Dart shows an unfamiliar number 11 in place of Bob's usual number 44.

While fast, Sir John Whitmore's works-supported Alan Mann Cortina Lotus failed to finish its Trans-Am debut.

Trans-Am points were awarded to both classes for first through sixth on a 9-6-4-3-2-1 basis. Points only were awarded to the highest finishing example of each make. For example, at Marlboro two points were earned by the Johnson/Yeager Mustang which finished ninth overall and fifth in class.

The Pan American 6-Hours at Smithfield, Texas, was a grind. Located near Dallas, the 1.6 mile Green Valley track is little more than a drag strip with connecting loops and miniscule esses as it passes the pits.

Of the thirty-four runners, the over-2 forces rose to ten, thanks to an Oklahoma Falcon that wound up seventeenth. The 6-Hours was won by the John McComb/Brad Booker Mustang with a 65.306 mph race

Jim McKay of ABC-TV's Wide World Of Sports with Sebring winner Jochen Rindt at the 1965 Le Mans where Rindt was to win his first major event.

Rindt's Alfa Romeo GTA shows signs of his roll-over during practice for the 1966 Sebring Trans-Am. Cam Warren/Road & Track

average; the second-place Andrey/Kwech Alfa was six laps off the pace.

After Bob Johnson's Barracuda won the pole, he teamed up with Charley Rainville to finish third. Californians Ron Grable and Miles Gupton brought their Dart home fourth. Texans Kysar and Gertz earned fifth in their Cortina and the Tullius/Adamowicz Dart managed sixth. The seventh- and

ninth-place Cortinas were separated by a Mini-Cooper; tenth place went to the Don Pike/John Timanus Mustang.

That long rainy day at Green Valley made racing history as two of the drivers were to become key figures in the future of pro racing. Charley Rainville would serve as IMSA's technical director and John Timanus continues to act as technical manager of the SCCA's professional racing. Of the many changes Timanus has seen, one of the more significant may have been a ten-time increase in the $1,200 first-place prize money won by the Mustang at Green Valley.

Hollywood could not have done better: Going into Riverside, the last race of the year, Ford and Chrysler were tied with thirty-seven points.

The Trans-Am came of age at Riverside on September 18, 1966, when Carroll Shelby put Lew Spencer, one of his Cobra drivers who also happened to be a good administrator, in charge of Ford's semi-official team of three Mustangs. Still, Shelby's effort may

Winner of the 1966 Bryar 250 was Allan Moffat's Lotus Cortina.

Overall Sebring winner Rindt with the first Trans-Am trophies. Being beat by a 1600 cc Alfa on a long airport course stunned Detroit brass.

Tony Adamowicz (left) and Bob Tullius confer with race officials prior to the Marlboro 12-Hours Trans-Am. Covering a record 689 miles, the Tullius/Adamowicz Dart finished four laps in front of the Charley Rainville/Scott Harvey Barracuda. Pete Luongo/Bob Tullius collection

have been fruitless if someone hadn't remembered to get a late entry for Jerry Titus.

At that time Jerry, a pleasant, small, unassuming man, was editor of *Sports Car Graphic*. He also played a good enough jazz trumpet to sit in with some of the big bands. And it hadn't been too long before that he had worked as a mechanic on Shelby's Maserati. Back in New York he had been with the legendary Bill Frick of Fordillac fame. Above all, Titus was a racer.

The under-2s were again in the majority at Riverside. But fourteen of the thirty-four-car entry were V-8s, and eight of the fourteen were Mustangs. Being California, the thin 7,500 gate (a good crowd for many Trans-Am circuits, but a poor one for the popular desert course) was treated to such exotica as a Hino, NSU Prinz, two Ford Anglias and a Sunbeam Imp. But it was the eight Mustangs that made news.

Ford of Britain was back with three/Cortinas for Frank Gardner, fellow Aussie Harry Firth and the hard-charging Sir John. Having already earned the overall Trans-Am championship, Alfa gave five of its six cars to California drivers. Only the Andrey/Kwech GTA had factory support.

Because the 1966 Riverside Trans-Am was run on a 2.6 mile short course that varied slightly from that used by NASCAR, practice and race time comparisons were meaningless. But that didn't stop Titus from blasting a 91.854 mph qualifying lap that was a full two seconds faster than the old sedan record.

FORD MUSTANG, 1966-67 (SHELBY)
Engine: ohv V-8, 289 ci (4737 cc), 350-375 hp (440 hp in 1968 with tunnel-port heads), single 4-barrel carb
Transmission: 4-speed
Brakes: front, disc; rear, drums
Suspension: front, independent upper and lower A-arms, coil springs; rear, live axle, leaf springs
Weight: 2700 lb
Notes: Street car was the Mustang GTA, 289 ci, 271 hp (300 hp with tunnel-port heads), 2905 lb.

Battered number 4, the Tullius Dart, gets fueled while Tullius, in silver helmet, confers with Adamowicz. Pete Luongo/Bob Tullius collection

Mustangs filled the grid's first three spots with Pete Cordt's Falcon fourth, followed in fifth place by Ron Grable's Dodge Dart. Best of the Team Starfish Barracudas was Bob

David Pearson.

Johnson's 1:46.2, good enough for eighth on the grid.

The Titus Mustang won. But it wasn't easy. Following a Le Mans start, Titus flooded his engine. Playing catch-up saw him move from thirty-first to fifth within five laps. Ron Dykes' Mustang had been the early leader and he had been challenged by the Johnson Barracuda and Tullius Dart.

While making a two-car pass closing in on the leaders, Titus hit, or was hit, by an errant course marker that broke an oil line and his oil filter. Following a pit stop he again worked his way through the field.

Taking the lead on the ninety-fifth lap, Titus held it for forty more to win with an 87.29 mph race average. One indiction of how hard he drove is that his best race lap, 92.58 mph, was considerably faster than his qualifying record!

Forty-eight seconds behind the winner was the Tullius/Adamowicz Dart followed by the Dykes/Froines Mustang. Under-2 honors went to the fifth-place Whitmore/

Driver Horst Kwech, extreme right, helps Alan Mann's crew service the Jacky Ickx/Hubert Hahne Cortina Lotus, which failed to finish the 1966 Marlboro 12 Hours. Ford Motor Company

Gardner Cortina that finished a full lap up on the Kwech/Andrey Alfa Romeo.

As the series heated-up the rule bending began. Still in the future were acid dips, lowered front ends, hard-to-detect shifting of weld points and huge, deep wraparound roll cages that nearly eliminated body/chassis flexing.

This was the beginning of the big-tire era. Getting lots of rubber on the road was the way to go. But FIA sedan rules allowed wider wheels only when homologated and available through the car maker's dealers. Detroit was soon to catch up. But no one wanted to wait. Teams simply bent fenders out of the way or made crude fender flares. Although blatantly illegal, such infractions were so common that enforcing the rules would have eliminated entire fields.

Because the races averaged 370 miles, all seven of the first-year Trans-Ams were true endurance races. Entry lists indicated more, but the average first-year starting field was thirty-three cars. Total prize money amounted to $37,000 and the cars represented nineteen different makers. Of the 240 drivers in the Trans-Am's maiden year, twenty-three were from overseas. Final 1966 points were as follows:

Over-2 liters

Ford	46
Chrysler-Plymouth	39
Dodge	33
Chevrolet	3

Under-2 liters

Alfa Romeo	57
Ford of Britain	36
BMW	3
Volvo	2
Fiat	1

During 1966 Carroll Shelby used many independent Mustang drivers. Tom Yeager and Bob Johnson were first at VIR and Mid-America, John McComb and Brad Booker won the 1966 Green Valley and Milt Minter was to earn points for several teams.

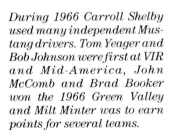

Stock car racing's legendary Curtis Turner joined David Pearson, Wendell Scott and Richard Petty in the 1966 Virginia International Race- way (VIR) Trans-Am, but only Turner was around at the finish.

Frank Gardner, whose Cortina Lotus was third under-2 and fifth overall at the 1966 Bryar 250. times.

Chapter 4

Playing his own game

Dated April 27, 1984, the Automobile Club de l'Ouest (ACO) press release read: "20 Ans Après: Le Router De Jaguar," After 20 Years: The Return of Jaguar.

Within days of getting the ACO mailing, I learned that Bob Tullius would pass up several IMSA GT races to prepare for the 1984 24-Hours of Le Mans. Then I heard that he was putting the Group 44 Jaguars through twenty-four-hour tests at Pocono Raceway in mid-May.

It wasn't only because Bob Tullius was high on my "must see" list of Trans-Am drivers, I also have a special interest in Americans at Le Mans. When I called Bob's shop in Winchester, Virginia, to tell him about this book, I asked for a date and suggested meeting him at Pocono.

"Sure," he said. "Come up early Friday afternoon. We're running right through Thursday night. By Friday afternoon we should have time to talk."

Bob Tullius was an experienced driver before the Trans-Am began. Born in Rochester, New York, in 1935, he is an Air Force veteran who has long found it practical to meet his commitments by flying his own plane.

Tullius, who still limps from a college football injury, had planned a teaching career. But he started racing a TR3 in 1961 and has never turned back. Early in his career, he

The venerable Dodge Dart that Bob Tullius drove to big wins at Daytona and Marlboro in 1966 and 1967. Bob Tullius collection

tried stock car racing, driving for such veterans as Buck Baker and Jim Pascal as well as trying Walt Hansgen's Falcon sedan.

But it was Bob's own immaculately turned-out Group 44 cars, with their attention-getting reversed 44s, that reflected their handsome owner and enabled him to carve out an unusual spot in American racing. A five-time SCCA national champion, Tullius developed, and got the backing for, a contradiction—a professionally run, amateur race team. When the lines between club racing and professional racing finally began to blur, Group 44 was in the right spot.

It was a treat driving up to Pocono along the Delaware Canal past clouds of flowering white Dogwoods and blossoming fruit trees. But when I got to the track it had that desolate test-day look that goes with miles of windswept empty grandstands.

There was a single car droning around the track. Typically, all the activity was confined to a small area in the center of pit row. Directly across the track from Group 44's pit was the ever-present decrepit ambulance.

There were three motorhomes, Group 44's own huge transport, a Goodyear truck, one race car, three drivers and several dressed-up guys—some of whom wore vests and pointy shoes.

The workers were the ones with dirty hands. They handled the tricky, flat-bladder fueling rig, changed tires, fiddled with the suspension and engine, and got the job done. Workers too were Bob's elegant Pam, who is skilled in the care and feeding of race drivers, and Lee Dykstra, who had designed the big Jaguar and was timing and recording its every lap.

Doc Bundy was on the course when I arrived and Bob was suiting-up in readiness for his turn. "I'll be out about one-hour and 15 minutes," he said. "Go see Pam and get something to eat. Then we'll talk."

Until I got close enough to read his jacket patch, I had failed to recognize the tall bearded crewman. As he was acting like he knew the ropes, I should have guessed that it was Brian Fuerstenau. A mechanical whiz kid, demon driver and Bob's good companion. Brian had left racing for other fields. "I've taken a leave of absence," Brian said. "After all how could I miss this!"

Waiting for Bob in his trailer with a cool drink and one of Pam's sandwich specials, I

Tullius with co-driver, mechanic and friend, Brian Fuerstenau, in 1967. Pete Luongo/Bob Tullius collection

Bob Tullius.

wondered if Bob realized how good he looked in overall Trans-Am statistics.

Following the 1971 Trans-Am season, when the SCCA began making drastic rule changes and added a driver's championship, three drivers—George Follmer, 1972 and 1976; Peter Gregg, 1973 and 1974; and Bob Tullius, 1977 and 1978—have been double Trans-Am driver champions.

Tullius did not run the Trans-Am in 1983. Nevertheless, his total Trans-Am appearances up to the 1984 season numbered sixty. Only George Follmer's sixty-three and Mark Donohue's fifty-two are close. More meaningful, Donohue leads the Trans-Am in total career victories with the twenty-nine. Bob Tullius is next with twenty-one, followed by Follmer's thirteen and Peter Gregg's eleven.

Figuring out who won the most money involves trying to compare 1960 and 1980 dollars. Without 1984 earnings, Follmer led with $124,366; Tullius was next at $120,366. As will be later documented, Greg Pickett, who had $104,032 at that time, took over the lead at the close of the 1984 season.

After Bob compared notes with Doc Bundy, he settled down with one of Pam's creations, and talked. "There's just no question about the early Trans-Am being great. What I liked best about them were those long four-hour races when I could get out there and drive them by myself.

"It became obvious," he continued, "that the Trans-Am appealed to a broader base of the population than sports cars. The SCCA should have realized what they had when NASCAR took the same cars and started their Grand American series. The only difference was that NASCAR ran them on half-mile ovals. What was unbelievable was the way Detroit supported the series . . . I think that you have to say that the Trans-Am succeeded in spite of the SCCA."

Having finished his sandwich, Bob spoke of his experience as a member of the SCCA's national board of directors. "I'd been elected to be a governor of the SCCA by the Washington region. And I really tried very

A top contender on the Camel GT circuit, Bob's Jaguar has nine career victories in 67 starts.

hard to work with the board. But I just simply could not take it. So I resigned.

"Individually," Bob went on, "they are probably bright people with lots of talent, but there wasn't any leadership. The way they tried to run the club simply wouldn't work. Their philosophy was wrong . . . Democracy is fine, but you still need leadership.

"I think that one of the most interesting experiences I ever had was at Daytona just before the first 1967 Trans-Am. I'd been getting help from Chrysler during 1966. Plymouth had been giving support to their Team Starfish and Dodge had been left out.

"When Dodge did find out about the Barracudas, they became real jealous to think they had a deal and I didn't. So they insisted on getting me some help. And it did make a difference in maintaining my shop.

"We were underpaid and overworked. Tony Adamowicz and I did almost all the work ourselves on both the Dart and on our Lotus Cortina."

Then Bob recounted how he went to Detroit to see Chrysler about 1967, the coming year. "Scott Harvey, who worked for R&D at Chrysler, and who did a lot of rallying for them, went with me to see the Chrysler PR people. Only Scott went into the meeting and I was asked to wait outside.

"I was wondering how soon I'd get into the meeting when Scott came out. I asked him how we had done and he shocked me by saying, 'We didn't, we were shot down. There isn't one dime in the budget for your Dodge.'

"By the time we got to Daytona in February of 1967 I was strictly on my own. The people at Dodge had managed to send me some engine parts for the Dart, but nothing else.

"The night before the Daytona Trans-Am we went to one of those pre-race cocktail parties. You know how they are. You stand around talking with a group. It just so happened that some Goodyear people were a part of the group I was with. And one of them was Tony Webner in charge of Goodyear's racing PR.

"Tony asked how I was doing. So I told him about losing my Dodge help and said that I'd probably have to drop out of the Trans-Am after Daytona. We then talked about other things for a couple of minutes and then he asked me how much I would need to stay in the series. I told him that I thought I'd be able to get through the year if I could get $10,000. That was all that was said.

"Just a few days later, right after I got home from Daytona, there was a letter from Goodyear. It was in one of those envelopes with a clear window; the kind that usually contains a bill or a legal notice. Inside was a check for $10,000. No letter, no instructions, just that beautiful $10,000 check.

"To have had the race turn out the way it did, then to get that Goodyear check, unquestionably made the 1967 Daytona Trans-Am weekend one of the high points of my life!"

From left to right: one of England's postwar racing greats, Duncan Hamilton, Jaguar engineer Peter Batten, the author and Bob Tullius in Coventry, December 1981. Andrew J. A. Whyte

Chapter 5

Big guns

Late in 1966, SCCA Competition Director Jim Kaser issued a statement regarding the club's 1967 Trans-Am plans. What follows are his comments as they appeared in *Sports Car* magazine.

"We again plan to limit the series to about 8 races . . . After Daytona will be a 4-Hour Trans-American race at West Palm Beach on Friday, April 1, 1967. The big news being that this event is being moved from Sebring to a new facility."

Only it didn't happen that way. The SCCA sanctioned twelve Trans-Ams in 1967. The West Palm Beach race was never held. The second race of the season was run at Sebring. "Sedan" was dropped from the series name. Of the twelve events, only nine could be counted toward the championship.

Alfa Romeo defended its title. But it used mostly stateside drivers. Having reclassified the Porsche 911 as a sedan tended to reduce interest in the under-2 series and focus on the hotly contested "big" cars.

What had been a trickle of factory help in 1966 turned into a flood in 1967. Ford's Lincoln-Mercury Division created a three-car Cougar team prepared by long-time Ford stock car loyalist Bud Moore, of Spartanburg, South Carolina. Moore's drivers, Dan Gurney, Parnelli Jones, David Pearson, Cale Yarborough, LeeRoy Yarbrough, Peter Revson and Ed Leslie, were an awesome lot.

Continuing the direct involvement that began with the 1966 Riverside, Carroll Shelby put the Ford Mustang program on the front burner. Jerry Titus and Doc Thompson, with random support from Milt Minter, Ronnie Bucknum and Jim Adams, were Shelby's drivers.

This put a lot of the testing and a big racing load on Jerry Titus. But that was the

---

MERCURY COUGAR, 1967 (BUD MOORE)

Engine: ohv V-8, 289 ci (4737 cc), 350-375 hp, single 4-barrel carb

Transmission: 4-speed

Brakes: front, disc; rear, drum

Suspension: front, upper and lower A-arms, coil springs; rear, live axle, leaf springs

Weight: 3350 lb

Notes: Street car was Cougar GT, 289 ci, 271 hp, 3800 lb. Very limited number of Cougar Eliminator models were produced with Boss 302 engine in 1970.

From left, 1967 Cougar drivers Ed Leslie (the Monterey auto dealer was an experienced sports car driver), Parnelli Jones and Dan Gurney. Deke Houlgate collection

way he wanted it. He was soon to leave *Sports Car Graphic* and would probably put in more time in Shelby's Mustangs than the other drivers combined.

Daytona 1967 saw the first Trans-Am Camaros. Two of the four Z-28s were Penske cars for Mark Donohue and Craig Fisher. Roger West and John Moore had the other Z-28s. Who did what for them, and how certain GM divisions managed to circumvent the firm's "no racing assistance" policy, is a study in Byzantine intrigue. Later, this book will document some of what went on.

As it was introduced in the fall of 1966, the Camaro lacked an engine suitable for the Trans-Am. You could order a Z-28 with a 250 cid six, 327 V-8, 350 V-8 or, a bit later on, a big 396 cid V-8.

CHEVROLET CAMARO Z-28, 1967-69 (PENSKE)

Engine: ohv V-8 (Traco-built), 302 ci (4950 cc), 440-460 hp, dual 4-barrel carb (later, single 4-barrel)
Transmission: 4-speed
Brakes: 4-wheel disc
Suspension: front, independent upper and lower A-arms, coil springs; rear, live axle, leaf springs, Panhard rod, Positraction
Weight: 3250 lb
Notes: Street car had 302 ci, 290 hp, single 4-barrel carb (dual 4-barrel and 4-wheel disc available as kits).

But Chevrolet engineering boss Vince Piggins could be talked to. Soon the 327 cid became the ideal 302 cid, 4950 cc Trans-Am mill. Sporting close-ratio transmissions, dual exhausts and steel wheels, 600 Z-28 Mustang-eaters were produced by Chevrolet in 1967.

American Motors had yet to make its move and Chrysler was represented at Daytona by a single, tired Barracuda and the Group 44 Dodge Dart. But Ford and Chevrolet came to Daytona "loaded for bear."

The February 3 Daytona 300 had thirty-four starters, nineteen finishers and a surprise winner. The Parnelli Jones and Dan Gurney Cougars earned the first two places on the grid with identical 104.86 qualifying times. Also in the 104 bracket was Jerry Titus. Bob Tullius, eighth on the grid, was 3 mph slower than the pole-sitting Cougars.

But seventy-nine laps around the 3.81 miles of chassis-testing high banks and brake-killing twisty infield is a long haul. The Mark Donohue-Parnelli Jones rivalry, which turned touchy by season's end, may have started here when Mark took the early lead from Parnelli. But Mark's Camaro suffered ignition failure and retired early.

Gurney enjoyed a brief lead, but pulled in to check his failing oil pressure. Titus then got out front but bumped an errant Porsche and thereafter suffered from excessive tire

Gurney, Bud Moore, Parnelli Jones and Fran Hernandez (left to right) looking over Cougar engine. Ford Motor Company

Team Cougar with Parnelli's original Cougar.

wear. Doc Thompson's Mustang then had the lead but blew an engine when tapped by the brakeless Gurney Cougar. Jones then

Ford's corporate racing boss, icy but efficient Jacque Passino.

Bud Moore, the quiet, hard-working Spartanburg, South Carolina, stock car builder quickly adapted to road racing's oddities.

Works Alfa Romeos on the high banks during the 1967 Trans-Am. Peter Gregg's 911 made off with under-2 honors.

had things his own way until shortly after the halfway mark when his engine began slowing from a broken rocker arm.

When the flag fell, the evergreen Bob Tullius and his sturdy Dart finished a full lap up on the Fisher Camaro. Two laps back was Parnelli Jones, with Jerry Titus a distant fourth. Both the Jim McKeon Lotus Cortina and Kwech Alfa had qualified in front of Peter Gregg. But they retired early and Gregg's 911 captured under-2 honors.

Bob Tullius carried on. But even with Goodyear's $10,000, his 1967 season became a lost cause without factory support. Daytona was to be the Dart's last hurrah.

For only slightly different reasons, both Dan Gurney and A. J. Foyt say they regard the spring of 1967 as the high points of their racing careers. Two weeks after A. J. won his third Indy 500, he and Gurney won the 24 Hours of Le Mans to become the first Americans to win Le Mans in an American car.

Dan Gurney's magic spring of 1967 was equally rewarding. Two weeks after winning Le Mans, Dan drove his All American Racers Eagle to win the Belgium Grand Prix at Spa in record-smashing time with a 148.81 mph race average. Making his victory especially noteworthy is that Dan became the first American driver to win a Grand Prix in an American car since Jimmy Murphy captured the French Grand Prix in a Duesenberg in 1921.

Sebring's Four-Hour International, the Trans-Am that wasn't supposed to happen, pulled a record sixty-one entrants. Twenty-six were over-2 liters, and thirteen of those twenty-six were Camaros!

Jerry Titus "owned" Sebring on that last day of March. He qualified fastest with a record 98.53 mph. He led all but two of the seventy-three laps, and he covered 400 solo miles with a record 94.824 race average.

Only Mark Donohue's Camaro, which finished close to a full lap behind the Mustang, had been able to maintain a serious race-long threat. The Thompson and Minter Mustangs came in third and fourth, with Leslie's fifth-place Cougar the sole Lincoln-Mercury entry to go the distance.

In tenth place, four laps off the pace, the Gregg/Posey Porsche led the under-2s as thirty-four of the sixty-one starters survived.

Jerry Titus' Mustang leads Mark Donohue's Camaro. The 1967 Daytona saw the first Z-28 Trans-Am Camaros. Of the four, two were Penske cars for Mark Donohue and Craig Fisher. Donohue retired but Fisher finished second to the Tullius Dart, albeit a full lap behind.

Team Cougar got its act together at the Green Valley 300 on April 16. Thompson's Mustang and Gurney's Cougar were up front with identical qualifying times. Third on the grid was Parnelli Jones, only the blink of an eye slower. Titus almost didn't make the party as he clobbered a haybale during practice and flipped. He was required to win a consolation race for the privilege of starting twenty-ninth in the thirty-car field.

Titus might have won this one too, but the intense heat forced him to pit on lap forty. Refreshed by a water bucket shower, he stormed back through the field and, with help from Ron Dykes, finished fifth.

Gurney won over Jones in what probably was the closest finish, less than a yard, in Trans-Am history. Gurney's 75.9 winning average was the same as that of second-place Jones. After Titus had given up the lead on lap forty, Gurney ran first from laps forty-one to 188 with Jones on his rear bumper. Thompson and Donohue were third and fourth with under-2 laurels going to the seventh place John Pauly/Bill Bowman 911.

Shown here are Gurney and Jones who had earned the 1967 Daytona pole with identical times.

Parnelli was leading the 1967 Daytona Trans-Am until he suffered engine problems at the halfway mark, but still finished third.

Winning the 1967 Daytona Trans-Am in his own Group 44 Dart gave Bob Tullius his greatest racing thrill.

A memorable shot of Jerry Titus controlling a cut-tire-induced slide. Repeated tire failure dropped Jerry's Mustang to a fourth-place finish in the 1967 Daytona Trans-Am. Deke Houlgate collection

A grinning Bob Tullius and co-driver Tony Adamowicz start their lap of honor after winning the 1967 Daytona Trans-Am.

Peter Gregg's 911 finished first in under-2 and fifth overall. Predictably, Gregg's remarkably fine drive was ignored as photographers mobbed the winning Dart.

The May 30, 1967, Trans-Am moved east to sylvan Lime Rock Park. The curving 1.53 mile up-and-down track in northwest Connecticut's Berkshire hills had gone through growing pains but now was in the capable hands of the veteran driver, Jim Haynes.

Cougar's big guns were at Indy where Parnelli Jones had his second 500 in his pocket until lap 196 when he retired. Andy Granatelli lost the big one when a dime part broke and shattered the turbine's transmis-

Washington Dentist Dick Thompson brings the Grady Davis Mustang home third in the 1967 Sebring Trans-Am.

Bill France, Jr. (center), congratulates Peter Gregg (left) and Bob Tullius (right), the under-2 and over-2 winners of the 1967 Daytona Trans-Am. Alice Bixler/Road & Track

The Mark Donohue/Bruce Winterstein Camaro finished second in the 1967 Sebring Trans-Am. Sharing team ownership with Penske at this time was Terry Godsall. Roger Penske collection

Jerry Titus (left) gets Carroll Shelby's best wishes after winning the 1967 Sebring. Jerry's tactics were to get out front on the first lap and stay there for the next 73.

sion. Dan Gurney, who had qualified second, retired his Eagle on the twenty-first lap with a burnt piston.

Lincoln-Mercury's hired gun, Peter Revson, made his first Trans-Am a memorable one by bringing Cougar its second consecutive victory. Averaging 87.3 mph, Revson left Donohue and Titus two laps behind as eighteen of the thirty starters completed 330 miles.

Horst Kwech lifted Alfa's hopes by winning under-2 with a fourth overall while beating a strong Porsche entry headed by Peter Gregg and Bert Everett.

Mid-Ohio held its first Trans-Am on June 11. After 300 miles, only half the thirty-two-car field was still running. NASCAR's David Pearson had earned the pole with a record 81.20 lap. But the only race lap he was to lead was the first, as Jerry Titus stormed out front and stayed there for the next 125 laps.

Star-to-be George Follmer made his Trans-Am debut at Mid-Ohio as a replacement for

Green Valley Raceway, 1967. What may have been the closest finish in racing history is still recalled vividly by both Parnelli Jones and Dan Gurney. That Parnelli's bumper is caved in could have had a bearing on the finishing order of the two Cougars.

Not a new type of air brake. A first-lap accident in the 1967 Lime Rock 400 Trans-Am forced Dick Thompson to crawl back for repairs to his number II Mustang. Ed Leslie's Cougar and Bob Johnson's Mustang retired, as did Thompson's Mustang. Deke Houlgate collection

Mark Donohue. Bringing Penske's Camaro in third, albeit three laps behind the leader, got Follmer off to a solid start.

Mid-Ohio saw the two Ford teams lodge protests that canceled each other out. Team Cougar protested the winning Titus Mustang on the basis of Jerry having received outside assistance getting back on the course following an off-track excursion. Shelby in turn protested the second-place Pearson Cougar for having left the engine running while taking on fuel. As both acts were clearly against Trans-Am rules, Solomon-like, the race judges let the results stand.

Twelve-laps into the August 6 Bryar 250, what had been a light drizzle turned into a race-long downpour. As only Ed Leslie was on rain tires, the Monterey car dealer moved from the back of the pack to overtake the race leaders, Bert Everett and Peter Revson.

But Leslie was to lose his engine and Revson got his Cougar past Everett's Porsche to bring Lincoln-Mercury its third win. The Pennsylvanian finished second overall and first in under-2 liters as Doc Thompson's Mustang came in third, four laps behind Revson.

The wet track resulted in both Donohue and Titus going out early with crunched cars, as five of the first seven finishers drove under-2s.

Standings following six events, the halfway mark in the twelve-race 1967 season, saw Cougar with thirty-nine points, Mustang thirty-five, Camaro twenty-seven and Dart nine. Porsche, which had opened the year with three straight wins, led Alfa Romeo, forty-six to thirty-seven. Only the marvel of the Tullius Dart at Daytona prevented Ford Motor Company from sweeping all six firsts.

Retained by Lincoln-Mercury to pinch hit for Dan Gurney, who had chores at Indy, Peter Revson won his first Trans-Am at Lime Rock Park on May 30, 1967. Averaging 87.3 mph for 330 miles was fast enough to leave both Jerry Titus and Mark Donohue two laps behind. Here, Revson's Cougar, number 15, is about to lap the Dockery Mustang. Deke Houlgate collection

Marlboro's August 12 Double 300 saw the Maryland circuit drop its customary 12-Hours in favor of running *separate* 300-mile races for each class. As each event was to last about five hours, many drivers opted to run in both the over and under enduros.

The Everett/Titus 911 led the fourteen under-2s that finished. There had been a total of twenty-five runners, the veteran pair beating such sterling Porsche competition as Gregg/Posey, Herb Wetson/Jennings and Thompson/Moore. Mysteriously, all three Alfa GTAs retired ten laps from the finish while on the same lap.

Only eight of the thirteen over-2 starters went the distance. But history was made as Donohue and Fisher brought Roger Penske's Camaros their first win. Rubbing it in, Donohue/Fisher finished two laps in front of the Minter/Moffat and Titus/Adams Mustangs. Hometowners Tullius and Jennings' fifth-place Dart was good enough to earn two points for Dodge.

Prominent among big-car DNF's were Bud Moore's Revson/Leslie and Yarborough/Yarbrough Cougars. Race times for the 177 laps run by both classes were close: 4 hours 45 minutes 30 seconds for the over-2s, com-

This wild crash at Bryar in August 1967 was triggered when Mustang number 47, driven by Ken Duclos, hit Titus' number 17. Slamming into a sandbank, Jerry spun back onto the track and continued whirling, half airborne, for eight revolutions. Barely getting by (lower right) were

Craig Fisher, number 77, and Bert Everett, number 14. Revson brought Cougar its second win at Bryar with Bert Everett's 911 liking the rain well enough to finish second overall and first under-2. Deke Houlgate collection

pared to 4 hours 53 minutes 5.4 seconds for the under-2 liters—a 61.62 versus 63.23 mph race average.

A new venue, the twisty 2.66 mile Continental Divide Raceway at Castle Rock, Colorado, was the scene of the seventh 1967 Trans-Am.

Minter's Cougar took the pole. But the Titus Mustang led all 250 miles, averaging 75.40 mph for ninety-four laps. Leslie's Cougar was second, a lap up on the third-place Minter/Bucknum Mustang. Doc Thompson's

Lincoln-Mercury recruited Cale Yarborough and LeRoy Yarbrough, two of stock car racing's winningest drivers, for the Marlboro Double 300, but neither good old boy lasted the distance. Shown here is Cale Yarborough (right) and Peter Revson.

Mustang rounded-out the top four, as sixteen of the twenty-three starters saw the checker.

In fifth and sixth place, the Monty Winkler and Kwech Alfas nosed-out Everett's seventh-place 911, which in turn was one lap ahead of Donohue's ailing Camaro.

On September 10 the Trans-Am ran another new course, the three-mile circuit at the US Naval Air Station in Crows Landing, California. Staged in a blazing sun, it was here that the over-2s outnumbered the under-2s for the first time.

A thin, twenty-one-car field saw Jerry Titus earn the pole, run an 89.91 mph fastest race lap and lead all eighty-six laps. Only Revson's Cougar stayed on the same lap as the leader. Donohue brought the Sunoco Camaro in third and Winkler's Alfa edged-out Everett to win under-2.

Riverside's September 17 Mission Bell 250 was a blow to Mustang's title hopes. Titus had won another pole with still another lap record. But David Pearson had matched it and went on to win when Shelby's Mustang lost its brakes and Titus retired early.

Ed Leslie's Cougar followed Pearson with Bob Johnson's Camaro coming in third. Tony Settember, a budding star that never blossomed, DNF'd Penske's Camaro while

Cale Yarborough trying his Cougar at the 1967 Marlboro.

Donohue was back East blowing an engine in the Bridgehampton CanAm.

With but two races to go, winning Riverside enabled Cougar to pick up a full nine points, as it dropped Marlboro, where Lincoln-Mercury's cat had not placed. Score: Cougar sixty points to Mustang's fifty-nine.

Riverside also saw Bert Everett give Porsche its sixth win as twenty-two of the thirty-four starters ran the full 249 laps.

Trans-Am number eleven was a tough 350 miles of night racing on the three-mile Stardust Raceway in Las Vegas. Parnelli Jones and Mark Donohue shared the front row with identical 98.18 mph lap times, with the Bucknum and Titus Mustangs lying third and fourth on the thirty-one car grid.

Jones started by running away from the field. But the abrasive surface, coupled with his hard charging, added up to the car suffering from excessive tire wear. Donohue moved the Penske Camaro into the lead when the Cougar pitted, and went on to win with a 94.8 race average.

The Bucknum and Titus Mustangs came home second and third, with Jones fourth. Under-2 honors saw Kwech bring Alfa its fifth, and last, win. Among the eighteen retirements were the Revson Cougar, Tullius Dart and Minter Mustang.

Thanks to Donohue's win and Bucknum's

Peter Firestone (center) congratulates Bert Everett (left) and Parnelli Jones for having won their classes in the Paul Revere 250, an unofficial Trans-Am night race at Daytona in July of 1967. Bert Everett collection

Jerry Titus on his way to winning the Continental Divide 250. Milt Minter's Cougar had taken the pole, but Jerry's Mustang would lead all 94 laps. Deke Houlgate collection

The 1967 Crow's Landing Trans Am. Behind Ed Leslie and Peter Revson, left, and Bud Moore with Fran Hernandez, lies the US Naval Air Station, providers of a three-mile circuit in the shimmering desert heat. Judy Stropus collection

second place, after dropping two lower scores, Mustang entered the final only a single point behind Cougar.

The October 8 Kent, Washington, 300 had it all. Cougar entered cars for Jones, Gurney, Moffat and, in reserve, Leslie. Carroll Shelby went with Titus, Bucknum and Minter.

But it was Mark Donohue who won the pole, the race and Carroll Shelby's gratitude. Titus had flipped and badly damaged his car in practice. After borrowing a private entry, he was out before the halfway point.

Milt Minter was gone by lap eleven with no oil. But Ronnie Bucknum managed to beat Dan Gurney for second place. Bud Moore's strategy had been for Gurney and Jones to

The Jerry Titus Mustang and David Pearson's Cougar led the 1967 field into Riverside's turn seven. Titus had earned the pole but Pearson and Ed Leslie brought Cougar a one-two win. Cam Warren/Road & Track

run side by side behind Donohue. This would keep the Mustangs away and put one of the Cougars in the best position to nip by Donohue in the final laps. But Gurney was slowed by a leaky gas filler and Jones failed to restart after a routine mid-race pit stop.

The final point standings were as shown below.

Over-2 liters

Mustang	64 (74)
Cougar	62 (67)
Camaro	57 (64)
Dart	11 (11)

Under-2 liters

Porsche	75 (89)
Alfa Romeo	59 (63)
Ford of Britain	5
BMW	2
Volvo	1

The 1967 Trans-Am pulled an estimated 102,000 admissions. Prize money of $67,660 was said to have been equaled by manufacturers' contingency funds. Starting fields averaged thirty-three cars. The average event ran 298 miles, but more than four out of each ten starters failed to go the distance. Races averaged 3.5 hours. All but a few of the 300 drivers were Americans, and 207 of the 393 starters were over-2 liters.

Both Mustang and Cougar added muscle for Kent: Shelby going with Jerry Titus, Ronnie Bucknum and Milt Minter; while Bud Moore put Allan Moffat in Leslie's car, keeping Ed in reserve. But Mark Donohue won the race and Shelby's gratitude. Bucknum had managed to beat Gurney for second place as both Jones, who dropped out, and Gurney were slowed by mechanical problems. Bucknum, number 31, is shown passing the 911 as Mustang took the 1967 championship. Ford Motor Company

Broken windscreen in Gurney's Cougar at Kent, the 1967 season's final event, where Dan finished third. Leon Beauchemin/Road & Track

Ford honors Carroll Shelby and Jerry Titus for winning the second consecutive Trans-Am title. Scene was Ford Motor Company annual Motorsports Dinner. Standing behind number 17 (left to right) is Jerry Titus, John Bishop (then executive director of the Sports Car Club of America), Carroll Shelby and Jacque Passino (manager of Ford's special vehicles). Ford Motor Company/Deke Houlgate collection

A practice crash destroyed number 17, the Jerry Titus Mustang, at Kent. Jerry borrowed Brad McComb's car but retired from the 1967 finale. Leon Beauchemin/Road & Track

Chapter 6

Blackbird pie

The 1968 Trans-Am lost the Lincoln-Mercury Cougar, gained the American Motors Javelin and benefited from a batch of new regulations.

Two Pontiac Firebirds came aboard late in the season. But their arrival was complicated by so many homologation problems that their creditable showing was obscured by red tape.

While not drastic, the rule changes were significant. Over-2 liter cars could weigh no less than 2,800 pounds as raced, but without fuel. Rim widths for over-2s were not to exceed eight inches; seven inches for under-2s.

Wheelwells and fender flares could be legally altered to accommodate the larger tires. The substitution of plastic or aluminum bumpers was allowed. Knock-off wheels were forbidden.

Over-2 engines could be bored-out to a full 5000 cc (305 cid). Engines could be left running during fuel stops. In May, after the season started, the SCCA made the use of safety fuel cells mandatory.

Race purse minimums were increased from $5,000 to $10,000. Not unexpectedly, Trans-Am sanction fees (the charge levied by the SCCA on promoters holding Trans-Am races) went from $750 to $1,500.

Thirteen events, fourteen if you count the separately held under-2 race at Sebring, were held in 1968. War Bonnet, Bridgehampton, Meadowdale, Canada's Mt. Tremblant (or St. Jovite, as it was often called) and Watkins Glen were added to the 1968 schedule. Marlboro, Green Valley and Las Vegas were dropped.

The relative stability of driver assignments that had characterized the Trans-Am's first two seasons, became a game of musical chairs in 1968. Except for Mark Donohue's by now hallowed relationship with Roger Penske (and Penske was only to run one car in nine of the thirteen races), you literally could not tell the players without a program.

Mustang driver Peter Revson and Camaro regular Craig Fisher joined George Follmer in Javelins. Fisher left Javelin in mid-season

---

AMC JAVELIN, 1968-69
Engine: ohv V-8 (Traco-built 1968, Kaplan-built 1969), 290 ci, 375 hp (later, 435 hp with cold-air pack), single 4-barrel carb (later, dual 4-barrel with Edelbrock manifold, 480 hp)
Transmission: 4-speed (Borg-Warner)
Suspension: front, independent upper and lower A-arms, coil springs; rear, live axle, leaf springs
Notes: Street car had 290 ci, 225 hp.

PONTIAC FIREBIRD, 1968-69 (T/G RACING)
Engine: ohv V-8 Camaro Z-28 (Bartz-built), 304 ci (4950 cc), 410-420 hp, dual 4-barrel carb
Transmission: 4-speed
Brakes: 4-wheel disc
Suspension: front, independent upper and lower A-arms, coil springs; rear, live axle, leaf springs, Watts linkage
Weight: 3350 lb
Notes: Street car had 400 ci Ram Air IV, 345 hp, 3350 lb. The Firebirds ran with Chevrolet engines in 1968 and 1969 because they were sold in Canada with those engines! Pontiac had no suitable small-block engine. There were a small number of 303 ci engines built and sold; they featured tunnel-port heads, forged cranks and ram intake manifolds.

for a Firebird. Sam Posey drove both Camaros and Mustangs. Alfa Romeo ace Horst Kwech joined Shelby's Team Mustang. Dodge loyalist Bob Tullius drove both Porsches and Mustangs. And Jerry Titus, Mr. Trans-Am himself, closed his frustrating Mustang season in a Firebird.

The series opened on an unfamiliar note when the first two events ran as parts of other races, the February 2 and 3 24-Hours of Daytona and the March 23 12-Hours of Sebring. Combining the events was a mixed blessing.

Knowledgeable Trans-Am followers liked the idea of seeing how their Detroit favorites would fare against the world's best, the big Ferrari, Ford and Porsche prototypes, as well as watching them go head-to-head with state-of-the-art GT cars such as Porsche Carreras and Corvettes. But casual race fans only had eyes for the European and big Fords, although the small American sedans made up a third of Daytona's sixty-three-car entry.

Donohue, the fastest of Daytona's Trans-Am qualifiers, was a respectable twentieth on the grid. Jerry Titus was twenty-second. Making an even stronger statement for the entire Trans-Am concept, the Titus/Bucknum Mustang finished the 24-Hours fourth overall.

Ford's pony car covered 629 laps, versus 673 run by the winning Vic Elford/Jochen Neerpasch/Jo Siffert Porsche 907. But Ford started the year with nine big points.

On the high banks and going through the infield, Mark Donohue in the 1968 season opener at Daytona. Bill Warner/Roger Penske collection

In spite of making repeated sick-engine-induced pit stops, the Donohue/Johnson/Fisher Camaro made 565 laps. This was good enough for twelfth overall and six points for being second in class. Sweden's Sten Axelsson helped Daytona master Peter Gregg to a sparkling ninth overall and first under-2 liters.

New in 1968 was a group of real-world regulations that accepted the facts of life. Wheelwells and fender flares could be *legally* altered to accommodate larger tires. The substitution of plastic or aluminum bumpers was allowed, although knock-off wheels remained forbidden. Over-2 engines could be bored-out to a full 305 cid, 5000 cc. And engines could be left running during fuel stops. Then, soon after the 1968 season started, the SCCA made the use of fuel cells mandatory. Over-2 rim widths were not to exceed eight inches and the weight of over-2s could be no more than 2,800 pounds as raced, but without fuel.

Both the Daytona 24 Hours and Sebring 12 Hours included full fields of Trans-Am cars. That Detroit's pony cars did as well as they did against the world's fastest automobiles, the Ferrari, Ford and Porsche prototypes, and beat many of the big GT cars, such as Porsche Carreras and Covettes, was not overlooked by the motoring press.

Donohue, who was twentieth on the Daytona grid, was fastest of the Trans-Am qualifiers. Jerry Titus was twenty-second. Making the Trans-Am come up roses for Shelby was that Titus and Ronnie Bucknum won the 24-Hour Trans-Am by coming in fourth overall.

The Donohue/Fisher/Johnson Camaro finished twelfth overall, good enough for second in the Trans-Am.

After running the under-2s as a separate event on Friday March 22, Sebring also combined the FIA Manufacturers Championship with the Trans-Am. Unlike Daytona, where he had qualified fastest of the under-

Bert Everett earned the pole and went on to win the under-2 Trans-Am over John Moore's 911 and Horst Kwech's Alfa GTA. Run on Friday prior to the 12 Hours, several drivers entered both events. Dennis Koelmel/Bert Everett collection

Bert Everett with a demure race queen in victory lane after winning the Sebring 1968 Governor's Cup Trans-Am. Bert Everett collection

2s, only to retire early with a broken rod, Bert Everett stuck his 911 on the 3-Hour pole and went on to win. John Moore's 911 was second and Horst Kwech's Alfa third.

Being surrounded by sixty-seven of the world's fastest cars seemed to inspire Penske's drivers as they dominated the Trans-Am class by coming in third and fourth overall. The winning Siffert/Hans Hermann Porsche 907 recorded 237 laps over the rough 5.2 mile circuit, the Donohue/Fisher Camaro covered 221.

As the Titus/Bucknum Mustang was fifth overall and third in the Trans-Am, the rivals went into their regular season with Chevrolet leading Ford, fifteen to thirteen. Twelfth overall and fourth among the Trans-Am sedans was the Tullius/McComb/Richards Mustang.

The 1968 Sebring was American Motors' first Trans-Am. The team manager was Jim Jeffords, a Milwaukee advertising man who had raced sports cars. One of them was a rather special Corvette in which Jeffords had won the 1958 and 1959 SCCA B-production title. He is best remembered for driving the Corvette Purple People Eater.

Winner of the 1968 Daytona 24-Hour Trans-Am was the Titus/Bucknum Mustang with a fourth overall.

Late in 1967 when AMC decided to enter the Trans-Am, it was Jeffords who arranged to have the Javelin development work done by Ronny Kaplan, a Chicago race car builder. Kaplan made good moves in turning to Traco Engineering to convert AMC's 290 cids into raceworthy 305s, and in hiring George Follmer to be the test driver.

At Sebring, Follmer was joined by Peter Revson and mechanic/driver John Martin. Covering 193 laps in their very first Trans-Am, they finished thirteenth overall and fifth in the Trans-Am. The Janet Guthrie/ Liane Engermann/Bill Haenett Javelin ran 144 laps to finish thirty-third.

In mid-race, while the pretty Dutch girl

Shelby's number 2 Mustang. Driven by Allan Moffat and Horst Kwech, it failed to finish the 1968 Daytona.

Donohue and Craig Fisher, in number 16, won the 1968 Sebring with a third overall, covering 221 laps to the Siffert/Hermann 907's 237.

Engine-builder Frank Coons in the Penske pits during the 1968 Sebring. Meticulous record keeping for both cars was typical of the Penske/ Coons operation.

was driving, the Javelin brushed a French 911 that, in turn, nudged the Paul Hawkins/ David Hobbs GT40 into the boondocks. (Being a vicar's son had done little to limit Hawkins' vocabulary following the incident!)

The May 12 War Bonnet 250 in New Mannford, Oklahoma, had eleven over-2s, three Camaros, two Javelins, five Mustangs and one Dart, plus nine under-2 liters.

Parnelli Jones, who was driving for Ford, took the pole and an early lead. But the combination of a rough course, rough driving, an argument with a race stewart and a wet track brought him nothing but trouble and a third-place finish.

Jerry Titus, in the other works Mustang, retired with a blown engine. Neither the John McComb nor Sam Posey Mustang was a contender. Javelin drivers Follmer and Revson finished second and fourth. Horst Kwech impressed Ford when his Alfa beat the Adamowicz 911 to win under-2.

As Penske was to enter only one car for nine of that year's thirteen races, it was, as ever, all up to Mark Donohue. War Bonnet had been stopped when Malcom Starr's Mustang went into the crowd and injured two spectators. The restart resulted in a

With Penske's second Camaro taking fourth place, the 1968 Sebring saw Chevrolet take the Trans-Am lead. Driven by Bob Johnson and Joe

Welch, number 15 nosed-out the Titus/Bucknum Mustang for fourth place. Taylor Warren photo/ Roger Penske collection

scoring mixup that saw a rash of final position protests. But no one questioned Mark's Camaro being in first place. He won with an 82.549 race average for 110 laps over the 2.3 mile circuit, fast enough to give him a forty-five-second advantage over second-place George Follmer.

There were twenty-one cars in the May 30 Lime Rock, but it was Camaro all the way. Donohue won the pole and led the entire 256 laps. Second-place Titus and third-place Peter Revson were both two laps back. The Mustang and Javelin had come together and Titus was fined following Revson's protest over Jerry's rough driving.

Brought in to replace Parnelli Jones, who was at Indy watching George Snyder finish thirty-first in Parnelli's Ford Special, David Pearson was out early with failing oil pressure. And Tony Adamowicz gave the Milestone 911 a fine ride to finish fourth overall and first under-2.

Both Mark Donohue and George Follmer, who were at Mosport running one of the early Indy-car road races, missed qualifying for the June 16 Mid-Ohio 250. The Javelin and Camaro team bosses solved the problem quite differently.

Roger Penske allowed that Mark wouldn't be terribly handicapped by starting in the back of a nineteen-car field. But Javelin manager Jeffords gave Follmer's ride to John Martin, who went out and stuck number 16 on the pole. With Revson's Javelin second fastest, the front row was a blaze of red, white and blue.

Jerry Titus, whose catch-up efforts in Shelby's Mustang included trying everything but cutting across the infield, made it into second place. Helping to make Mid-Ohio a trying experience for Team Mustang was the presence of Jacque Passino, Fran Hernandez and other Ford racing brass.

What made the weekend even more difficult for winner Donohue's opposition was Mark's casual prerace comment that he figured on getting into first place by the eleventh or twelfth lap. In fact, he was there in ten.

In winning under-2 at Mid-Ohio, Bert Everett broke his own one-year-old under-2 record. Yet his 911 averaged 76.19 against the 83.32 record made by Donohue. Almost three laps off the pace was third-place Revson's Javelin which was followed by a second Camaro, driven by Bob Johnson.

Famed engine builder and designer Smokey Yunick had trouble getting his Camaro, number 81, through Tech. Driven by Lloyd Ruby and Al

Unser it had tied Donohue for the pole at Daytona, shown here, but failed to finish Sebring or Daytona.

The crowd was announced at 15,000. Winner Donohue earned $1,500; Bert Everett, $1,000. Each also collected accessory awards. Even for 1967 that kind of money was peanuts.

Automobile racing came to Bridgehampton in 1915. Following a long lapse, in 1949 the Bridge began running sports car races over a four-mile combination of village streets and nearby country lanes. As in the first Watkins Glen (October 1948), an Alfa won the June 1949 first Bridgehampton. Dreams became reality: Allards, the first Ferraris, old Bugattis, new MGs, the amicable families who lived along the old town's pleasant tree-lined roads, picnicked as they watched.

Could it have gone on if the two ladies who sat with their legs in the road hadn't ignored the motorcycle policeman's request that they move? The humpbacked bridge, the out-of-shape Allard, then the wail of sirens. When the 1953 race was red-flagged, Phil Walters' 1.5 Osca was just short of overtaking Bill Spears' 4.9 Ferrari.

The aborted 1953 Bridge was the last on public roads. The story was the same at Elkhart Lake, at Watkins Glen and at Pebble Beach. Perhaps unruly crowds are inevitable.

The present 2.855 mile Bridgehampton Circuit opened in 1957. Bending around giant sand dunes that overlook Long Island Sound and the old whaling port of Sag Harbor, the track constantly changes elevation from 132 to 265 feet. Climbing slightly, the half-mile-long pit straight abruptly falls into a heart-stopping 150 mph, sharply downhill right-hander. It was a brake-tapping gearing-down turn until Walt Hansgen found he could take it flat-out, which explains why it's known as Hansgen's Bend.

Originally a community-backed effort, Bridgehampton soon was managed by others than those who owned the now nearly priceless land. Long under-capitalized, Bridgehampton is a mass of contradictions.

According to many drivers, including some of the world's finest, "If you'd only pave the bloody thing it would be this country's best circuit." It also is lacking in the most primitive of amenities. It is hard to reach, lacks sufficient parking and fails to supply even the rudiments of pit or garage facilities.

But what a course! Perhaps Jo Siffert, even though his English was limited, said it best. Until the Swiss GP star ran the 1969

Peter Revson/John Martin/George Follmer introduced the AMC 1969 Javelin at the 1968 Sebring, finishing thirteenth overall and fifth in the Trans-Am. AMC collection

CanAm for Porsche, which Stuttgart acknowledged was designed to see what its three-liter 917 needed to beat CanAm machines that had double the Porsche 917's displacement, Jo had never seen the Bridge.

I believe it was a Wednesday and that Porsche had arranged for Jo to practice before the track was officially open. I was alone in the press shack (the poorest equipped press room I'd ever seen, but the best located, being opposite the pits and directly over the start/finish line) when Jo climbed our rickety outside steps.

We weren't friends, but he'd seen me around and I thought highly of the quiet Swiss. He was fast and smooth and got the most out of everything he drove. Jo had made a few slow laps so we talked about CanAm times while looking at a course map.

"I think I will do better here," Jo told me. "The Bridge is more like what I am used

Savoring victory at the 1968 Sebring. Left to right are mechanic Roy Gaines, Craig Fisher, Mark Donohue, crewman Al Holbert and, looking up at Bill Mayberry, young Kip Penske. Taylor Warren/Roger Penske collection

David Penske, Roger's younger brother (seated left with outstretched arms), directs 1968 Lime Rock pit stop. Randy Hilton, co-sponsor of the

Sunoco Camaro and (at extreme left) a Sun Oil executive (right, behind fuel hose) look on. Road & Track *photo*

Sam Posey joined Penske's Trans-Am team for several events during 1968. Roger Penske collection

to—more like good European courses. Here you keep moving. You watch. Here I might surprise some people."

He did. Siffert's 917 finished third, on the same lap with Bruce McLaren and Dennis Hulme, for his highest finish in the entire 1969 CanAm.

In theory Bridgehampton was New York's home track. Being 100 traffic-clogged miles away didn't do much for the gate. But New York City was also the home of many sponsors, and their publicity people used the Bridge to host many nice parties.

Nowhere—Saturday afternoon down King's Road, Paris fashion shows or even Monaco at GP time—was there more exquisite "bird" life. Perhaps the biggest contradiction of all was the track's Circuit Club. For a $5 "membership" fee you got unsurpassed viewing of the pits, most of the course and sailboat racing on Gardner's Bay; comfortable deck chairs under a green-striped awning; and when it was run by Southampton's famed Herb McCarthy, good food and fine drinks.

The veteran Bob Grossman in his two-year-old Mustang at the 1968 Bridgehampton Trans-Am. Ford Motor Company photo

A case in point is that during its CanAm years, the Bridge was the only track where the world-class drivers stayed around for the award ceremony even when they didn't finish in the money.

During its first four years, only Dan Gurney and Mark Donohue had been able to dent the monopoly that overseas drivers held on the CanAm. By coincidence, both Mark and Dan won their CanAm races at the Bridge.

The June 23 Bridgehampton 3-Hours was the sixth Trans-Am of the 1968 series. Ford, Chevy and AMC would have two-car teams on the eighteen-car grid. Roger Penske put Sam Posey in his second Camaro and Horst Kwech became Titus' Mustang teammate.

Ford was still suffering from its prolonged 1967 labor troubles. During 1968, those drivers who had tried both the Mustang and Camaro usually gave the Z-28 the edge. Ford's long-planned 302 was still a year away.

Kwech blew an engine on race morning. Titus retired his Mustang with a broken transmission on the eleventh lap. Donohue and Revson shared the front row. It would be up to the Javelins to make a race of it. But Peter was only able to stay with Mark until the sixty-third lap when his Javelin lost its gearbox. Mark's winning average was 94.372; he ran the fastest race lap and seemed to win as he pleased. Follmer hung it all out but still finished one-and-a-half minutes back, but on the same lap. The Posey and Rusty Jowett Camaros filled third and fourth.

AMC and Ford entered strong teams at the 1968 Bridge, but Mark ran the fastest lap, finishing almost two minutes in front of Follmer's Javelin. Shown here are Mark (left) and Roger in a familiar pose. Roger Penske collection

Sam Posey wheeled his Penske Camaro home third in the 1968 Bridgehampton 3-Hours, the season's sixth Trans-Am. Pete Luongo/Roger Penske collection

Adamowicz's 911 racked up another under-2 win, arch-rival Everett finishing last of the twelve runners with a sick engine.

Going into Meadowdale, seventh in the thirteen-race series, found Camaro and Porsche far out front with identical fifty-one-point scores. But Ford and AMC kept plugging away. Before the season was over the Mustangs made two more trips to victory lane and Javelins developed better reliability. Alfa then gave Porsche fits by winning the last two under-2s.

Meadowdale Raceway, a born-again 3.2 mile course in Carpentersville, Illinois, near Chicago, had been known for its car-breaking Monza Wall. Refurbished and partly repaved, the organizers were lucky, as race day stayed clear until minutes before the start.

Donohue averaged 87.053 mph to earn nine more points. A lap back was Revson's Javelin with Posey's Camaro coming in third. Titus had started next to Donohue on the front row, and he recorded the fastest lap, only to finish eleventh.

Meadowdale had two other firsts: Canadian Craig Fisher drove a Pontiac Firebird into fourth place. And George Follmer was disqualified for rough driving, having been observed barreling into a Mustang's right rear. Tony Adamowicz brought his 911 in fifth, as sixteen of twenty-two starters finished.

The Pontiac Firebird Trans-Am entry was complicated by an engine line-up that included a small six and several V-8s that were much too large. Although it raised some questions, the SCCA allowed the Z-28 mill to be used, as Chevrolet engines were standard in Canadian Pontiacs.

To further confuse matters, the Pontiac Trans-Am Firebird, which didn't come along until late in 1969, originally failed to have a 5000 cc 305 cid engine. It's well known that Pontiac pays the SCCA a $5.00-per-Trans Am royalty.

What isn't so well known is that back in 1966 John Bishop had the foresight to copyright such club names as CanAm and Trans-Am, and that the long-accumulated Pontiac dollars helped to keep the SCCA afloat. Consequently, it's ironic that several members of the 1966 Board of Governors objected to Bishop incurring the expense of obtaining these copyrights. (Come to think of it, one wonders when the Automobile Club de l'Ouest, or the city fathers of Le Mans, are going to see a lawyer about Pontiac's long-time use of the word LeMans.)

Off-season Bridgehampton test day. The two figures in the new Pontiac GTO are Car and Driver's *David E. Davis and Walt Hansgen. John Hearst of* Autoweek *(on right) and Steve Smith of* Car and Driver *(in dark glasses) are talking with Hansgen.*

Perhaps Parnelli (left) figured it was Ford watchdog Homer Perry's turn to buy. Ford Motor Company

The Trans-Am crossed the border for Les Trois Heures du Circuit Mt. Tremblant. But the results stayed the same. Revson's Javelin shared the front row of the grid with Donohue and he started to make a race of it. But Revson's Javelin and Dick Bauer's Volvo came together and Revson retired.

Then Follmer took up the chase over the hilly 2.70 mile ski slopes surrounding the course. But Donohue just cruised on to his seventh win as Follmer's Javelin finished a distant second, a full lap behind.

Bert Everett blew an engine and Tony Adamowicz, who had earned the under-2 pole, went on to take fifth overall and first under-2. Sam Posey's Camaro was third and Craig Fisher gave his countrymen a little to cheer about with a fourth-place finish, six laps off the pace.

Neither Mustang ran the distance, although Titus was technically considered a finisher as he limped in fourteenth, the last of twenty-two starters. Donohue's average for 260 miles was 86.419 mph.

Two American Motors Javelins competed in the 1968 circuit. They were powered by modified 290 V-8s, bored out to 304 cubic inches, with red, *white and blue color schemes. Drivers were Follmer and Revson. AMC collection*

Cutting the August 4 Bryar Trans-Am from 250 miles to 200, did nothing to alter the results. Donohue breezed to an easy win, four laps in front of second-place Follmer, while Adamowicz took advantage of the 911's liking for the third-gear course to come in third overall and first under-2.

Fourth was John McComb's Mustang, followed by Everett's 911 and Posey's Camaro. Titus and Kwech did manage to break Donohue's lock on start-to-finish leads by running 1-2 for the first fifty laps. But Kwech departed with a blown engine and Titus, who set a 77.31 mph race lap record, lost his rear end.

Both the Penske and Shelby crews routinely distinguished themselves by making ten- and eleven-second pit stops. If tires were changed in addition to taking on fuel, a couple of seconds were added. At Bryar the Ford crew performed the minor miracle of giving Titus a new rear in less than nine minutes.

Fourteen of the twenty-one starters completed Trans-Am number nine which saw American Motors slip past Ford to take over second place in the standings, forty to thirty-seven.

To everyone's delight—it was said that even Roger Penske was relieved—Jerry

St. Jovite, 1968. Donohue, number 6, and Revson, number 3, lead the pack off the line. Peter, who was sidelined by an errant backmarker, failed to finish. AMC collection

Titus broke Mark Donohue's eight-race winning streak in the August 11, 114 lap, 262 mile, Watkins Glen 500.

Good will ran amuck at the upstate New York track that weekend. Winner Titus said that he never would have been able to catch Donohue if the Camaro had been healthy.

Fifth overall and under-2-winner Tony Adamowicz stated that it had been his crew's faster pit stops that enabled him to beat Bert Everett.

Donohue did manage to make the fastest race lap. And runner-up Sam Posey pushed to within nine seconds of the Mustang at the finish. Donohue came in third, Revson fourth, Adamowicz and Everett fifth and sixth, and Follmer's Javelin, eighth.

Bob Tullius didn't have much luck at the Glen in his 911. But he was better off than Dan Gurney, who had been given Kwech's ride. After pitting early to exchange a smoking differential, Dan was forced to pull in for good with a broken engine five laps later.

Predictably, as both Javelins had fared poorly, American Motors President Roy Chapin was in the AMC dealer-packed hospitality tent.

Displaying vigilance, the stewards disqualified Jacques Duval's 911 for failing to meet under-2 specs, and they fined Herb Swan, whose BMW finished tenth overall and fourth under-2, for being thirty-seven pounds underweight.

Mark Donohue's Camaro en route to his seventh 1968 Trans-Am win, followed by Revson's Javelin. Scene is St. Jovite's notorious bridge dip. Pete Luongo/Roger Penske collection

Mark Donohue returned to his winning ways at the Continental Divide 250 on August 25. Only ten of the meager seventeen-car entry survived this dispute-filled weekend.

Disagreement over the lack of evenhandedness in rule enforcement resulted in both the Penske and Shelby teams threatening to withdraw. There also were arguments over the legality of certain Javelin parts, although Revson's disqualification was for getting a push-start on the course. Then Fred Baker's under-2-winning 911 was found to be *150* pounds underweight.

Although Titus made the fastest race lap, neither he nor Gurney was around at the finish. Donohue tooled to an easy three-lap win over Craig Fisher's Canadian Firebird and the third-place John McComb Mustang. Adamowicz was another DNF as under-2 honors remained with Baker's Porsche.

At Riverside Donohue made more news by failing to win, than Horst Kwech did in winning. Penske kept Donohue busy racing in everything in sight, and that was the way Mark wanted it. Although Mark's comment in my June 1967 *Road & Track* profile, "The USRRC was fine but it's like playing tennis with your wife," was uncharacteristically cynical, Mark's great satisfaction was from pinning back the ears of Jones, Gurney, Follmer, Titus, Revson and company.

Donohue's FIA rides with Walt Hansgen, his two trips to Le Mans for Ford and his experience in the CanAm—in 1968 he won Bridgehampton and finished the series in third place, a single point behind Bruce McLaren and eleven points ahead of Jim Hall—convinced Mark, and apparently Roger too, that Mark would win against the world's best.

Riverside's September 8 Mission Bell 250

Riverside's Mission Bell 250 saw Donohue and Titus share the front row, shown here going through a turn. But there were two long-shot winners, *Vic Provenzano's Alfa and Horst Kwech's Mustang.* Road & Track

had a strong thirty-two-car field and two long-shot winners. Donohue took the pole with a record-smashing 100 mph lap over the 2.6 mile sedan course. Once again he shared it with Titus' Mustang.

Early in the race the Mustang and Camaro exchanged the lead. First Titus and then Donohue suffered terminal engine ailments. Horst Kwech stuck the second works Mustang out front and stayed there to bring Ford its third 1968 win to Chevrolet's nine.

Under-2 was such a hard race between the 911s of Adamowicz and Everett that they left the door open for Vic Provenzano's Alfa after both Porsches lost their engines. Revson's Javelin finished a close second. Craig Fisher brought his Firebird from thirty-second up to third, and dirt-track-driver Jon Ward's Camaro wound up fourth, six laps off the pace and one lap up on the under-2-winning Alfa.

The big news at Kent wasn't that Mark Donohue won his tenth race in the final 1968 Trans-Am. It was that Jerry Titus had left Ford. Terry Godsall, a young Canadian businessman, offered Jerry a chance to run a team of his own Pontiac Firebirds.

Replacing Jerry was Peter Revson. By coincidence, Peter had recently bought a Lincoln-Mercury dealership with Peyton Cramer. Peyton and Ray Geddes were the two whiz-kids sent to Shelby-American by Ford. Neither of them returned to Dearborn, which tells us something about the appeal of California, or motorsports, or both.

Lother Motschenbacher was hired to drive Peter's Javelin. Skip Scott, Peter's driving partner in Skip's successful Essex Wire GT40, drove a Camaro. And Ronnie Bucknum, who had finished eighth in a Mustang at Riverside, was back in a pony car for Kent.

Dick Guildstrand's Camaro led Tony Settember's Camaro and Ronnie Bucknum's Mustang in the early stages of the 1968 Riverside Trans-Am.

Only number 18, the Mustang, went the distance.
Road & Track

Once more the Mark-and-Jerry show saw them start side by side. Only it was Titus who had taken the pole at Kent with a time that was close to two seconds under Donohue's old record. Paired off neatly behind the leaders were the Revson and Kwech Mustangs and Follmer and Motschenbacher Javelins.

Titus battled Donohue for the lead and actually ran first until the Pontiac's engine failed before mid-race. Follmer's bump-and-shove methods earned him a reprimand and a fine. But he was able to continue racing while his opponent, Kwech's Mustang, was too badly damaged to go on.

Staying out of trouble, Fisher's Firebird came in second, followed by the Bucknum and Hall Mustangs. Fifth overall and first under-2 was Ed Wach's Alfa, which had been the slowest of all under-2 qualifiers. Only ten of the twenty-six starters were still running at the end of the season's finale.

Shown here at Mid Ohio, Mark visited victory lane ten times during the 1968 13-race Trans-Am season. Pete Luongo/Roger Penske collection

Based on "best ten out of thirteen finishes," Chevrolet and Porsche were tied with ninety points. Runner-up Ford had fifty-nine, American Motors fifty-one and Pontiac—all Fisher—twenty-two. Alfa Romeo followed Porsche with forty-three points while BMW had nine, Volvo four, BMC three and Lancia three.

The racing year had seen some not always good natured ribbing between Roger Penske and Jerry Titus. A master salesman who routinely picked up major sponsors such as Sun Oil, Penske conveniently overlooked his Chevrolet connections to stress the problems caused by his independent status while having to battle the giant Ford Motor Company.

Jerry Titus, who had a puckish sense of humor, had teased Roger about Daytona, where Jerry was first to Donohue's fourth, in a letter to *Competition Press*. The following letter, reprinted here from the April 20, 1968, *Competition Press*, indicates that Roger won this round.

"We at Penske Racing lead a tenuous existence. We work in the shadow of Ford's monstrous vans, struggling painfully against a tide of factory support. Our independence has compensations — living poor, we subsist on a meager diet, and the crow that Jerry Titus had us eat at Daytona tasted almost like roast turkey.

"We wonder if Mr. Titus, living as he does the rich life on the Ford factory gravy train, found his double dose of large blackbird pie at Sebring equally digestible. (signed) Roger Penske Racing Philadelphia, Pa."

LANCIA FULVIA HF
Engine: sohc V-4, 66.5 ci (1300 cc), 87 hp, single 2-barrel Weber carb
Transmission: 4-speed
Suspension: front, upper and lower wishbone, transverse leaf springs; rear, rigid axle, elliptic leaf springs, Watts linkage
Chassis: front engine, front-wheel drive
Weight: 2150 lb
Notes: Street car had 1300 cc, 75 hp, 2280 lb.

Chapter 7

"It wasn't easy"

The index of Mark Donohue's 1975 book, *the unfair advantage*, reveals that Don Cox is mentioned at least one time on thirty-one of its 305 pages. Except for Mark himself, only Roger Penske (who was both Mark's and Don's boss) and Peter Revson have more listings.

My experience with automotive engineers is that most of them are more interested in the "test bed" aspects of automobile racing than in the sport itself. But Don Cox turned out to be a roaring exception.

The man's quiet demeanor hides a car nut. An enthusiast since childhood, Don is a General Motors Institute graduate who thoroughly enjoyed the exceptional circumstances that have enabled him to combine his engineering training and General Motors background and use them in racing.

While still in college, long before he had met, or may ever have heard of, Roger Penske or Mark Donohue, Don had built a race car. "Two of my GM classmates were Bob Stout and Lee Dykstra. All three of us became interested in building a sports car. So we pooled our resources and made something we called the SCD Special."

Don believes that Stout is no longer involved in auto racing; Lee Dykstra, of course, most assuredly is. Following Lee's stint at Kar Kraft, where he worked under Roy Lund on Ford's big Mark IIs and, not so well publicized, on the Trans-Am Mustangs, Lee has moved to the forefront of American race-car design.

Don Cox became aware of Penske Racing while still with Chevrolet Research & Development. As Don observed, he probably would not have become a part of the General Motors-Penske picture if it had not been for Roger's friendship with John DeLorean.

Following his outstanding record at Pontiac, it was inevitable that DeLorean would be rewarded by moving up the GM corporate ladder. The plum was Chevrolet, and that's where DeLorean soon succeeded Pete Estes as general manager. "Up to this time," Don stated, "Roger simply never got the support from Chevrolet that they gave Jim Hall."

Cox went on to say, "There was no question but that Hall had the inside track." Don did say that Penske was not entirely neglected, as he got some help from the Chevrolet Engineering group. "But it was peanuts compared with what Hall got from R&D.

Penske's Newton Square, Pennsylvania, shop was one of Mark Donohue's "unfair advantages." From left, Karl Kainhofer, Al Holbert and Roy Gaines. Road & Track/Albert Bochroch photo

Chevrolet really treated Roger like an orphan."

One reason for this, Don explained, was that "Research & Development had much more money to spend than Engineering. But Jim Hall himself stood very high at R&D.

Don Cox said, "I guess the best way to describe what I did for Roger is to say that I acted as the liaison between GM Research and Penske Racing." Road & Track

Characteristic Penske quality.

Roger was an outsider . . . R&D were accustomed to working on many of Jim Hall's projects. In fact, I was working on Jim's 2H, the vacuum-cleaner car, before I started to help Penske."

Until recently Don had been an executive with one of Roger Penske's companies, the Philadelphia-based General Motors power distributorship. After Roger decided to divest himself of that business, it was bought by Don and two of his colleagues.

After commenting on how difficult it had become to talk about the brilliant John DeLorean of those earlier days—the DeLorean case was in the news at the time—Don discussed how he came to work with Penske Racing while still at GM, and how he eventually joined Roger as a member of his staff.

"As I had mentioned," Don continued, "Roger and John DeLorean were good friends. This wasn't only in business, they

would often see each other when Roger came to Detroit. During one visit, shortly after DeLorean had been made manager of Chevrolet, he and Roger got together and, naturally, Roger talked about the Trans-Am situation.

"This probably was late in 1968 and by then the Trans-Am was becoming important around Detroit. It was obvious," Don said, "that Roger needed help to keep the Z-28 competitive."

Apparently, one of the first steps taken by Chevrolet's new general manager was to assign Don Cox to the job of seeing that Penske Racing got more factory assistance.

"It was in March 1969," Don went on, "that I got the word. I guess the best way to describe what I did is to say that I acted as the liaison between GM Research & Development and Penske Racing. Even though the Z-28 was a good car, it was not a race car.

After all, no new car out of a dealer's showroom is ready to race.

"Less than a year later, in December of 1969, I left General Motors and came to work for Roger full time. There was a lot to do. As you know, Roger's Z-28s did very well. They won the Trans-Am championship in both '68 and '69. But they did take a lot of work. Even with DeLorean's help it wasn't easy.

"Then, American Motors came to Roger with such a good offer that he really didn't have much choice. When I told Jim Musser, my old boss at General Motors, that I understood that American Motors would pay Roger $2,000,000 to run their Javelin program, Jim simply said, 'If that's the kind of offer he got, there's no way that we can keep him.'"

"No," said Don in reply to my question, "I don't go to races anymore. I'm still inter-

Roger directs Camaro pit stop from front. Note vinyl top and controversial soaring fuel rig. In stands to right are both Road & Track's *Jim*

Crow, in dark glasses leaning on VW sign, and Car and Driver's *David E. Davis, well to Crow's right, with moustache. Penske collection*

ested, but I just don't have the time. There is one exception, though. I go to Indy each year and while I'm there I work on Roger's cars as a part of his crew."

If you watched the 1984 Indy on TV, you may have seen a crewman in a white shirt start to hand Roger a sheet of paper. It was during a tense moment on the track and Roger failed to take it.

Later, near the end of the 500, the camera caught Roger and the same crewman, Don Cox, standing quietly, side by side, along the pit wall. Within minutes they would see the long-standing 162.962 mph 500 race record set by Mark Donohue in Penske's Sunoco Special in 1972, broken by Rick Mears, another Penske driver, when his Pennzoil Z-7 averaged 163.612.

The make changed but Roger, with fire extinguisher in front, still ran a smooth, fast show. Race driver and journalist Pat Bedard, with clipboard, behind Roger. Richard George photo/ AMC collection

Chapter 8

Mark and Parnelli in hit show

There are many ways to measure the popularity of a race series. Prize money, number of races held, the number of cars entered and, the one that counts, paid attendance, all showed gains for the Trans-Am in 1968. Of the year's 316 car total entry, 173 were over-2 liters. Twenty-four cars made up the average field.

Organizers gave the drivers $152,350. Industry shelled-out an additional $52,650, almost all of which went to well-placed finishers who agreed to endorse their products and use their decals on their cars and uniforms.

If we assume that promoters inflated their attendance figures by the same percentage in 1968 as in 1967, Trans-Am gates climbed from 102,000 paid admissions for twelve events in 1967 to 171,000 for thirteen races in 1968.

The 1969 twelve-race series included four new courses. Two of the four dropped were Daytona and Sebring, the SCCA having decided that while the Trans-Am was an endurance series, twenty-four-hour and twelve-hour races were not what it had in mind.

Marlboro, which was on its way to becoming a building project, also was dropped. And Continental Divide chief Syd Lansgan said that he couldn't afford to hold another Trans-Am. Appropriately, the 1969 Championship season opened near Detroit at Michigan International Speedway (MIS).

In addition to MIS, the 1969 series raced at the great Laguna Seca course near Monterey and at two new circuits—Donnybrooke Speedway at Brainerd, Minnesota, and in the hills above Sonoma, near California's wine country at Sears Point International Speedway.

Driver assignments made news. After assuring Ronnie Bucknum that his Z-28 would be equal to Mark Donohue's in every way, Penske announced that he would run a second Camaro. Ford fielded two two-car teams. Bud Moore, whose Spartanburg, South Carolina, based Cougar team came close to shooting-up Shelby's 1966 corral, prepared a pair of Mustangs for two untamed tigers, Parnelli Jones and George Follmer. Shelby went with Peter Revson, who had replaced Jerry Titus in the 1968 final, and Horst Kwech.

Ford also announced a new engine for its Boss 302. Although the engine's over-the-counter pieces remained in short supply

---

FORD MUSTANG, 1969-72
(BOSS 302, BUD MOORE)
Engine: ohv V-8, 302 ci (4942 cc), 460 hp (as high as 475 by mid-1971), dual 4-barrel carb until rules change (inline 4-barrel was used at one point)
Transmission: 4-speed
Brakes: 4-wheel disc (Kelsey-Hayes)
Suspension: front, upper A-arms, coil springs; rear, full floating live axle, adjustable antisway bar, track bar
Weight: 3240 lb
Notes: Street car had 302 ci, 290 hp, front disc/rear drum, 3600 lb. The Boss 302 engine was created by combining the Windsor 289 block with the Cleveland 351 heads. Also included were a solid-lifter camshaft, high-rate valve springs, 4-bolt main bearings, forged pistons, forged steel crank, H-D rods, deep oil pan with windage tray and low-restriction exhaust manifolds for the street version. During the course of development, Ford made many purpose-built parts for the race program, such as the inline 4-barrel carb and forged connecting rods from the 4-cam Indy engine.

until mid-summer, Ford did build 1,300 of the 302s and received their homologation papers before the 1969 season began.

Javelin stayed with John Martin, who had filled a dual driver/mechanic role. And it took on Ron Grable, a young Californian with several SCCA national titles to his credit.

In going with Pontiac, Jerry Titus found that he was handicapped by the need of a great deal of development work, especially on the engine. Pontiac had made a handful of legal 4960 cc, 303 cid engines that were based on its 6560 cc 400s. But less than a month before the first 1969 race, the SCCA rejected Pontiac's bid to have it homologated, as production had failed to come anywhere near the required 1,000 minimum.

Introduced in March of 1969, the Pontiac Firebird was a neat car. But Pontiac had trouble getting its act together. Not until 1972, when the Trans-Am began its slide into the doldrums, did a Firebird record a Trans-Am win.

When Pontiac introduced the Trans Am Firebird, it lacked a suitable engine for the series. Pontiac thought enough of the Trans-Am to name a car after it (and pay the SCCA five dollars per car), but its engine line-up was an unsuitable six and the big 6560 cc 400 cid V-8.

But Jerry and his partner Terry Godsall, pushed on. For a time they ran three updated 1968s for Craig Fisher, Milt Minter and Jerry.

In 1969 neither the Daytona 24 Hours or Sebring 12 was to include the Trans-Am. One wonders if having Mustangs and Camaros finishing fourth and fifth overall in 1968 may not have discomfited the promoters. Also dropped in 1969 were Marlboro and Continental Divide Raceway. Added to 1969's 12-race schedule were Michigan International, California's testing, Laguna Seca and two new circuits, Donnybrooke in Brainerd, Minnesota, and, an hour north of San Francisco, Sears Point. Bud Moore lost his Lincoln-Mercury Cougars but gained two new schoolbus-yellow Boss 302 Mustangs for Parnelli and George Follmer. Shelby began the year with Peter Revson and Horst Kwech, while Jerry Titus started his ill-starred relationship with Pontiac. Backed up by Ronnie Bucknum, Roger Penske and Mark Donohue sailed into 1969 without missing a beat.

The May 18 Michigan opener was a disaster: A spectator was fatally injured. The SCCA timers and scorers miscalculated *both* the under-2 and over-2 winners. And it rained.

The accident occurred on the eighth lap when Kwech spun, although one report said he was ticked, onto slick wet infield grass. Slamming through the retaining fence, Kwech crashed into a spectator's parked car. An American Motors employee, Durward Fletcher, was killed, and a dozen spectators injured.

Qualifying, which had been held in rain and sleet, resulted in the two Bud Moore Mustangs on the front row. Next fastest were the Donohue Camaro and Titus Firebird. Everett's 911 and Revson's Mustang shared the third row. Because they lacked practice times, the last row of the large forty-five-car field, was taken by the Martin and Grable Javelins.

Shelby's number one driver for 1969, Peter Revson. Ford Motor Company

Run for four hours over a new 3.61 mile MIS road course, winner Parnelli Jones completed 104 laps, one more than Donohue and Titus, to register an 85.99 race average. Bob Tullius was fourth in a 1968 Javelin, and under-2-winner Fred Baker's 911 wound up tenth overall.

But these results were not known until more than five hours after the checker fell. Originally, the SCCA posted Donohue and Gary Wright as the winners. But the Bud Moore pits, as well as Penske's (as it turned out), knew that Jones had won. It was a simple error. The scorers had missed Mark's tire change on lap eighty.

Reviewing the race charts also revealed that the under-2 results were wrong. But half the occupants of Detroit's front offices went home thinking that they had congratulated the winners. As very few of the press hung around, most of the nation's newspapers also had the wrong results.

Undoubtedly the MIS fiasco simply was a coincidence. However, the SCCA was entering a period that saw incessant staff changes. John Bishop had gone and soon formed IMSA. Later that year, after it moved to Denver, the SCCA changed executive directors and department personnel with bewildering frequency.

A road accident prevented Ronnie Bucknum from running as Mark's teammate for much of the 1969 season. Roger Penske collection

John Martin, number 4, and Don White started 1969 as Javelin regulars. AMC collection

69

As it conflicted with Indianapolis, pony car regulars Jones, Bucknum, Donohue and Revson missed the May 30 Lime Rock Trans-Am. NASCAR at first refused the suggestion that Richard Petty and Cale Yarborough race Fords at Lime Rock. Then it was rumored that Bill France changed his mind. By then it was too close to race day, so Penske and Ford made other arrangements.

Shelby hired Sam Posey, and Bud Moore called on Swede Savage and Canada's John Cannon. Bob Johnson and Ed Leslie sat in for Donohue and Bucknum.

A strong thirty-car grid headed by Sam Posey and Horst Kwech put on a good show that saw twenty finishers. A native of nearby Sharon, Connecticut, Posey averaged 87.27 mph for 219 miles to win his first major

event. Swede Savage's Mustang was second, Johnson's Camaro third, Cannon's Mustang fourth, Minter's Firebird fifth. Following a race-long battle with Andrey's Alfa, the Adamowicz Porsche captured under-2 honors.

Out at the 500, Revson qualified his underpowered Repco-Brabham thirty-third and finished fifth. However, Peter failed to win the coveted Rookie of the Year award. That honor went to Mark Donohue, who qualified Roger's Lola fourth and finished seventh.

News that would add worry-hours to the Jerry Titus program was that his partner, Terry Godsall, was pulling out. Saying that the SCCA was inconsistent in its rule enforcement policies, the young Canadian

Ronnie Bucknum's Camaro leads tail-end of pack at the 1969 Michigan. Number 54 is the Van Camp Porsche 911, number 72 is the Dunn/Harley Firebird, number 85 is the Dick Long Camaro, number 41 is Gary Wright's Porsche, number 77 is the Campell/Gifford Porsche and number 36 is Wilbur Pickett's 911. Cars shown represent less than half the 45 car field. Roger Penske collection

Ron Grable's failure to qualify his Javelin saw number 3 grid last in the 1969 Michigan Trans-Am. AMC collection

Subbing for ailing Ronnie Bucknum, Ed Leslie failed to finish the 1969 Lime Rock Trans-Am. Note vinyl top. Roger Penske collection

had tried in vain to enlist other teams in his crusade. Now Jerry would carry the administrative as well as the driving responsibilities, for his team.

Ford had registered back-to-back wins going into the June 8 Mid-Ohio 240 where Donohue was fastest of the thirteen drivers (he beat his old record). The thirty-five starters weren't far into the 100 laps when Jones and Follmer had rough-driving complaints filed against them.

Mark and Parnelli were never more than a few yards apart during the first half of the race. Then Mark crawled back in with a broken wheel bearing. Jones stayed out until his second refueling stop, which allowed Bucknum to take over. Jones stormed back

out, but the Camaro held on to finish thirteen seconds in front of the Mustang. Ronnie's 83.53 race average was still another Mid-Ohio record.

Everett's Porsche led the under-2s until his gearbox let go and Peter Gregg's 911 went on to nose out Fred Baker's Porsche. The Follmer and Revson Mustangs filled third and fourth, with fifth place going to Ron Grable's Javelin.

Before the June 22 Bridgehampton 250, 1969 standings showed Mustang with twenty-four points, Camaro eighteen, Firebird six and Javelin five. Bud Moore's Mustangs owned the Bridge that weekend. Par-

Mid-Ohio 1969. Ronnie Bucknum, behind Mark in number 9, was to bring Camaro its first 1969 win. Roger Penske collection

nelli and George shared the front row and Follmer won by eighty-six seconds, the exact margin that Donohue had won by the prior year.

Starting thirty-first and last, because of a car switch, Mark had stormed through the field and was only seconds behind the leaders by lap twenty. Running as a tight troika until lap eighty-one, when Jones retired with an ignition fire, the Mustang and Camaro finished in that order.

Transmission failure sidelined both Kwech and Revson. Grable's Javelin retired with a broken axle and Martin blew his engine. Pete Hamilton, the young New Englander who had been named NASCAR Rookie of the Year in 1968, and whose Camaro was dominating the Grand American series, repeatedly went into the sand, finally flipping on lap fifteen.

Starting fifth on the grid, the Titus Firebird finished a strong third behind Donohue. Independent Rusty Jowett's Camaro was fourth; Revson's Mustang fifth; and seventh overall, Peter Gregg's 911 drove off with under-2 honors.

Dave Tallaksen, the SCCA's chief steward for the Trans-Am series, had his share of detractors. But I can vouch for his sense of humor. . . .

It is minutes before the start. Circling over the Bridge is a high-wing Cessna 206 without a door. In it are four skydivers hired by American Motors. The drill calls for them to land on the track in front of an overflowing AMC hospitality tent.

The pilot's radio-equipped ground guy is standing next to me on the press room deck. Directly below us, on the start/finish line, Tallaksen has been holding an endless driver's meeting. The pilot has been telling his man that he can't hold position much longer. I repeatedly implore Dave to end the meeting and allow the jump. But he can't be hurried.

Just as the jump is about to be scrubbed, Tallaksen whirls, looks up and calls "Okay!" Split seconds later, after four forms had tumbled out of the plane and were in their free fall, Dave wheels about, throws up his hands, and yells, "Hold everything!"

After a race-long tussle with Parnelli Jones, it appeared that the new three-mile Donnybrooke raceway would see Mark's first 1969 win. But a broken crankshaft forced Mark to park on the seventy-ninth lap of the eighty-four-lap race.

Ted Roberts' Javelin, number 55, was to come in sixth at the 1969 Bridgehampton and Donnybrooke. Gordon Means/Road America

Donnybrooke pulled a thin but classy nineteen-car entry. Lloyd Ruby drove a Camaro. Ed Leslie subbed for Ronnie Bucknum (injured in a highway accident). The under-2s were down to five cars, including Peter Gregg, Bert Everett and Fred Baker. Follmer gave Mustang the pole with a 102.46 lap that saw Mark only a hair slower. Donnybrooke was fast, a horsepower course.

When the bunched leaders—Jones, Kwech and Donohue—all pitted together on the sixtieth lap, only Parnelli needed tires. Had Mark's engine stayed healthy, the chances are that Parnelli's tire change would have cost him the race.

Ed Leslie prevented Ford from making it 1-2 by barely beating Revson for second place. Fourth fell to the Titus Firebird as both Javelins retired. Fifth overall and first under-2 was Bert Everett's 911.

Donnybrooke also was the scene of The Great Vinyl Roof Rumble. Two weeks earlier, at Bridgehampton, Roger had been warned to remove the vinyl before the next event. Roger had not done so. At Donnybrooke he was advised that he would not be allowed to race with vinyl-covered roofs. Roger's reply was to say that he would withdraw if forced to do so.

Many conferences and long-distance calls later, Roger was given an exception until the July 20 Bryar. When Javelin and Ford learned of this, they in turn threatened to withdraw.

Bets were being taken on what was under the crinkled vinyl. Under the roof would be found space-age metals; the roof's texture exerted downforce. It would be made of paper-maché, or cheese cake. One observer has suggested that a bar magnet commonly found in a mechanic's tool box would not stick nor display any attraction to the top when laid against the vinyl.

Milt Minter's ailing Pontiac makes an unscheduled stop during the 1969 Bridgehampton. Empty sand dunes in back of paddock indicate the event pulled a small crowd. Carroll Shelby, in dark western hat and white shirt, watches Minter pass.

Actually the Penske Camaro's wrinkled vinyl roof had nothing to do with weight, or aerodynamics, or handling. It was cosmetic.

Acid dipping, or "chemical milling" as it is sometimes called, was used by many Trans-Am teams to lighten body panels. Although the acid-dipped machine still had to meet minimum weight requirements, the weight that was saved could be distributed in places that gave the car better balance or a more desirable weight distribution. In this case, the acid dipping had left unattractive ripples. Being a neat freak, for appearance sake, Roger had the roofs covered.

What seemed to settle the matter at Donnybrooke was that Follmer took the pole from Donohue.

Of all the front-runners, only Parnelli Jones raced on Firestones. Teammate Follmer frequently used Firestones when qualifying, but George often raced on Good-

Revson's Mustang takes on fuel during 1969 Bridge Trans-Am. Shelby team manager, Lew Spencer, is in short-sleeved white shirt on right.

Penske's vinyl roof rhubarb reached its peak at the 1969 Donnybrooke where Mark had one of his rare DNFs. Roger Penske collection

years. Not only was Parnelli's all-out style hard on rubber, there were times when Firestones didn't measure up to Goodyears.

Complicating Jones' problem was his relationship with Firestone. He was a Firestone tire distributor, he owned several Firestone stores in Torrence, California, and his ties went back to Indy when Firestone helped him win the 500. In view of the final 1969 results, Parnelli's loyalty may have been a factor in Ford's defeat.

Mark snapped his losing streak when Penske Camaros filled the first two places in the July 20 Bryar 200. Gaston Andrey's Alfa made news by running away from five 911s on this tight, hilly, 1.6 mile handling course.

Donohue and Jones, by now less than best buddies, again shared the front row, followed by the Leslie Camaro and Revson Mustang. Indicating his intent, Andrey's Alfa GTA out-qualified Porsche hot shoes Gregg and Everett by a full second.

Bryar is where the SCCA got its technical inspection act together, when chief scrutineer Walt Hane and series steward Tallaksen made the rules stick.

Jones took an early lead with Donohue so close to the Mustang's tail that when Parnelli spun off on lap fifteen, Mark's Camaro went with him.

Mark was able to make an immediate restart but Parnelli had trouble getting

underway. Unable to make up the lost restart time, Parnelli finished second, Revson, third, Follmer fourth and the battered Titus Firebird fifth.

Bob Tullius, who had come to Bryar as a spectator, drove a Titus Firebird as only twelve of the twenty-four starters took the checker.

Javelin had another rough day. Grable crashed in practice and Martin went out early with ignition failure. The good news was that Donohue earned $3,500 and that an overflow crowd filled every foot of the New Hampshire hills.

Entering the August 3 St. Jovite 3-Hours with six races down and six to go, Ford had forty-six points, Chevrolet forty, Pontiac fifteen and Javelin eight.

For Ford, St. Jovite was bad news. Jones was sidelined early when a fourteenth-lap pile-up eliminated fourteen cars, including the three works Mustangs. Donohue and pole-sitter Follmer had been running nose-to-tail when the Mustang's engine let go.

Spinning in his own oil, George flew into the guardrail, only to bounce back onto the circuit just as the pack rounded a blind curve. Carnage. The race was stopped for the first red flag in Trans-Am history. One corner worker was seriously injured. Several drivers were hospitalized and held for observation. But the race restarted with twenty-three of the original thirty-seven on the grid.

Donohue won his second straight. The Titus Firebird took second, Leslie's Camaro and Motschenbacher's Javelin were third and fourth with Rusty Jowett's Camaro finishing fifth. Eighth overall was good enough to give Gregg's 911 the under-2 win. Indy ace Johnny Rutherford, Tony Adamowicz and Bert Everett joined the DNF's with nineteen of the thirty-seven starters going the distance.

Milt Minter's Firebird finished fifth in the 1969 Laguna Seca Trans-Am. Road & Track

Ford, with overtime from Shelby-American, Bud Moore Engineering *and* Kar Kraft, managed to replace three of its four cars in only four days. Of the Mustang regulars, only

Horst Kwech lacked a car for Friday practice at Watkins Glen.

Donohue was on a roll. When Mark won his third in a row he had finished 117 laps with a 107.3 mph race average that brought him in a full lap ahead of Parnelli. Although Parnelli had to change tires, if the charts can be believed, this time he was on Goodyears.

Jones and Donohue again shared the front row. But Parnelli only led until his first fuel stop. They were still close when Parnelli stopped for tires. This time Mark went past for good.

Leslie tapped Revson, sending Peter into a spin that left his Mustang hanging helplessly on a curb. Then both Parnelli and Mark were black-flagged and brought in to be dressed-down for passing on the yellow that had resulted from Leslie's brush with Revson.

But Mark was soon to retake the lead and went on to win from a slowing Jones. Rusty Jowett's and Craig Fisher's Camaros finished third and fourth with Ron Grable's Javelin fifth. Gregg's 911 earned nine points, as sixteen of the thirty-two starters completed the distance. Rutherford, Leslie, Revson, Follmer, Minter and Titus were a few of those who fell by the wayside.

Laguna Seca is another of America's better road courses. Lying completely within the grounds of the Fort Ord Army Base on the Monterey Penninsula, the 1.9 mile circuit rises from 700 feet in the pits, to 940 feet along its back straight. The Trans-Am ran on few tracks that called for better driving than Laguna's Cork Screw and turn nine.

Donohue and Jones at Riverside in 1969—the ultimate shoot out. Bob Tronelone/Road & Track

Ford was desperate. Penske's Camaro's had won three straight. Shelby hired his old AAR (All American Racers) partner, Dan Gurney. Daring Dan was every bit as much of an apple-pie-All-American-boy as Mark and, depending on your predilection, a better driver. But the best Dan could do at Laguna was to qualify eighth, behind Follmer, Jones, Donohue, Titus, Grable and Revson, in that order. At Laguna both of Bud Moore's front-row Mustangs stayed shod with a new type of Firestone tire.

New faces at Laguna included the often-underrated Scooter Patrick, fastest of the under-2 qualifiers, and Elliott Forbes-Robinson, whose future was to include a Trans-Am championship. Also at Laguna was Steve Griswold in a 1966 Alfa GTA. Young Griswold didn't make news, but his name did— his father Frank had won the first Watkins Glen.

Except for agreeing that Mark Donohue's Camaro was first, tech and scoring protests filled the day. Shelby team manager Lew Spencer protested Penske's cars as being underweight. They weren't. Penske protested that both the Bud Moore and Shelby fueling rigs were beyond the legal height. They were.

Once again, not until the fans and press had long gone did final results become official. Ed Leslie was second, not Gurney, who was third. Revson's Mustang finished fourth. Minter's Firebird fifth and under-2 went to Gregg's Porsche.

By averaging 90.43 mph for 227 laps, Mark gave Chevrolet an eleven-point lead, sixty-seven to fifty-six, with three races to go.

His highway accident injuries healed, Ronnie Bucknum returned to the Trans-Am wars at Seattle in time to deal Ford a crush-

Ed Leslie, who substituted for Donohue, during 1969 Lime Rock pit stop. Road & Track

ing loss. The September 8 Kent 300 also saw Horst Kwech ready to jump in. But, with Gurney and Revson handling Shelby's pair, and Bud Moore naturally staying with Jones and Follmer, the Australian became Ford's backup driver.

Donohue's 1:27.8 Kent qualifying record was broken by seven drivers, with his own 1:25.2 and Jones' 1:25.3 sharing the front row. Jerry Titus, who had hired the former SCCA tech manager, Walt Hane, to look after his cars, sat next to Follmer on the second row, with the Gurney and Revson Mustangs filling row three.

Again, fastest of the independents was Rusty Jowett's Camaro. Grable's Javelin broke during practice and Jerry Grant took the other AMC entry. Roy Woods drove a Camaro in the first of his many Trans-Ams.

Neither of the Ford teams managed a full quota of practice laps—the entire Mustang entourage had food poisoning! But race day found them at the barricades, sufficiently recovered from what the pits, with apologies to Montezuma, called Roger's Revenge.

Jones got a fast start and by lap ten was six seconds up on Donohue and Follmer. First Follmer, then Donohue made unscheduled tire stops and Jones slowed his pace. Cutting the apex of Kent's turn six resulted in littering the track with sharp-edged stones. Both Bud Moore cars were on Firestones, but the problem hit teams using Goodyears as well.

Mark called it a day after taking a stone through his windscreen at the same time his engine began to go sour. Jones, Gurney and Bucknum were running close in that order when Parnelli pulled in for two rear tires. He got back out in time to take third, but in the meantime Bucknum had passed Gurney.

With Penske's crew giving Bucknum five-second fuel stops, the Camaro stayed in front until overtaken by Jones at the halfway point. Bud Moore and Carroll Shelby must have aged twenty years in the next twenty minutes!

Gurney's dif went bad. While it was being replaced, Follmer roared in for two new tires. Still running 1-2, Jones and Bucknum pulled in for fuel on lap seventy-three at the same time. Jones had a ten-second lead when he came in. But Penske's crew got Ronnie out first and Jones was never able to make up the difference—each time he closed in, the Mustang had tire problems.

Then Gurney, who had raced hard to make up much of the time he lost getting a new rear, got a rock through his windshield. Jones was now in fifth place; he never let up, but both he and Follmer were to have still more tire troubles. Being a prudent man, Bucknum slowed down to finish more than a lap ahead of Jones.

Titus brought his Firebird home third. Revson was fourth, Craig Fisher's Camaro fifth and tenth overall and first under-2 was Peter Gregg's 911. Only twelve of the strong, thirty-seven car field, completed the full 303 miles.

An appropriate heading for a report of the September 14 Sears Point 200 would have been, "Penske's Pits Clinch Title." The penultimate 1969 Trans-Am saw Jones with a new car. As Shelby only had one car ready for Sears Point, Kwech was to take Gurney's place in the Bud Moore car.

Again, Jones and Donohue sat on the front row. Only this time the Ford was a remarkable two full seconds faster than the Camaro. Follmer and Titus were followed by Kwech, Bucknum, Revson and Grable.

Dan Gurney didn't show up for Sears Point practice. The rumors flew. Dan had quit. Ford racing boss, Jacque Passino, who was at Sears Point, had ordered Carroll to fire Dan. One possible reason for Dan's behavior may have been the result of "secret" tests that showed Bud Moore's cars to average a full second faster than Shelby's. Dan would be back, but not with Ford.

The story of the race is a simple one: Jones led for sixty-nine of the eighty laps, Jones' single fuel stop took fourteen seconds. Replacing his two rear tires consumed fifty-two seconds. Jones' two pit stops took sixty-six seconds. Donohue made three pit stops. The two for fuel took 5.1 and 3.3 seconds. His tire change lasted 26.5 seconds. The three Camaro pit stops totaled 34.9 seconds, 31.1 seconds faster than the Mustang's two stops. Jones' losing margin was *2.17* seconds.

Sears Point had been a tough weekend in many ways. Bert Everett's post-race protest against Javelin driver Ron Hunter "for unprovoked contact" was upheld. Hunter was fined $50.

Follmer, Titus and Bucknum filled the three spots behind Donohue and Jones. First under-2 and eleventh overall was Elliott Forbes-Robinson's 911.

It all came to boil at Riverside in the Mission Bell 200 on October 5, the final Trans-Am of the season.

Mark and Parnelli had never been friends, but they had shown each other mutual respect. There had been a couple of Moore/Penske rough spots before. One, as Mark admits in his book, had been his fault.

Firestone had a sort of secret new low-profile tire that Mark wanted to try. As Mark relates, he was not happy with the way he went about borrowing a set. That the Firestones proved faster, but were subject to more wear than Mark's Goodyears, got lost in the storm.

Firestone accused Mark of spying. Penske, Goodyear, Ford and Jones were annoyed at his lack of judgement. As Mark wrote, "I couldn't blame Firestone for their reaction, but at the time, if they were that concerned they should have kept closer control over the tires." Mark tried to apologize at Kent, but Jones was too upset to accept.

Feuds between race drivers go back to the beginning of the sport. Although it usually takes the form of tactics, not contact. The rivalry between Barney Oldfield and Ralph DePalma is a cornerstone of racing folklore.

What follows is how Mark and his collaborator, Paul Van Valkenburgh, describe the stalking and showdown at Riverside.

"Parnelli was so furious at Kent that he couldn't even talk to me. We had been friends—at least professionally—up to that point, so I went up to him to apologize for the way things turned out with the tires. That was really the end of our friendship, though. He reckoned that I had knifed him in the back when it came down to the point where our success, and our jobs, were on the line. I can't say for sure, but that could have had something to do with a bash Parnelli and I got into at Riverside.

"Follmer was leading the race there, and when I came out of the pits after a fuel stop, I was right ahead of Parnelli. Going down through the esses I was a lot heavier, and since I still had fuel running off the rear of the car, I was relatively slow. Going into turn six, which is the slowest turn on the track, I put my brakes on normally—and Parnelli came up and rammed me in the back. I thought, "Christ! Now what did he do *that* for? Did he skid on my spilled fuel, or is this the big showdown?" I knew it couldn't have hurt me very much, and I figured it didn't hurt his car either. So I continued on. But I looked back and I couldn't see him any more. A few laps later I went into the esses—and there was Parnelli again, going real slow. I thought he must have gotten a flat tire or something, so I started around on the outside—and he turned into my path. I pulled up behind him, and then he put on his brakes! I ran right into him. I spun off the track and stalled my engine, while Parnelli drove around to the pits.

"However, we had built those cars from the very beginning to take that kind of punishment and keep running. Naturally we wanted most of the weight to the rear for better handling, but we also made sure there was nothing vulnerable in the crush space in the nose. The oil coolers were back in the fenders behind the front tires, all electrics were isolated, and there was no sharp objects ahead of the radiator that could puncture it in a collision. I took a tremend-

Bob Tullius did drive a Javelin at Michigan, but it was number 33. AMC collection

ous hit, but everything flexed around and there was no serious damage.

"Follmer was still in the lead, but I was running quicker by then. Finally I unlapped myself from him, and as I passed I gave him a sign to indicate that I had one lap to make up yet. I guess he got incensed at that somehow. He started trying harder, and he took himself out of the race. He broke a front wheel in a turn and limped all the way around to the pits on the brake disc—where he ran into the pit wall and destroyed his car. I came in first, with Bucknum second, and we won the Trans-Am Championship again.

"In the meantime, Parnelli had gone to the press and complained that I put my brakes on and busted his radiator intentionally. He told everyone that I was really a dirty guy, when in fact he had obviously waited around to finish me off. I hadn't meant to cause trouble, but what he had done was totally unnecessary. I was kind of pissed when I heard that, but racing is racing, and we had won after all, and Homer Perry was looking bad. So I went down to their pits to apologize. I guess that was the wrong thing to do at that point, but I figured that if Parnelli was so mad he was going to punch me in the nose, it was better now than waiting for it. Everyone had been drinking it up, though, and they became very, very nasty. What stands out in my mind is that they said I had a halo reputation with the press and the public, but really I was a rotten SOB underneath. All I could do was just stand there

J. A. Lagod's 1968 Camaro of Michigan. Flimsy catch fencing, seen behind the car, contributed to severity of the accident in the wet. Road America

and take it like a man. Parnelli had already left by then. The next day I tried to call him at his Firestone tire dealership to apologize, but he wasn't in. I really made an effort to reach him, but he was not here . . . and not there . . . so I finally gave up. Much later I heard a rumor from one of his guys that there was nothing really wrong with Parnelli's car—he was just so mad that he drove it in and parked it. He and I raced against each other some in the next year's Trans-Am. We would say hello occasionally, but we never really had any conversation after that."

The Parnelli-and-Mark show shared the front row at Riverside. This time the Firestone-shod Mustang was a full second faster than Penske's Camaro. Follmer and Revson filled row two. The Titus Firebird and Bucknum Camaro were next. Al Unser's Bud Moore Mustang sat next to Jerry Grant's Javelin on row four. Midway down the thirty-six-car grid, future Trans-Am champion David Hobbs made his pony car debut in a 1968 Firebird.

Riverside's short sedan course had been repaved and now measured 2.5 miles. The new surface also proved to be very abrasive and tire wear during practice was excessive.

Repeating the season-long script, Jones and Donohue pulled away from the field. Moore's pits got busy on lap twenty-two when Unser coasted in with a smoking engine. Minutes later Parnelli pulled in with a flat tire. Two laps later, he stormed back in to have his wheel lugs tightened. What this sort of oversight cost in time can be measured. What it did to Parnelli's morale is something else.

The stewards called Jerry Titus in for rough driving. But Jerry didn't get either an official reprimand or a fine when he explained that his actions had been the result of a sticking throttle.

Jones was out of the race on lap thirty-four. Follmer had gotten two good five-second fuel stops and was running thirty seconds ahead of Donohue at the two-thirds mark. Minutes later, on lap sixty-seven of the 100 lap race, the leading Mustang lost a wheel. Follmer tried to make the pits but barged into a wall head-on.

Donohue, who tooled in with a 95.76 mph race average, was followed by the Bucknum Camaro, Titus Firebird, Revson Mustang and Jowett Camaro. Alan Johnson's 911 picked up first in under-2 and $2,500.

The 1969 final standings were Chevrolet seventy-eight, Ford sixty-four, Pontiac thirty-two and American Motors fourteen. Under-2 showed Porsche with eighty-one points to Alfa Romeo's twenty-eight, BMW nine and BLMC (Austin/Morris) four.

Even though Porsche ended the year with eleven wins, the pleasure was short lived. Effective January 1, 1970, the 911 lost its sedan classification. Revised FIA/SCCA sedan interior measurements eliminated the 911.

For Penske's Camaros to have come back after losing four of the first five races was as much a tribute to Roger's meticulous preparation and his precisely drilled pit crews, as it was to Mark's superb driving.

Ford's reaction to losing the 1969 championship was to come out swinging. Dodge and Plymouth fielded new factory teams in 1970. Penske announced his intention to run Javelins. Displaying numbers 1 and 2 on his Camaros, Jim Hall carried the colors for Chevrolet.

The 1970 Trans-Am shaped-up as the ultimate Detroit shoot-out.

Chapter 9

For Ford less is Moore

The 1970 Trans-Am began to generate news in October of 1969 when Dan Gurney told a packed Los Angeles press conference that he had signed to drive for Chrysler.

Dan said that he would be making "a concentrated effort" and that testing would soon start at Willow Springs and Riverside. Destroked 340 cid, 5570 cc engines were to power the Plymouth Division's new AAR Barracudas. Dan would not be using Keith Black's Chrysler engines; almost all of the work would be done in Dan's own shop.

All American Racers' second Barracuda would be driven by Dan's great young proté-gé, Swede Savage. When questioned, Dan admitted that he had been approached by several other manufacturers but stated, "The lack of politics at Plymouth will allow me to devote more time to a complete racing effort."

One week later American Motors announced that Roger Penske had signed a three-year contract to develop and race a two-car team of AMC Javelins. The Sun Oil Company, at the time Roger's largest sponsor, said that it was coming along and that the Penske Javelins would be painted "Red, White and SUNOCO blue."

Never one to make rash statements, Jim Hall confirmed that Firestone Tires would help to support Chaparral Racing's factory-blessed Camaro project in the 1970 Trans-Am.

Weeks earlier Dodge had started a search that narrowed down to Bob Tullius and Sam Posey. One Dodge Challenger was involved and Salesman Sam was the winner. Ray Caldwell, a well-known Formula V builder/driver and long-time Posey associate, would maintain Posey's Dodge.

Until the time of Ford's year-end announcement, it had been assumed that the Ford Motor Company, in its eagerness to regain the Trans-Am title, would redouble its Trans-Am effort. Then Henry Ford II dropped a bombshell. Ford's 1970 racing

---

PLYMOUTH AAR 'CUDA (ALL-AMERICAN RACERS) AND DODGE CHALLENGER T/A (AUTODYNAMICS), 1970
Engine: ohv V-8, 303.8 ci (Keith Black-built), 440-450 hp (destroked 340), single 4-barrel carb
Transmission: 4-speed
Brakes: 4-wheel disc
Suspension: front, independent upper and lower A-arms, torsion bars; rear, live axle, leaf springs
Weight: 3000 lb
Notes: The street cars were the AAR 'Cuda and Challenger T/A, 340 ci, 290 hp, dual 3-barrel carb, 3-speed automatic or 4-speed manual, front disc/rear drum, 3250 lb. The 303 Trans Am engine was derived from the 340 "six-pack" engine block with big port heads, forged-steel cross-drilled crankshaft, forged rods, 4-bolt main bearing.

AMC JAVELIN, 1970 (PENSKE)
Engine: ohv V-8 (Traco-built), 305 ci (destroked 360), 375-440 hp, single 4-barrel carb
Transmission: 4-speed (Borg-Warner)
Suspension: front, independent upper and lower A-arms, coil springs, Koni adjustable shocks; rear, live axle, leaf springs, Panhard rod, antisway bar, Koni shocks
Weight: 3050 lb
Notes: Street car was the Javelin SST Mark Donohue Special 3500, 360 or 390 ci, 290 or 304 hp, 3200 lb. AMC developed special engine pieces as did its "Big 3" rivals. These included aluminum intake manifolds, H-D crankshafts and 4-bolt main blocks.

budget was to be cut by seventy-five percent.

Ford would not disclose how much the company had spent on racing in 1969. He simply said that all Ford racing programs would have to make do with one quarter of their 1969 total.

It first appeared that Ford's 1970 effort would be limited to a single Bud Moore Mustang for Parnelli Jones. Confirming this, in late November Parnelli was seen testing a 1970 Mustang at Sears Point.

A couple of major privateers were in the wings. Owens-Corning Fiberglas announced that it would sponsor a team of two Camaros. Tony DeLorenzo, the son of a reportedly embarrassed GM vice president, and a Chevrolet project engineer, Jerry Thompson, were to drive the Owens-Corning cars. The Toledo glass maker also announced plans to sponsor a Corvette entry in Daytona and Sebring. But the company made it clear that its major effort was to be the Trans-Am.

Atlanta Firestone distributor Gene White, a backer of the Indy cars, was readying a Camaro for the veteran oval track and sports car racer Lloyd Ruby. Jerry Titus decided to forget building Pontiac Firebirds for customers and concentrate on his own race cars.

In the end, big-buck, well-managed independents such as Owens-Corning and Gene White had few good placings—an indication of just how tough the Trans-Am league was.

New for 1970 were over-2 specs that allowed 3,400 pound minimum weight when filled with fuel, or 3,200 pounds dry. New sedan homologation requirements that affected NASCAR as well as the Trans-Am called for 2,500 units, or 1/250 of the 1969 model's total production.

As the larger figure became the base for all the higher volume, more popular cars such as the Mustang and Camaro needed to show that they had produced 6,500 units within the first quarter.

By early April, just a couple of weeks before the season opener, only the AMC Javelin had its papers in order. However, postponements were granted to both Ford and Chevrolet, and verifications were eventually made.

But Ford lost its bid to homologate the new carburetor setup it had planned for the 351 Cleveland engine used in the Boss 302 Mustang. Ford had met the 500 minimum production, but was turned down because the carb was not available through Ford dealers.

Also new in 1970 was the rule that transmissions have no more than four speeds forward and that Trans-Am transmission

Follmer's Boss 302 going through 1970 Laguna Seca Tech. Fran Hernandez, with glasses, is on the left; on the right, Bud Moore. Cam Warren photo/Road & Track

---

**CHEVROLET CAMARO Z-28, 1970
(OWENS-CORNING TEAM AND CHAPARRAL)**

Engine: ohv V-8 (built by Competition Services, Owens-Corning, Gerald Davis, Chaparral), 302 ci, 440 hp, single 4-barrel carb

Transmission: 4-speed

Brakes: 4-wheel disc

Suspension: Owens-Corning team relocated the rear pickup points for the leaf springs and added an anti-sway bar.

Weight: 3300 lb

Notes: Street car had 350 ci, 370 hp, single 4-barrel carb, 3650 lb. For 1971 dry-sump lubrication was allowed, the Owens-Corning team duly installed this, along with a new intake manifold. The rear suspension came in for much change as well, with the fuel tank becoming a part of the rear sub-frame, allowing solid mounting of the rear antisway bar and Watts linkage. The T/G Racing Team converted one of its 1970 Firebirds to 1971 Camaro sheet metal to be able to run the Chevrolet engine again.

Laguna Seca 1970. First lap, season's first race. Parnelli Jones and Mark Donohue had shared the front row but Jones is already out of sight. Donohue's number 6 Javelin leads the number 16 Follmer Mustang, number 48 Gurney Plymouth, number 77 Posey Dodge, number 1 Hall Camaro, number 8 Titus Pontiac and, dark car on left, Revson Javelin.

1970 Laguna Seca, Jones in pits. Hustle shown by Bud Moore crew member was typical of effort made by entire Ford crew during the 1970 season. Cam Warren/Road & Track

Jones' Mustang taking Leslie's Camaro on Laguna's corkscrew. Road & Track

modifications be available from dealers as advertised options.

John Timanus became an exception to the SCCA's revolving-door antics, bringing stability to the club's technical inspection procedures. In May, savvy Burdette Martin of Chicago replaced Dave Tallaksen as the Trans-Am's chief steward. Prize money and promoter sanction fees again increased. Most drastic of all, the character of the series was changed when the SCCA banished the under-2s. Beginning in 1970 all under-2 races were separate events.

———————

Trans-Am racing reached its peak in 1970. The Dan Gurney/Swede Savage works Barracudas, Jim Hall's factory-blessed Camaros, an official Dodge for Sam Posey, Roger Penske's American Motors-supported Javelins, plus strong privateers such as the Owens-Corning Fiberglas Camaros and Jerry Titus Pontiac, all had the same objective: beating Bud Moore's Mustangs.

New for 1970 were regulations calling for no more than four forward speeds and all transmission modifications to be advertised options or dealer available. Also new in 1970, the under-2 series ran as separate events.

———————

Ford's drastic budget cut wasn't racing's only bad news. General Motors suffered a sixty-five-day strike that contributed to an eight-year low in total domestic auto sales. But the sale of imports, of which ninety percent were from Japan, showed 1,230,931 units in 1970, against 1,061,617 in 1969.

Terms such as "emissions" and "environment" became commonplace. US Transportation Secretary John Volper became critical of Detroit advertising that featured "speed and muscle cars."

Yet the ambivalence that marked GM's attitude toward auto racing—originally Chevrolet had been reluctant to produce the 1,000 Z-28s required by an earlier Trans-Am homologation rule—was gone. The company began using ads with such headings as, "We'll take on any other two cars in this magazine," and, "A word or two to the competition: You Lose!"

During the winter of 1969-70, Mark Donohue became involved in launching a new racetrack, Chesapeake International Race-

Turn nine Laguna Seca 1970. Revson is in number 9, Savage number 42, Titus number 8. Note: numbers 9 and 42 lean slightly, while number 8 reflects Jerry's preference for a rock-hard setup. Deke Houlgate collection

way (CIS). Planned as a $5,000,000 computer-designed three-mile circuit on a 410 acre site near Elkton, Maryland, the SCCA had promised CIS a full calendar of race dates. Mark was more than a personality lending his name to the venture, he worked at it; but it never flew.

Everyone complained about not being ready for the April 19 season opener at Laguna Seca. But most of it was talk. Detroit was "loaded for bear."

Jim Hall had two immaculately prepared white Camaros, number 1 for himself and number 2 for Ed Leslie. Chaparral's twenty-five-man shop at Rattlesnake Raceway had spent the winter building and testing the gleaming coupes. It looked as though Chevrolet had come out of the Penske/Hall switch smelling like a rose. But Chevrolet only won a single race.

Just when it seemed that Ford was to go with one car for Parnelli Jones, Bud Moore added a schoolbus-yellow Boss 302 for George Follmer. Friends and rivals since their Morgan and Elva days, Peter Revson joined Donohue as Penske's second driver.

Donohue put a large number 6 on his red-white-and-blue Javelin. Swede Savage and Dan Gurney were in fast but fragile Cudas. Sam Posey introduced his acid-green Challenger. Still battling with the problems of being an independent, Jerry Titus was back with a new Firebird.

On April 18 a sparse fourteen-car field of imports was the curtain-raiser for a big over-2 season.

Californian Lee Midgly's Alfa averaged 83.27 to win over Nels Miller's BMW. But the post-race inspection revealed the BMW to be illegal, so second place went to Don Pike's similar make. Horst Kwech, whose Alfa sat on the pole, and who was the only former under-2 winner in the field, suffered from tire trouble.

PONTIAC FIREBIRD, 1970-72
Engine: ohv V-8 (destroked 400), 305 ci, 450-480 hp, single 4-barrel carb
Transmission: 4-speed
Brakes: 4-wheel disc with hydraulic servo assist, increasing line pressure and curing brake troubles from 1969
Suspension: forged-steel spindles added to front

Titus number 8 Pontiac leads Posey Dodge during 1970 Laguna Seca. Deke Houlgate collection

1970 would be Jerry's last season. One of the most popular drivers of his time, Jerry Titus exemplified the best in motor racing. Deke Houlgate collection

The year's first Tech session stirred up a storm. Both the Hall Camaro's and Firebird's rear-deck spoilers were tossed-out for failing to be homologated. Bud Moore's clever use of headlight vents for brake cooling also was disallowed and Titus was required to remove his Firebird's air scoop (although approved for the Trans-Am Firebird, the air scoop was not listed for standard Firebirds).

Both Bud Moore and Jim Hall disagreed with Tech. Hall practiced with and without the spoiler. Still unhappy over being stuck with a single Holley Ford carburetor, Bud Moore took his problem to the chief steward, but to no avail.

The Mark-and-Parnelli show picked up where it had left off with Jones' 1969½ Mustang and Marle's new Javelin sharing row one. Follmer's Mustang and Gurney's Bar-racuda lined up behind them. Posey's Challenger and Leslie's Camaro occupied row three and they were followed by the Titus Firebird and Savage Cuda. Hall's and Minter's 1969 Camaros were on row five. Last of the pros was Revson's ailing Javelin, eighteenth on the twenty-one-car grid.

Both Hall and Gurney retired early with engine troubles. Parnelli pulled away from Donohue and stayed out front until the Mustang went in for tires on the thirty-third lap. Bud Moore's cars again were on Firestones. But this year's Firestones were competitive and Moore's pit work was fast.

Jones was able to overtake Donohue, setting the fastest race lap in doing so. Gradually pulling away, Parnelli covered ninety laps with a record 91.375 race average, the Mustang getting the checker forty seconds before the Javelin.

BMW 2002, 1969-72
Engine: sohc inline 4, 124 ci (2032 cc), 200 hp, dual 2-barrel Solex carb
Transmission: 5-speed
Brakes: 4-wheel disc
Suspension: front, struts, coil springs, antisway bar; rear, independent semitrailing arm, coil springs, antisway bar
Chassis: front engine, rear-wheel drive
Weight: 1975 lb
Notes: Street car had 122 ci (1998 cc), 95 hp, single 2-barrel, 4-speed, front disc/rear drum, 2200 lb.

ALFA ROMEO 1750 GTV/GTAM, 1970-72
Engine: dohc inline 4, 110 ci (1810 cc), 205 hp, dual 2-barrel Weber carb
Transmission: 5-speed
Brakes: 4-wheel disc
Suspension: front, upper and lower A-arms, coil springs; rear, live axle, coil springs
Chassis: front engine, rear-wheel drive
Weight: 2245 lb
Notes: Street car had 1725 cc, 132 hp, 2400 lb.

Swede Savage (left) and Dan Gurney practice at Lime Rock 1970.

Savage (left) and Gurney in pits, Lime Rock 1970.

In third, one lap back, George Follmer finished in front of Swede Savage, who was followed by Milt Minter and Sam Posey. For a team whose international reputation was made as much on reliability as winning, it must have been difficult for Jim Hall when both Chaparral Camaros failed to go the distance.

Most impressive had been the improvement in Bud Moore's pit work. Hauling his entire supply of race cars, two untried 1970s and the updated 1969, Parnelli had switched to the older car when one of the 1970 engines went off song.

The second Trans-Am in the eleven-race series had been scheduled for April 26 at the new Dallas Raceway in Lewisville, Texas. Heavy rains had flooded the circuit, and the surrounding grounds were seas of mud. First the event was postponed, then it was dropped.

More critical than the flooding and mud was the basically poor design of the track. Much of the circuit was run alongside sharp drop-offs with only a narrow berm between the track surface and parallel ditches. As one expert who tried Lewisville said, "It was like running on the edge of a tea cup."

Gurney number 48 and Savage number 42, at speed Lime Rock 1970.

Taking a leaf from NASCAR's successful Grand American Championship, in which both Javelins and Camaros shone, April of 1970 saw USAC launch its own thirty-race pony car series over mid-western ovals.

Seventeen imports entered the May 9 under-2 at Lime Rock. Swiss-born Gaston Andrey gave Alfa its second win after a race-long struggle with Kwech's Alfa and Don Pike's BMW. But the Pike BMW was one of five BMW's, one of which was disqualified for illegal heads, to DNF.

The following day's feature saw Jones nurse a sick engine to an easy full-lap win over Leslie's Camaro. Donohue and Gurney had earned the front row, followed by Jones and Leslie. The Savage Cuda, Revson Javelin, Follmer Mustang and Titus Firebird filled the next two rows. Hall and Posey sat on row

Jim Hall's Camaro. Note Chaparral nameplate on hood. Road & Track

Hall Camaro number 1.

Parnelli's Mustang on teammate Follmer's tail. Lime Rock practice, 1970. Ford Motor Company

Posey team manager, Ray Caldwell, and Sam with Dodge.

Note engine-builder Keith Black decal on block of Posey Challenger. Sam said that the engine was the strongest part of the car. Road & Track

Posey Dodge leads Hall Camaro, 1970 Lime Rock. Sam Posey collection

five in front of solid privateers Craig Fisher and Paul Nichter in older Camaros. Because of inadequate practice times, the touted Tony DeLorenzo Owens-Corning Camaro started twenty-third and last.

Tech saw fewer than the usual number of hassles. Only days prior to Lime Rock, the Automobile Competition Committee for the United States (ACCUS) had approved both the Camaro and Firebird rear deck spoilers.

In the beginning, Lime Rock had been a good tight race with Donohue and Jones running close for thirty of the 146 laps. But Mark began to fall back and retired with falling oil pressure on lap seventy-six.

Then Jim Hall and Ed Leslie had messed-up pit stops that required both of their Camaros to revisit the Chaparral pits to pick up missing gas caps. Lap forty-six saw Revson's big number 9 make life miserable for himself and the entire field when his engine let go and dumped all of its oil on the track, squarely in the middle of the pit entrance.

Gurney, who had fallen back with a smoking engine, drove hard to get back up to sixth. But the fumes made Dan ill, forcing him to retire on lap seventy-six. When asked if Swede Savage, who had fallen out with a busted engine, could take over Dan's Cuda, the race stewards refused.

At the end of 2.5 hours only ten of the twenty-three over-2s were still running. Ed Leslie came in second, more than a lap behind Parnelli, with home-town-hero Posey in third. Jim Hall finished fourth and two privateers, Paul Nichter and Vince Gimondo, brought their 1968 and 1969 Camaros home fifth and sixth.

What may have made Parnelli's 88.91 winning average especially sweet was that post-race inspection revealed his Mustang had faulty brakes and a broken pushrod.

The May 31 Bryar 2-Hours was held the day following Indy where Donohue had finished thirty-two seconds behind winner Al Unser who had driven Jones' Johnny Lightning Special. Keeping it in the family, Gurney finished the 1970 500 in third place. Both Revson and Follmer qualified for the 500, but broken engines prevented them from going the distance.

Using corporate aircraft, the Speedway brigade had shuttled between New Hampshire and Indiana. Then, after running the Trans-Am, many of the teams returned to Indianapolis for the first million-dollar-plus awards dinner.

Bryar saw Mustang win its third straight. But this time it was Follmer who came up from his seventh spot on the grid to finish ninety-three laps, three in front of the

First lap, 1970 Lime Rock. Jones Mustang, Donohue Javelin, Leslie Camaro and Gurney Plymouth lead the pack. Road & Track

second- and third-place Javelins driven by Revson and Donohue, respectively.

Swede Savage had stuck Dan's big blue number 48 on the pole. And with Parnelli's yellow Mustang the front row looked like an Easter parade.

The combination of Chrysler's racing cutbacks and Bruce McLaren's tragic accident saw Dan Gurney return to other forms of racing, mostly in Formula One and the CanAm for Team McLaren. Swede Savage ran out the season in what was largely a single-car effort. But at Bryar the Cuda lost its transmission on lap thirty-three of the ninety-three-lap 150 mile event.

Donohue pits during 1970 Lime Rock Trans-Am. Penske, crouched in front of the Javelin, directs his customary smooth pit stop. Note Judy Stropus behind pits board on truck. Road & Track

Follmer's Mustang takes on fuel at Lime Rock, 1970. Road & Track

Follmer Boss 302, Lime Rock practice.

Parnelli had opened a good lead only to be black-flagged off the course on lap sixty-two after his Mustang lost its hood. Freelancer Gordon Dewar brought his 1969 Camaro in fourth. Jim Hall finished fifth and veteran Bob Grossman's Camaro was sixth, as only twelve of the twenty-five starters went the distance.

BMW won its first Trans-Am when race-leader Kwech's Alfa suffered fuel-pickup problems while leading until the fortieth lap of the forty-five-lap under-2 feature. Kwech refueled to come in second, eight seconds behind Peter Schuster's Bavarian bread box.

Except for their failure to make the front row of the starting grid, an honor earned by Donohue's Javelin and Leslie's Camaro, Bud Moore's Mustangs turned the June 7 Mid-Ohio 180 into a Ford benefit.

Only when Jones and Follmer came in for fuel, Parnelli's stop was timed at twelve seconds, did the Mustangs lose their lead. On one occasion, when Jones was slowed by a shunt with a private Mustang, Follmer slowed so as not to pass the team leader, a display of discipline undreamed of in George's earlier years.

Sixty-eight seconds behind Jones was Donohue's third-place Javelin. Maurice Carter's Camaro, Posey's Challenger and Warren Agor's Camaro filled fourth through sixth.

The dreaded "client in attendance" gremlins struck again. Owens-Corning company brass packed Mid-Ohio only to watch Jerry Thompson destroy his Camaro in practice and watch Tony DeLorenzo bring his battered Fiberglass Special in tenth.

Porsche regular, Bert Everett, who had never sat in an Alfa until two days before the June 7, under-2 at Mid-Ohio, brought the Italian coupe its third 1970 win. Not entered until late Thursday, Bert told *Competition Press*, "These are much faster cars than my Porsches ever were."

With fourteen under-2s on the grid, both Everett's and Kwech's Alfas and the Hans Ziereis BMW broke the under-2 qualifying record set by Tony Adamowicz in a Porsche. Only eight under-2s completed the seventy-two miles, as Alfas filled first through fourth. Craig Fisher's 1100 cc Fiat-Abarth was fifth and Bob Lazebnik's BMW was sixth and five other BMW's retired with broken engines.

Inevitably the Penske-Donohue combination of meticulous preparation and brilliant driving would see Mark boot a Javelin into victory lane. As Mark points out in his book, *the unfair advantage*, it didn't happen a moment too soon, as AMC had planned to cancel Penske's contract until Mark won at Bridge.

The 1970 Donnybrooke saw Milt Minter bring Roy Woods' 1969 Camaro into victory lane, becoming the first independent to win a Trans-Am since February 1967 when Bob Tullius won Daytona in his Dodge. Pete Luongo photo, Road & Track

Tony Adamowicz (center) with Posey (left) and Ray Caldwell at 1970 Mid-Ohio. Ron Lathrop/ Road & Track

The Javelin's first Trans-Am win was all the sweeter because Mark snapped Ford's four-straight skein in a driving rain on his "home" circuit before many of his fans.

Finishing a solid two laps in front of Follmer and Jones made the AMC's maiden win look easy. It wasn't. During the early stages of the June 21 Bridgehampton 200, Donohue had been pushed by both Jones and Savage. Only after the Barracuda and Mustang faltered was he able to break free and cruise home with, for conditions, a fast 90.55 race average.

On the pole with a 1:43, 100.01 qualifying lap, Swede Savage immediately stuck the Cuda out front, leaving Jones and Donohue fighting for second place. But the rain that started on lap ten gave Mark a chance to show his mastery of the rolling Long Island circuit.

While all three front runners made good first pit stops, Mark was out first. Parnelli overcooked things trying to catch the Javelin and wound up in the dunes with two left-side flats.

By mid-race Mark had a thirty-six-second lead over Swede. Then the Cuda lost its differential and Follmer moved into second place. The race stewards then made the error of black-flagging Follmer, rather than Jones, for having had too many men over the wall during his tire change. So Follmer not only lost second place, but had slid back to fourth before the mistake was realized.

Donnybrooke winner Milt Minter. Road & Track

Drivers meeting, Road America 1970. Ed Leslie, left, Jim Hall, center, Tony DeLorenzo, center with glasses. Gordon Means/Road America

Drivers meeting, 1970 Road America. At left, Parnelli Jones (an unknown at the time) and pensive Sam Posey. Gordon Means/Road America

Follmer flew to regain his runner-up spot by the finish. Jones had also stormed back to finish third, with Jim Hall's Camaro fourth, Maurice "Mo" Carter's Camaro fifth and Peter Schwartzoot's 1969 Camaro sixth. Sam Posey and Jerry Titus were among the DNF's; eighteen of the twenty-eight starters lasted the full 200 miles.

Hans Ziereis gave BMW its second under-2 win when ten of the fifteen starters completed the hotly contested June 20 Bridge opener. Kwech's Alfa gave the German-born BMW driver a race-long challenge, but the weaving Hans proved difficult to pass and won the 100-miler by three seconds. Everett's Alfa and Pike's BMW both retired with failing oil pressure.

Donnybrooke became a genuine donny-brook on July 5 when Milt Minter survived seventy laps of bumps and grinds to become the first independent since Bob Tullius in

Mark Donohue brought the AMC Javelin its second-straight win at the 1970 Road America Trans-Am. Gordon Means/Road America

Parnelli chats with Indy veteran, George Snyder, prior to start of 1970 Road America Trans-Am. Gordon Means/Road America

"I've heard it all before," with Bud Moore before start. Gordon Means/Road America

Fran Hernandez, left, and Bud Moore appear perplexed, while George catches 40 winks prior to start of 1970 Road America. Gordon Means/ Road America

1967 to win a Trans-Am. Minter also gave Chevrolet its first 1970 look at the checker, his 1969 Roy Woods-American Racing Associates (ARA) Camaro succeeding where Chaparral and Owens-Corning had failed.

Follmer's second-place Mustang was followed by Roy Woods in the other ARA

Parnelli prior to start of 1970 Road America Trans-Am. Gordon Means/Road America

Savage's office, Road America 1970. Note that the tubing appears smaller than in the Donohue Javelin. Road & Track

Jones and Follmer Mustangs were 1-2 on the 1970 Road America grid. Gordon Means/Road America

Camaro. Savage took the Donnybrooke pole. Jones sat next to the Cuda with Leslie's Camaro and Follmer's Mustang filling row two. Posey's off-song Challenger and Donohue's Javelin were fifth and sixth. Indy winner Joe Leonard was in Jim Hall's Camaro, which shared row four with winner Minter.

After holding the lead until the two-thirds mark, Savage fell back when his gearbox locked in second. Follmer and Minter had closed in and neither would give any ground going into the last lap. Gentle George and mild Milt barely touched, but this time it was the Mustang that bobbled just long enough to let the ARA Camaro home first.

Following the race Follmer filed a "rough driving" protest against Minter. However,

the race stewards not only denied Follmer's motion, they levied a $100 unsportsmanlike conduct fine on him!

Once again the Titus Firebird and Posey Challenger were early retirements. The difference at Donnybrooke was that they were joined by Jones and Donohue, while Revson never made the start.

Going into Road America, round seven in the eleven-race series, saw Ford with forty-eight points, Chevrolet twenty-six, AMC twenty-five, Dodge seven, and Plymouth five. Alfa Romeo led the under-2s with fifty-one points. BMW had thirty-three, Fiat-Abarth three and BMC three.

With so much going for it—fine people, wonderful scenery and great food (Road America's bratwurst and fresh steamed corn are light years ahead of most racetrack grub)—it seems meanspirited to carp about the shortcomings of this well-maintained Wisconsin circuit. But the track itself has little to recommend it. Perhaps Denny Hulme, who saw the four-mile layout for the first time when he won the 1968 Road Amer-

Pit stops during 1970 Road America Trans-Am. Gordon Means/Road America

ica CanAm, said it best when he described it as "nothing but a series of connected drag strips."

With George Follmer and Parnelli Jones clearly the fastest of the thirty-six-car over-2 entry, it looked as though Ford had the July 19 Road America 200 in its pocket.

Even though Jerry Titus had qualified his troublesome Firebird, he was out again on Saturday morning when he crashed into the bridge abutment in Thunder Valley.

Originally thought to be showing improvement, Jerry had been listed as "satisfactory" as late as the day before his death, but Jerry died in Milwaukee's St. Joseph Hospital on August 5, seventeen days after his accident. Jerry Titus was forty-one. He left a wife and two teenage sons. The team said that it would carry on with John Cordts. But Jerry was Mr. Trans-Am. No one would ever take his place.

The 1970 Road America was where Penske/Donohue and company first tried starting races on less than full tanks. By staging other than normally timed pit stops, they gave themselves a clear track and a pit row free of traffic. Not only did it confuse the enemy, it worked. With his pits flashing a phoney oil sign, Mark pulled in after only ten laps, and again, twenty laps later.

On lap one Ed Leslie tried to squeeze between Jones and Follmer at the first turn. All three cars went sideways with Jones'

recovering. Follmer's car was damaged beyond repair, and Ed Leslie's was black-flagged.

Jones lost the lead because he had to go in for two tire changes. In the meantime, Sam Posey took the Dodge into the rarefied, for it, atmosphere of first place, tailed by Savage, Revson and Donohue. Posey enjoyed a

Savage blasting out of turn 12 at 1970 Road America. Road America

Warren Agor's Camaro, Road America 1970. James Ward/Road America

twenty-five-second lead until fuel-stop time when Donohue sailed past.

Revson retired with a broken driveshaft. But Donohue brought Javelin its second win as he led the Savage Barracuda, Posey Challenger, Hall Camaro, Jones Mustang and Minter Camaro over the line. Having pit stops out of sync paid off!

Under-2 saw Horst Kwech bring Herb Wetson, the Long Island Hamburger King, another Alfa win, beating Schuster's BMW by four seconds.

After Donohue brought his Javelin home first at St. Jovite, American Motors closed-in on Ford, forty-three points to fifty-six. It was Mark's third win in the last four races and it sent Ford back to the drawing boards.

Not unexpectedly, Ford had entered a third Mustang for the Canadian race. And

none other than A. J. Foyt was the driver. But the extra effort failed to pay off as Foyt's "yellow school bus" handled so poorly that Jones, who was helping Bud Moore set up the extra car, badly damaged it when he went off course.

Once again Parnelli and Mark shared the front row of the grid. Follmer's Mustang and Leslie's Camaro were in row two, with Posey and Savage behind them.

Next to Revson on row four was England's Vic Elford, a new face that was to become a fixture in American road racing. Realizing that his horrendous crash in the 1968 Stardust CanAm had left him less than 100 percent, Jim Hall hired the former champion rallyist and respected endurance driver to substitute for him in the number one Camaro.

Consistent with the sloppy methods shown by the Canadian officials over the entire weekend, the thirty-seven starters, of which twenty-two were Camaros, took the green flag two hours after the scheduled starting time.

In the early stages at St. Jovite, Donohue was the meat in the Jones/Follmer sandwich. Following Mark's early, fourteenth-lap pit stop, the Javelin took the lead. After los-

Posey's Dodge digs into turn five during 1970 Road America Trans-Am. Road America

1970 Road America saw Posey's Dodge hold a 25 second lead until the first pit stop. Sam Posey collection

100

*Challenger coming out of turn 12, Road America
1970. Road America*

*Posey's spinning Dodge avoids Selton Racing's
Camaro in turn five at 1970 Road America
Trans-Am. Jim Drago/Road America*

ing it briefly to Follmer during his second pit stop, Mark went back out front to win with an 80.23 mph race average for the 85.5 miles. Follmer finished on the same lap, fol-

Jim Hall with crew chief prior to 1970 Road America Trans-Am. Gordon Means/Road America

lowed by Jones, Posey, Revson and Mo Carter.

Alfas dominated the sixteen-car under-2 field. Lee Midgely beat Kwech as the Italian coupes filled five of the first six places. After setting an under-2 record in practice and running a record 85.37 mph race lap, the Everett Alfa suffered a puncture and limped-in eighth.

Vic Elford backed-up Jim Hall's judgment with a big win at Watkins Glen. It was only the English driver's second Trans-Am, but he was quick enough to bring Team Chaparral its first pony car win.

With forty-five muscle cars trying for thirty-five starting positions, the Glen field turned out to be the season's largest. Donohue and Jones sat out front with Elford and Posey, then Savage and Revson, followed by Leslie and Follmer.

One third into the ninety-one laps saw Jones in front of Donohue by ten seconds. Then the fuel stops and rain arrived about the same time. Even the Penske and Bud Moore pits got a little messed-up in the confusion of taking on gas and changing to rain tires at the same time.

Jim Hall's Camaro during the 1970 Road America Trans-Am. Road America

Returning to the action in fifth place, with rain tires, Vic Elford showed that he was at home in the wet as he moved past the field into first place. When the sun reappeared the Britisher held onto first after a quick change back to dry rubber.

Elford won by ten seconds over Donohue who passed Follmer in the final seconds when George suffered from momentary fuel starvation. Jones, Revson and Savage took the next three places with twenty-one of the thirty-five starters still running at the finish.

Kwech's Alfa had an easy time winning the August 16, under-2 feature—one full minute ahead of Lee Midgely's GTA. Kwech had everything his own way after Everett's pole-sitting GTA turned sick. Having a field of twenty-three under-2s gave the Glen the biggest starting field honors in both classes.

Ford locked-up the 1970 Trans-Am Championship at Seattle on September 20 when Parnelli Jones won the Kent 200. In beating Mark Donohue by nineteen seconds, Parnelli had averaged 90.93 mph. Sticking his Boss 302 on the pole, Jones had stayed out front for almost all of the ninety laps.

In fact, Parnelli had earned the pole twice. After recording a 1:25.7 in his own number

15, he then took out the team donkey and did a 1:25.5. Dan Gurney returned to the Trans-Am when a sponsor conflict inter-

Parnelli exiting turn 12, Canada Corner. Road America

Tony DeLorenzo Camaro, 1970 Road America. Gordon Means/Road America

fered with his McLaren CanAm ride. Sitting next to Dan in the second row was Follmer, with fifth-qualifying Elford's Camaro and Savage's Barracuda in row three, Posey's Dodge and Revson's Javelin filling row four.

Seventh on the grid was Ed Leslie's Chaparral Camaro, the last of those cars enjoying consistent factory support. However, the Kent grid included a second Challenger for Ronnie Bucknum, David Hobbs and John Cordts in Firebirds, the Milt Minter and Roy Woods ARA Camaros and the Thompson/DeLorenzo Owens-Corning Camaros, all of which benefited from extensive assistance.

In all, Kent's thirty-one-car entry included one Dart, three Javelins, two Firebirds, two Challengers, two Barracudas, four Mustangs and seventeen Camaros.

Parnelli Jones finished nineteen seconds up on Mark Donohue, with Sam Posey,

George Follmer, Vic Elford and Ed Leslie filling the next four places. Aside from both Plymouths retiring with blown engines, it was a good race for works cars.

But Jim Hall, a fair but hard-nosed man, filed protests against Bud Moore's Mustangs and the Penske Javelins. Hall cited the Fords for shortened exhaust pipes and for having brake-cooling vents. Hall's objections to the Javelins were based on illegal exhaust pipes and for covering the hood air scoops.

Both protests were upheld. Corrections were ordered before the next event. However, it was a Pyrrhic victory, as the race results were not changed, the judges declaring the violations had not affected the outcome of the race.

Bert Everett overcame sickening fumes (by driving with one hand out the window so as to deflect air into the cockpit) and a hard

Donohue, number 6 and Revson Javelins. Donohue won the 1970 Road America; Revson retired with a broken halfshaft. Gordon Means/ Road America

charge from Kwech. Everett's Alfa averaged 83.70 mph to lead sixteen under-2s and win $1,200.

One might think that having the title in its pocket Bud Moore's team would take it easy at the October 4 Riverside finale. Or that, being out of it, Penske's pair would just go through the motions. Nonsense. Anyone who knew Mark, Parnelli, George or Peter might suspect that they would go at each other harder than ever at Riverside. And they did.

For openers Parnelli set a record 103.67 mph qualifying mark. Then he averaged a record 100 mph for the 201.45 miles over Riverside's short sedan course.

All this in spite of number 15 taking such a hard whack on its right side from an errant back-marker that Jones became airborn as he flew off the course into the desert. By the time he scrambled back out of the scrub, he was in ninth place. Typically, it was while playing catch-up that Parnelli set the day's fastest lap.

Passing Follmer's slowing Mustang ten laps from the checker, Parnelli gave Ford its second 1-2 finish of the season.

Newcomers at Riverside included former under-2 champion Tony Adamowicz in the Dodge Challenger that Ronnie Bucknum drove at Kent, Dick Guildstrand in a Mustang prepared and entered by the students of Chaffey College, and Chevrolet engineer/writer Paul Van Valkenburgh in a 1967 Camaro.

Although Jones and Follmer had finished 1-2, with Donohue and Savage third and fourth, all four were ignored while fifth-place finisher Dan Gurney was mobbed by the post-race crowd and press.

After fifteen years of derring-do, lanky handsome Dan, the most versatile driver of his time, had unconsciously upstaged the big show by announcing his retirement on race-day morning.

Seventeen under-2s drove what turned

Jones Mustang tails Follmer. From the look of the crowd, this shot was taken during the warm-up lap, as Follmer was shunted off course during the first lap. Road America

Ed Leslie gives pits "thumbs up" sign. Picture was taken during practice or warm-up lap, as Ed was black flagged for squeezing between Jones and Follmer, with disastrous results, during the first lap of 1970 Road America Trans-Am. Gordon Means/Road America

out to be the very last under-2 Trans-Am. Following a torrid duel with Adamowicz, Kwech and Pike, the honor of winning the final went to Bert Everett. Averaging 92.4 mph for ninety miles brought Bert's Alfa its third win of the year and $1,700.

Helping to make Ford's 1970 title even sweeter than its 1966 and 1967 championships had been the caliber of the competition. There weren't any phoney fronts. None of the car makers hid behind dealer's skirts. Even Chevrolet was relatively outspoken about the assistance given Chaparral cars. Lost in the shuffle at times was recognition of the technical and financial help supplied by accessory firms such as Sun Oil, Castrol, Goodyear and Firestone.

Race purses increased in 1970. The big three—Jones, Donohue and Follmer—each

Riverside 1970, the season finale. Jones has been knocked out of the lead and into the desert. Follmer leads Gurney, Donohue, Savage and

Revson through Riverside's turn six. Gordon Chittenden/Road & Track

collected about $25,000. Milt Minter, the only independent to record a win, and consistently well-placed Maurice Carter each collected around $10,000.

Spectator turnout was a bit down—225,000 had been reported for twelve races in 1969, versus 200,000 for eleven events in 1970. The Trans-Am was held several times in conjunction with the single-seater Continental series. But schedule conflicts may have prevented more of these gate-building double-bills.

Ford, with seventy-two points and six wins, got away fast. But, as their fifty-nine points and three wins show, Penske's Javelins came on fast. Chevrolet finished with forty points and two wins; Dodge had eighteen and Plymouth, fifteen.

Trans-Am pros were busy. Following Bruce McLaren's fatal accident in June of 1970, Gurney returned to F/I in addition to running the CanAm and selected USAC races. Donohue, Revson, Follmer and Bucknum also drove in the CanAm. Jim Hall had been a CanAm regular. David Hobbs, Ron Grable,

Posey's Dodge would get by all three in a single pass to close in on Revson's Javelin with embarrassing results. (Riverside 1970) Gordon Chittenden/Road & Track

Sam Posey admits this was a dumb pass. He got around Revson, but sent both the Dodge and Javelin into the boonies. Posey recovered, Revson

did not. Harsh words and a little shoving in the Riverside 1970 pits followed. Gordon Chittenden/Road & Track

Bert Everett brings the Bobcor Alfa GTA home first in the 1970 2.5 Challenge at Seattle. Bruce Czaja/Road America

Posey and Follmer were steady Continental entrants. Savage was a USAC standby. Except for off-road racing, Jones stuck to the Trans-Am. But he was the active manager and co-owner of a successful Indy car.

It was too good to last.

After winning everything in sight—Le Mans, Indy, NASCAR 500's and the Trans-Am (all but the CanAm)—in November of 1970, Ford shocked the world of motorsports by dropping all racing support. Jacque Passino, whose icy but efficient management of Ford's American racing program brought results, refused transfer to a more mundane job and left.

Chrysler announced that it would drop both the Dodge and Plymouth Trans-Am projects. Then Jim Hall seemed to lose interest in the Chaparral Camaros. The following year saw Parnelli Jones run one race. George Follmer ran eight out of ten. But Roy Woods fielded a solid team and Roger Penske and his Javelins stayed with it. The Trans-Am lived!

Wacked hard enough to cave in the side and send the Mustang into the desert, Parnelli dropped from first to ninth place before clawing his way back. Playing catch-up resulted in the day's fastest lap and a big win. When asked what race he best remembers, Parnelli usually mentions the 1963 Indy 500, which he won, and the 1970 Riverside Trans-Am. Bob Mangram/Road & Track

Chapter 10

Two gentlemen and a lady of Connecticut

Back in the fifties, when Alistair Cooke still worked as a newspaper man, he began making a name for himself as a broadcaster. In addition to being the emcee on TV's *Omnibus*, he did a weekly BBC radio show in which he commented on the American scene.

One such broadcast was devoted to the spectacular fall foliage around the Lakeville-Salisbury stretch of the Housatonic Valley. What especially impressed the urbane Englishman was how little the northwest corner of Connecticut appeared to have changed since Colonial times.

My wife and I shared Cooke's enthusiasm. We had found an old inn that served great food. Good walks, including those up Selleck's Hill and Mt. Riga, a part of the Appalachian Trail, were close by. For concerts, Tanglewood was just over the Massachusetts line. Music Mountain, where John Fitch built his Pontiac-based Phoenix and Sprint, also was nearby.

Litchfield Hills and Lower Berkshires were sports car country too. As my XK120 had been delivered with a broken valve spring, I got to know George Cleveland's Wells Hills Machine Company. Miraculously, I also found Captain Huntington, the official starter of the thirties Automobile Racing Club of America (ARCA), tending bar in a nearby Sharon hotel.

Although George Cleveland handled a variety of makes, including Volkswagens, which were his biggest seller, his interest lay in more exotic directions. When VW ordered George to get rid of the other machines, he ditched the Beetle.

George asked one day, after we had spent hours with toothbrushes and solvent trying to get fresh tar off the Jag's wire wheels, if I would care to see where some friends planned to build a racetrack.

My first ride over Lime Rock's still-virgin hills was on a rented tractor driven by George Cleveland. Years later my second tour of the course was when Juan Manuel Fangio took me around in one of BMC's new Mini-Coopers.

New road courses invariably have rough going in their early years. Lime Rock's were

Judy Stropus with Mark Donohue. Standing behind Judy is the late Art Peck. Judy Stropus collection

made especially difficult by a local ordinance that banned Sunday racing. But the track had a lot going for it and Jim Haynes, a former driver with management talent, put the course on its feet.

Two of Lime Rock's assets are its pleasant surroundings and Sam Posey, its driver in residence. By coincidence, I was to write about both subjects, the Housatonic Valley and Sam, in consecutive issues, September and October 1967, of *Road & Track*.

Well-informed, articulate and opinionated, forty-year-old Samuel Felton Posey is an interviewer's dream. Because of his exposure as an announcer on ABC-TV's Olympic Games and as the principal commentator for the same network's coverage of the 1984 Indianapolis 500, chances are that you know that Sam is tall, slightly rumpled and boyish looking.

He is married to Ellen Griesedieck, a small, delicately beautiful woman who is a super photojournalist, and the father of a sweet son. Sam still lives in his native Sharon. A graduate of the Rhode Island School of Design, when his broadcast schedule permits, Sam continues to paint and build furniture.

Sam started racing with several handicaps. He was overweight and he spoke pure, New England prep-school English. The surplus avoirdupois is long gone, but the plumy vowels linger on.

How some of the racing world reacted to Sam's speech is illustrated by an incident during his first year at the Speedway. After I had been talking with him in Gasoline Alley, one of George Bignotti's crew wanted to know, "Who was that tall blond kid you were talking to? He's the one who talks funny." I believe that I replied that the "funny talk" was the sound of old money.

In 1972 Sam finished a solid fifth in the 500. But he lost the Rookie of the Year award to tenth-place finisher Mike Hiss. "Talking funny," plus Sam's characteristic candor, may not have helped his cause.

Sam had been racing about five years before it all came together. He had good finishes at Daytona and Le Mans and had placed well in both the under-2 liter and, during 1968, Penske's Trans-Am Camaro. But the big win had eluded him until May 1969. Then, within two weeks, he earned two of them: the Lime Rock Trans-Am and Laguna Seca F/5000.

A year-long championship contender in the 1968 F/5000 series, Posey's only Trans-Am during that year was his Memorial Day win in Peter Revson's Mustang. But that win had not gone unnoticed.

1970 Daytona 24-Hours. Judy Stropus in the Penske pits, with Roger (speaking) in the foreground. Pete Biro/Judy Stropus collection

Judy Stropus with Lee Sorrentino at Daytona. Information board is ready for start. Butch Sherwood/Judy Stropus

Aside from the modest help given the Tullius Dart and Team Starfish Barracudas, Chrysler had been sitting on the Trans-Am sidelines. As the last of Detroit's Big Four to join the pony car wars, in 1970 Chrysler jumped in with separate big-bore programs for Plymouth and Dodge.

Sam recalled that news of Chrysler's plans created a good deal of excitement. "Of course, we had heard that Dan Gurney would wind up with Plymouth. And we also understood that Dan would probably have a second car for Swede Savage. But the situation at Dodge was very much up in the air.

"There was a lot of maneuvering going on, but I thought that we had the advantage at Dodge because Peter Hutchinson, who was the guy making the decision, knew us.

"Pete," continued Sam, "was the son of a former important Chrysler executive. For a while Pete had worked at *Car and Driver*. While he was there he did a story about me and had come up to Autodynamics at Marblehead. So he knew a good deal about Ray Caldwell and about me.

"Well, we got the Dodge contract. We had hoped for a two-car team and I had already thought I'd ask Vic Elford to be our second driver. But it came down to a single car. Chrysler may have been slow to accept the Trans-Am, but when they did get in they did it right. From what I saw, they gave both teams, Gurney's and ours, full support.

Sam went on, "The budget they gave me was entirely adequate. Gurney did his own engine work at AAR, but Dodge supplied us with engines and they were simply great. In fact, the engines were the strongest part of our car.

"What Pete Hutchinson did was to have our engines prepared by Keith Black in California. He's the one who builds those great dragster engines for Chrysler.

"We ran the Challenger in all eleven 1970 Trans-Ams. But three thirds and a fourth, fifth and sixth was the best we could do. Our pit work was good. Our relationship with Goodyear was excellent and we didn't have any trouble with tires. The car's weakness was in the chassis and a lot of that was our own fault.

"For one thing we overdid the acid dip. Our cars would just flex and crack all over. Suspension mountings would buck and the frame almost collapsed. By the end of the season you could just about see through the cars.

"We also tried Ray Caldwell's idea of a different basic linkage than the standard one used by the factory. It didn't work at all. No, I didn't pick the Lime Green color, the factory did. But with those huge number 77s and the black top, it didn't look too bad."

After reflecting a moment on my question as to what one experience stood out during the year, Sam replied, "Actually, there were two that were outstanding: One was at Road America when I somehow managed to power past Parnelli coming down the long straight behind the pits. Normally I'd never have been able to get by him. But then my brakes began locking and both Mark and Parnelli finished in front of me.

"The second incident happened in the last race of the season at Riverside. We had already heard that Dodge were unlikely to return to the Trans-Am in 1971. Then, on race morning, someone from the factory told us that the only chance that we had for

Victory Lane, Daytona 1969. Judy in pits with Penske crew following the Donohue/Parsons win. Roy "Axle" Gaines, with cigarette, in foreground.

a renewal of our contract was to win at Riverside."

As Sam recounted, the Challenger's brakes, a year-long problem, were especially bad that day at Riverside. "It was early in the race. It happened when I tried to get by Peter. But the car's handling was terrible that day. The rear axle was hopping all over the place and the brakes grabbed and I hit Peter broadside and we both spun off into the sand. I managed to get back out first. But it was a bush-league thing for me to do.

"Then my differential broke and I walked back to the pits and sat on the wall. Soon after that Peter went out with a blown engine and I saw him walking toward the pits. Before I had a chance to apologize, Peter yanked me off the wall and had me on the ground, Carroll Smith and Jack McCormick broke it up before I got poked. But it was a near thing.

"Our troubles were never over and we worked very hard. But that didn't stop me from enjoying every minute of it. It was absolutely marvelous racing.

"Every one of the top eight or so drivers in the Trans-Am knew in their hearts that being picked for a factory ride in the Trans-Am was the American road racer's litmus test."

When Jim Jeffords, the advertising man who managed the American Motors Trans-Am teams in 1968 and 1969, finally met Judy Stropus, his opening remark was, "I'm sick and tired of hearing your name."

It seemed that no matter to whom Jeffords had talked, and his search for a good timer and scorer had been a thorough one, he was told, "Get Judy Stropus."

My own memory of Judy goes back to the mid-sixties when Art Peck brought her to Bridgehampton to handle his lap charts. Although well up the CBS corporate ladder, Peck did the Bridge track announcing simply because he loved both racing and Bridgehampton.

Jeff Scott, the CBS staffer who specialized in racing, replaced Art Peck at times. But as I found after I took over the press room, it didn't matter who was on the track's PA system, the press and announcers, as well as many of the race teams, took their information from Judy's charts.

She was a trim good-looking girl, who is now an even trimmer better-looking young woman. Whenever teams disagreed with official lap charts, Judy's work was accepted as gospel. (Cases in point were the Trans-Am scoring snafus at the 1969 MIS and 1971 Bryar.)

Judy opened her own PR office toward the end of 1973, and has since acted as PR counsel and consultant for such diverse clients as Armco Steel, CBS-TV, Volvo, the elite Road Racing Drivers Club, Dunlop and a long list of race teams that includes Bayside Imports, Holbert Racing, Group 44 and Toyota Motorsports.

"I had been timing for several years, but I'd not thought of it as a career." Then Judy related how the 1967 Marlboro Trans-Am changed everything. "It was at Marlboro

Sam Posey during the mid-1960s.

where Duke Manor, who worked for *Competition Press* as both a writer and a space salesman, introduced me to Ford's Fran Hernandez.

"Fran hired me on the spot. We settled on a salary plus expenses and the use of a rental car. For the rest of 1977 I worked all the Trans-Ams for Bud Moore's Cougar Team.

"I liked working for Bud Moore and I liked his drivers. But there was talk that Ford would drop Cougar in 1968. I knew that I didn't stand a chance with Carroll Shelby because he used Don and Ruth Nixon, and they were close friends of Shelby's manager, Lew Spencer. So when Jim Jeffords offered me the Javelin job for 1968, I accepted it."

Back then, Judy said, most of the teams didn't like the idea of having a girl as a regular member of their outfits. Even Roger Penske (with whom Judy worked from 1969 through 1973) was at first reluctant to have a girl on his team.

"Since then I've gone freelance. This," Judy explained, "enables me to sign up any number of teams. As timing and scoring requires that you keep track of all the cars in a race. I'm able to supply charts to anyone who pays my charge. I set a fee for each event. Then I charge each team a prorated share of my expenses. As you know, except for Indy, I've worked everywhere on all kinds of racing."

Judy not only conducts timing and scoring schools throughout the country, her book, *Stropus Guide To Auto Racing Timing*

Sam Posey at Road America 1970, flanked by Lola importer, Jay Haas (left) and team manager, Ray Caldwell. Judy Stropus collection

and Scoring, is the motorsport timer's standard work.

Judy feels that her years with Mark Donohue and Roger Penske were especially interesting. "Everybody worked very hard. Roger had cars in the CanAm and Trans-Am. And we went to all the endurance races at Sebring and Daytona. Then Roger tried NASCAR too.

"In 1971, Mark and David Hobbs went to Le Mans with that special Ferrari 512M that Roger got from Kirk White. That was my first Le Mans trip. But I've been there almost every year since, for BMW or Al Holbert or Hurley Hayward, and I did a lot of scoring for Peter Gregg at Le Mans.

"Those of us who knew Mark had mixed emotions about his retirement. He had become so involved in racing just after he left college that he never developed any hobbies or outside interests.

"After he stopped driving you could see that even the business side of racing didn't appeal to him. You could see that he was becoming restless. . . . As I cared for Mark, I was reluctant to advise him. But those of us who knew him well realized that racing was really all that Mark could do."

After so many years around racing, Judy said, "I began to wonder about a life outside of racing. I tried it. But it didn't work. The people didn't reach me. They just weren't as quick or as bright."

"Bob Sharp Racing/Parts and Accessories/Datsun-Ferrari/Serving Enthusiasts Since 1965/$3.00," read the front cover of the colorful brochure.

In profile, the top of his driving uniform embellished with sponsor patches, Paul Newman fills the upper right-hand corner. Running across the fold is the race driver-actor's number 33, a red, white and blue 280ZX. In addition to the big black Datsun lettered on its white Kaminari air dam

Posey Challenger at speed, Road America 1970.
Gordon Means/Road America

($249.95), number 33 is plastered with seventeen sponsor messages.

Parked next door, in front of Bob's Ferrari dealership, are two red Ferrari 308s. Sharing the folder's back cover is a special Datsun that looks as if it were an Italian coachbuilder's auto-show design exercise.

The catalog offers everything from a $1.50 Bob Sharp Embroidered Ferrari Jacket Patch, to a $1,848 bolt-on turbo system. What makes it a special treat is that all eighteen of its pages include small pictures and briefs on Bob's competition cars and racing years.

Sports car drivers turned import car dealers were routine by 1964 when Bob started selling and racing Datsuns. Few drivers, however, have grown to match Sharp's many-faceted complex in Georgetown, Connecticut. Tall, mid-forties and still pencil thin, Bob's long been regarded as a "neat" guy. Neat as in "orderly" or "immaculate" (his salesmen are required to wear jackets and ties), as well as neat as in "nice."

Although Bob is a six-time national SCCA champion, it wasn't until 1971 when Lime Rock impressario Jim Haynes asked Bob to give Paul Newman a ride around the course that Bob's fame zoomed. It doesn't bother Bob that he now may be better known for preparing cars for Paul Newman than for his own accomplishments.

Sharp's involvement in the Trans-Am had been spotty. He had taken his 510 to SCCA national championships in 1971 and 1972, as well as driving in many IMSA events. In 1975, when the Trans-Am was a single-class series, Bob earned one second and two thirds in his 280 at Nelson Ledges, Watkins Glen and Road America.

In 1982 Paul Newman set a track record in winning the Brainerd Trans-Am in a Bob Sharp Racing-prepared 280XZ.

Looking back to when Datsun was giving both Pete Brock and Bob Sharp factory support for the 2.5 Challenge, Bob remarked, "For its time the Trans-Am was a relatively expensive series for us to participate in. We did get some help from Nissan East. But, understandably, Nissan's big push was with Pete Brock's BRE on the West Coast. Not only was Nissan based in California, but Pete Brock had been set up to campaign the 510 nationally.

"I ran a few of the 2.5 Challenge series in a 510. And, of course, I was glad to win right here at Lime Rock. But, I think that most small-sedan drivers had come to prefer the SCCA nationals or IMSA.

"Actually," Bob continued, "none of the small-sedan drivers that I knew could see any future in the 2.5 Challenge. And it didn't help to have the SCCA treat those of us in the 2.5 like stepchildren."

Paul Newman ready to drive Bob Sharp's Datsun. Bob Sharp collection

Chapter 11

Javelin wins an empty bowl

The thirty-one machines that showed up for the 1971 opener at Lime Rock on May 8, looked about the same as their 1970 counterparts.

Permission to use dry sumps, which neatly took care of a chronic Javelin lubrication problem, was 1971's only significant rule change. Significant, too, was that in 1971 Roger Penske had the only team with direct factory support.

Roy Woods Racing, RWR, later known as ARA, American Racing Associates, developed a relationship with Team Penske that lead to ARA inheriting Penske's 1972 American Motors sponsorship. Penske had sold ARA the team's old 1970 Javelins with updated sheet metal.

Six of the ten new Javelin engines that Traco built for Team Penske also were sold to Roy Woods. As the 1970 to 1971 changes were minor, the combination of updated appearance and their new dry sump engines resulted in the Roy Woods Javelins being classified as 1971s. Of equal importance was an exchange of information between Penske and Woods.

For 1971 Penske planned to run a single Javelin for Mark Donohue. David Hobbs would be in reserve.

AMC JAVELIN, 1971-72 (PENSKE AND ARA)
Engine: ohv V-8, 305 ci (Traco-built), 440-460 hp
Suspension: front, new pickup points, revised spindles; rear, new pickup points (ARA used Ford rear axle)
Weight: 3100 lb
Notes: Street car was the Javelin AMX, 390 ci, 304 hp, 3300 lb. Dry-sump system cured previous year's oiling problems.

Bud Moore came to the Lime Rock 200 as an independent with two new school-bus-yellow 1970 Mustangs. Both of Moore's cars had been built in 1970 *after* the year's last event. While new, technically they were the previous year's cars. In fact, ten of the twelve Mustangs at Lime Rock had come out of Bud Moore's shop. The result of this model confusion saw new, late-1970 Mustangs considered as 1970s, while used, early 1970 Javelins became 1971s.

Parnelli Jones and Peter Gregg were Moore's drivers. But Bud Moore's Lime Rock appearance was a one-shot deal made possible by support from a group of New York and Connecticut Ford dealers.

The 1971 Lime Rock 200 had an incredible ending with Mark Donohue finishing *five laps* in front of the second-place Mustang driven by Tony DeLorenzo. It had rained, so Mark's skill in the wet on Goodyear's new Blue Streak rain tires played a part in the Javelin's runaway win. Still, Mark was not the only one on Goodyear's new rain tires.

The grid, with Mark sitting next to Parnelli on the front row, was a replay of 1970. Tony Adamowicz, who had been recruited to drive an RWR Javelin after Roy Woods got banged-up during practice for the Riverside Continental, sat behind Parnelli. Next to Tony was his RWR teammate, Peter Revson.

Row three was occupied by SCCA Rookie Of The Year Marshall Robbins in a 1971 Camaro and Tony DeLorenzo's 1970 Mustang. DeLorenzo's father, a GM vice president, was reported to have been disturbed when Tony raced Camaros. One wonders how he reacted to his son driving a former Parnelli Jones Mustang.

Troy Promotions, as the Jerry Thompson/ DeLorenzo team was known in 1971, had sponsorship from Marathon Oil. This is the same pair whose 1970 Camaros were supported by Owens-Corning Fiberglas. Thompson started the year next to Peter Gregg's Mustang on row four.

Except for the thirty-first (and last) car on the grid, a 1964 Pontiac Tempest driven by Bob Tullius, the remainder of the field was a mixed bag that ranged from talented young "pros" with good equipment, to backmarkers whose equally good equipment became year-long moving chicanes.

The last car in the field, the Tullius Tempest, which became known as the Gray Ghost, had an interesting history. Herb Adams, a Pontiac engineer who had raced a little and had some experience with the Jerry Titus/Terry Godsall Firebirds, was the project innovator. Joined by six other Pontiac engineer-enthusiasts, they proceeded, on their own time, to convert Mrs. Adams' daily transports into a race car.

It began when Adams learned that Pontiac had homologated the 1964 GTO. The fee had been $15 and it seems to have been the only time a Pontiac from around that time

<table>
<tr><td colspan="2">PONTIAC TEMPEST, 1971 (HERB ADAMS)</td></tr>
<tr><td>Engine:</td><td>ohv V-8 (389 bored to 400 then destroked to 303 ci to allow TRW forged pistons), 303 ci, 450 hp, single 4-barrel carb</td></tr>
<tr><td>Transmission:</td><td>4-speed (Muncie)</td></tr>
<tr><td>Brakes:</td><td>4-wheel disc (Corvette)</td></tr>
<tr><td>Suspension:</td><td>front, upper and lower A-arms, coil springs, Koni shocks, Trans Am stabilizer bar; rear, live axle, leaf springs, Koni shocks, Trans Am stabilizer bar</td></tr>
<tr><td>Weight:</td><td>3400 lb</td></tr>
<tr><td>Notes:</td><td>This car was actually a 1964 GTO two-door sedan before modifications!</td></tr>
</table>

Jim Travers, left, and Frank Coons of Traco Engineering, tune engine for 1971 Penske Javelins. The 305 cubic inch, 450 horsepower Trans Am V-8 was based on the standard 360 cubic inch engine used in the Javelin AMX.

*Mark Donohue (left) and Roger Penske, Daytona 1971. Motor Racing Graphics/*Road & Track

had been homologated. Consequently, Adams could legally convert the six-year-old family car into a racer.

The Adams group gutted the car. The body was acid-dipped, the fenders flared and every excess ounce discarded. A frame-stiffening roll cage was installed. The engine was moved back four inches and a Muncie four-speed gearbox was mounted to a new bolt-on cross-member.

Originally a 455, the engine was completely reworked and reduced to a 303. A new racing crankshaft, Carillo rods, intake manifold, twin Holley electric fuel pumps and a dual-feed Holly carburetor were only some of the modifications.

The rear end was reworked to give one degree of negative caster. Springs were cut down to lower the body by four inches. Koni shocks were used all around. Corvette discs with metal pads were added. A new instrument panel was installed and a twenty-gallon safety fuel cell lived in the trunk.

Built without any help from Pontiac, the Adams group went looking for a driver. Bob Tullius was selected and invited to Detroit. Bob liked what he saw, signed up and came

Mark Donohue. Roger Penske collection

very close to making racing history his first time out. When Tullius started last at Lime Rock, some fans assumed it to be the slowest car in the field. But last-minute engine work had prevented Tullius from qualifying.

By lap twenty-three Bob had passed twenty-five cars. On lap 100 he had the GTO in second place and was closing in on Donohue. Tullius was driving the race of his life.

Mark had led from the start. Parnelli Jones retired (forever, as it turned out) after a first-lap excursion into the mud that resulted in extensive body damage. Revson had held second for most of the race only to fall out with ignition troubles. And Peter's teammate, Tony Adamowicz, overran the escape road and he too became mired in the mud.

As if by magic the crowd packing Lime Rock's gentle green hills caught fire. Everyone, the personnel of other teams, race officials, children and vendors, were on their feet rooting for old number 49.

Then the witches of Litchfield went to work. On lap 123, less then ten minutes from the finish, Tullius pitted with an overheated engine. After hurriedly splashing in a pail of water, Adams had Bob out while he still held second place. But the head gasket then blew and number 49 crawled in on the next lap.

Cruelly, the Gray Ghost died one lap short of being classified as a finisher. All around the course the crowd was on its feet, waving, shouting and, it's said, shedding a few tears.

Donohue's out-of-sight 75.041 mph race average earned him $4,000. Five laps back, DeLorenzo's second-place Mustang collected $3,000 and Warren Agor's 1969 Camaro got $2,500 for third. Peter Gregg's pony car was a distant fourth, Marshall Robbin's 1971 Camaro was fifth and Paul Nichter's 1968 Camaro (which covered 124 laps, only one more than the wounded Gray Ghost) was sixth.

The 2.5 Challenge series got off to a familiar start with Bert Everett's Alfa on the pole and Horst Kwech's Alfa winning the eighty-five lap, 130 mile preliminary with a 69.55 mph race average. Kwech earned $1,500 first-place money, Everett became permanently stuck in the mud, and Ziereis' and Lazebnik's BMW's ended-up second and third.

Bob Sharp's Datsun 510 and John Buffum's Ford Escort Twin-Cam were interesting additions to the series as thirteen of the twenty-one starters went the distance.

Used as a curtain raiser for the Trans-Am or run as a preliminary for other SCCA professional races, and 2.5 Challenge survived without making many friends. The series name, 2.5 Challenge, was catchy but meaningless. Not once in its three years did a 2.5 entry list have a contender that would not have qualified for the old under-2 Trans-Am. If it hadn't been for Peter Brock's 1600 and 1800 cc 510 Datsuns, it's doubtful that the 2.5 would have gone beyond its first year.

Two weeks after Lime Rock, Bud Moore showed up at Bryar because Peter Gregg had secured partial sponsorship from a Jacksonville contractor friend. Along with George Follmer, Gregg was expected to make runaway Lime Rock winner Donohue work for his laurels.

When Donohue, Adamowicz and Follmer found themselves tied for the pole with identical 1:12 times, it was discovered that

```
DATSUN PL510, 1971-73
Engine:       sohc inline 4; 99 ci (1622 cc) 1971, 1800 cc 1972-73;
              175 hp 1971, 200 hp 1972-73; dual 2-barrel Hitachi-
              Solex carb
Transmission: 5-speed
Brakes:       front, disc; rear, drum
Suspension:   front, struts, coil springs; rear, independent trail-
              ing arm, coil springs
Chassis:      front engine, rear-wheel drive
Weight:       1980 lb
Notes:        Street car had 1622 cc, 90 hp, single 2-barrel, 4-speed,
              2100 lb.
```

Mark Donohue, left, laughing at the sight of Bob Tullius working on the Old Gray Mare at the 1971 Lime Rock. As Tullius said, "Mark didn't appear to take the whole thing very seriously until after the race." Image/Bob Tullius collection

Bryar's SCCA timers were working with hand-held watches that only registered to the nearest tenth of a second.

Drawing straws, another Solomon-like solution, sat Follmer's Mustang on the pole next to the Adamowicz RWR Javelin, with Donohue in the third spot. When asked, Mark said that he thought the drawing had worked out fine. Then it was learned that Penske's redoubtable scorer, nifty Judy Stropus, had known that both George and Tony had been faster than Mark.

Donohue and Gregg were in the field at Bryar only hours after Indy, where Peter had knocked Mark off the pole and had gone on to finish second—a reminder that Peter seemed more at home in single-seaters than in sedans. Follmer and Hobbs also ran the 1971 Indy. But they, along with Mark, failed to finish.

Until Donohue retired with a faulty carburetor on lap thirty-five of the ninety-five, his Javelin and Follmer's Mustang had run inches apart. Then Revson held second until Peter Gregg gave Bud Moore a 1-2 finish by nipping inside the Javelin on the final lap.

Follmer's 75.32 mph winning race average gave him $4,000 and handed Ford a fifteen to thirteen lead over AMC. Bob Tullius proved that his stirring drive at Lime Rock had not been a fluke by bringing the 1964 Pontiac home fourth. Warren Agor's 1969 Camaro and Marshall Robbins' 1971 Camaro filled fifth and sixth.

New faces at Bryar included John Paul, Sr., in a Challenger and Kiroshi Fushida, a well-regarded Japanese driver, in a 1971 Camaro.

Gaston Andrey kept Alfa out front in the 2.5 Challenge by finishing more than one minute in front of Don Pike's BMW. The Hans Ziereis BMW and Kwech Alfa were third and fourth. California's John Morton held down first place for most of the seventy-lap 2.5 Challenge. BRE's Pete Brock, who had contributed a good deal to the success of Shelby's Cobras, showed what his 510s could do, before Morton's 510 snapped a halfshaft with victory in sight.

George Follmer picked up a neat thirty-six second win over Mark Donohue at the June 6 Mid-Ohio Trans-Am. And once again,

Bob Tullius started the 1971 Lime Rock Trans-Am thirty-first, and last. When the six-year-old Pontiac challenged the leaders the crowd roared its support. Road & Track

Peter Gregg drove the second Bud Moore Mustang into third place.

Follmer and Donohue had qualified 1-2, the Mustang earning the pole with a 1:39.28, 87.04 mph lap that had the SCCA's new electronic timer catch Follmer at 149.99 going through the trap. Gregg and Adamowicz sat behind the front row, with DeLorenzo's and Warren Tope's Mustangs in row three.

Peter Revson's RWR Javelin lost its engine during practice and started last in the thirty-three-car field. Driving a 1970 Mustang, Pittsburgh's Bid Ed Lowther made his first Trans-Am appearance and former Chevy engineer-writer, Paul Van Valkenburgh *drove* his 1967 Camaro entry from Los Angeles to Mid-Ohio.

Heavy rains at the start, combined with Mark having brake problems, plus Follmer's Firestones working poorly in the wet, saw the 180 laps get off to a dicey beginning.

Neither of Roy Woods' Javelins lasted the distance. Revson had splashed his way through the field to take third, only to expire with a blown engine. Adamowicz went against a guardrail while running second.

When Tullius came from seventh on the grid to challenge the leaders, he again captured the crowd's fancy. By lap eighteen Bob was running a strong second and no one could believe they were watching a seven-year-old clunker closing in on the latest muscle cars.

But Tullius came to grief when he went in for dry rubber. After taking nearly four minutes to make the change, the Tempest was so far back that Bob had to fly to finish fifth, between the DeLorenzo and Agor Mustangs.

Follmer's seventy-five-lap, 77.51 mph race average over the 2.4 mile circuit was good for $4,000. After three races, uncaring Ford had twenty-four points to unhappy AMC's nineteen.

John Morton gave the 2.5 Challenge a new winner by booting his 510 Datsun home first, almost a full minute in front of the Kwech and Andrey Alfas. Making it look easy, John led the entire forty-five laps as eleven of the sixteen starters ran the distance.

The June 20 Edmonton Trans-Am drew the smallest entry in the Trans-Am's six years. With only fourteen of the big cars and six 2.5s entered, the Canadian promoters were critical of the SCCA's failure to attract

Owner Herb Adams gave his six-year-old Tempest a club racing win near Detroit. Image/Bob Tullius collection

Horst Kwech, number 3, and John Morton's BRE Datsun at the Road America 2.5 Challenge. Kwech's Alfa finished third, as Morton went on to win. Bill Jennaro/Road America

an adequate entry. Some wag posted a "The SCCA Slept Here" sign in his pit; that said it all.

Having lost four of their six engines, which Roy Woods had figured on lasting the year, the RWR Javelins stayed home to try to find some answers.

To no one's surprise, Edmonton's front row consisted of Donohue and Follmer. Peter Gregg put his Bud Moore Mustang in third place next to the fine Canadian independent, Mo Carter, who was driving one of Jim Hall's old Camaros.

Except for Carter, none of the thin field ran anywhere near the leaders. The Canadian broke a timing gear on the fifty-ninth of the seventy laps and Gregg's race ended on the thirty-eighth laps with a snapped crank.

Neither the Donohue nor Follmer cars stayed healthy. But both survived and Donohue brought American Motors its second win in 1971 with an 89.98 race aver-age over the 185.5 miles. Follmer finished on the same lap. But Joe Chamberlain's third-place 1970 Camaro was *six laps* behind the leaders.

John Morton had an easy time beating the six regulars and five grid-fillers that had been recruited from the club races held earlier in the day. The Everett and Ken Schley Alfas were second and third as nine of the eleven 2.5 challengers completed forty laps.

Although Ford still led American Motors by two points, thirty to twenty-eight, Mustang's Trans-Am future looked bleak. Following Edmonton, Bud Moore and George Follmer had revealed that the team had been trying to get along solely on their winnings. Now, they said, the lack of funds had stopped them from buying new engines. Moore's entire project was endangered.

Mark Donohue pulled another of his hat tricks over the weekend of July 3 and 4. He won the 500 mile Indy car race at Pocono as well as the Donnybrooke Trans-Am in Brainerd, Minnesota.

Averaging 97.672 mph for 210 miles, Mark dueled with pole-sitter Peter Revson before bringing Penske's red, white and Sunoco Blue number 6 Javelin home first at Donny-

The 2.5 winning Datsun starts lap of honor. Drummond-Roble/Road America

BRE Datsun's Pete Brock, driver Morton and race queen, Road America 1971. James Ward/ Road America

brooke by only 1:35 seconds in front of Peter's RWR Javelin.

Every other machine in the Donnybrooke field, which did not include either of Bud Moore's Mustangs, was lapped at least once by the two leaders. Tony DeLorenzo and Jerry Thompson's Mustangs were third and fourth. Warren Agor's and Mark Waco's former Jim Hall Camaros finished fifth and sixth. Missing from Donnybrooke was the crowd-pleasing, Tullius-driven 1964 Tempest GTO.

Following his double-win weekend at Pocono and Donnybrooke, Mark Donohue had something to say about Trans-Am purses. After mentioning that he had won $100,000 the day before and $4,000 that day, Mark went on to say that both races had been equally hard to drive, and that the team's car preparation for Pocono and Donnybrooke had been about the same.

Mark was never one to pop-off without reason. If the SCCA had listened to his comments about the club's poor Trans-Am purses, the series may have continued to be a showcase for Detroit's most innovative cars.

Perhaps, too, adequate prize money may have slowed the trend of sponsor support becoming more important than the gate. The quiet men who manage the 500, the racing world's most successful event, have never lost sight of the need to pack 300,000 people in the stands. Without that awsome turnout (and 300,000 is probably on the low side), Indy wouldn't get worldwide publicity in magazines, newspapers, radio and television.

Indy's amazing media blitz is what makes the 500's big-buck sponsor money possible. But it all starts with those paying customers who pack the Speedway every May.

Bert Everett kept Alfa in the 2.5 Challenge lead when his 1965 GTA averaged 89.475 to win the Donnybrooke 150-miler.

John Morton and Horst Kwech had taken early leads. But both retired to let Bert's crippled coupe lead Harry Theodorpopulous and Ken Schley to a 1-2-3 Alfa finish.

Five races into the new 2.5 series showed Alfa with thirty-nine points, Datsun twenty-one, BMW fourteen, Ford Escort three and Cooper two. The only new make to be a factor in the 2.5 Challenge was the 1600 cc Datsun 510.

Peter Gregg drove Follmer's old number 16 to a fourth at Road America in 1971. After Ford dropped all support, Peter obtained short-term *sponsorship for Bud Moore's team. Jerry Reis/ Road America*

Mark enjoyed another double-win weekend on July 17 and 18. Bud Moore's Mustangs returned to the series in time for the Road America 200, but they did not stop Mark from bringing his Penske Javelin home first.

Vic Elford, who had been recruited to drive one of Roy Woods' Javelins, sat next to fastest qualifier Donohue. The Follmer and DeLorenzo Mustangs were in row two, with Thompson and Tope extending pony car country to row three.

Warren Agor and Marshall Robbins put their Camaros in row four, while Tullius had his Tempest in the tenth spot. Peter Gregg, who blew two engines in practice, was the thirty-fourth of thirty-five starters.

Follmer made a race of it until the fourteenth lap when one of his Firestones went flat. Unfortunately, it happened just after George had passed the pits. By the time he crawled around the four-mile course and got back out, he was in tenth place.

Follmer stormed back to finish second. But Mark easily maintained his lead, reeling in fifty laps with a 92.119 race average. Jerry Thompson, Peter Gregg, Tony DeLorenzo and Warren Tope all drove 1970 Mustangs into the next four places. Oil-pump failure sidelined Elford's Javelin and the Gray Ghost expired on the first lap.

With six down and four races to go, Robin and Batman were solidly in control.

The day following Road America found Mark in Michigan's Irish Hills where he won the 200 mile Indy car race at MIS. For a change, the $5,600 won at Road America compared favorably with the $14,202 that Mark earned at MIS.

John Morton gave the BRE Datsun 510 its third 2.5 Challenge victory. Mike Downs' BRE 510 also was well placed until he was forced to replace his windscreen and settle for ninth. The Bert Everett and Horst Kwech Alfas wound up second and third and eighteen small sedans completed twenty-seven laps.

July 25 saw an extra 2.5 Challenge held in Olathe, Kansas, where it was the day's fea-

ture race. Following a full card of club events, John Morton's Datsun had everything its own way. Lee Midgely and Horst Kwech placed their second- and third-place Alfas in the vanguard of the sixteen small sedans that raced over an abandoned airport's rough 2.02 mile course. In spite of its late start, Datsun now showed thirty-nine points to Alfa's fifty-one.

While the 2.5s were in Kansas, Peter Revson was winning the Watkins Glen CanAm; Tony Adamowicz was fifth, Sam Posey sixth and Vic Elford eighth. Meanwhile, at the Glen, Donohue was having a miserable time. He was a nonfinisher in the CanAm and, with David Hobbs sharing the Penske/Kirk White Ferrari 512M, DNF in the World Championship of Makes 6-Hours.

But July 31 found Mark recapturing his winning ways at Mt. Tremblant where he won the pole and went on to take his fifth Trans-Am in seven starts. Covering 185.5 miles with a blistering 86.57 race average, Mark's Javelin gave American Motors a full nine point lead over Ford.

Even though race-sponsoring Player's cigarettes had arranged for Bud Moore to provide Mark with some competition, Mark still led from flag to flag.

George Follmer filled his usual place next to Mark. Peter Revson and Milt Minter put Roy Woods' Javelins on row two. The Peter Gregg and Warren Tope Mustangs which filled row three were again in front of the Warren Agor and Marshall Robbins Camaros. Rusty Jowett stuck the old Gray Ghost in the eleventh row, Bob Tullius running his Group 44 Triumphs at Nelson Ledges.

Because of improperly mounted shocks, both Revson and Minter suffered from excessive tire wear. But Revson came in fourth, while Minter retired with a blown engine. Follmer and Gregg brought Bud Moore's Mustangs home more than one minute behind Mark, with the Tope and Thompson Mustangs fifth and sixth. Lap seventeen saw Herb Adams' gutsy old Tempest blow its engine, although seventeen of the twenty-seven starters did survive.

After the August 15, 218 mile Watkins Glen Trans-Am, where Mark beat George by twenty-six seconds, Donohue said that he had won in spite of using the wrong gearing. Then Follmer, in his post-race interview, repeated what he'd been saying privately, "There's just no way we can beat the Javelins while the Mustangs are running last year's cars on last year's tires."

The front row of the Glen grid had the, by now, customary Trans-Am look, with Mark and George on the front row. Only this time the Mustang was on the pole with 111.490 mph versus 110.581 for Mark's Javelin.

Swede Savage returned to the series in A. J. Foyt's orange Camaro. Prepared for A. J. by the storied builder Smokey Yunick, Terry Godsall and company had been recruited to handle the Glen pits on a one-race deal.

Vic Elford and Swede Savage shared the second row. But both Elford's and Revson's Javelins were struck with constant engine troubles during practice. Finally, when his car ran a bearing, Revson was forced to start thirty-first, last, on the grid.

Mustangs driven by Gregg, DeLorenzo,

Thompson and Tope occupied rows three and four. Bob Tullius slipped the Gray Ghost into mid-field.

Follmer stayed in front of Donohue and the previous year's Glen winner, Vic Elford, until the sixty-sixth lap when he pitted for fuel and fresh rubber. Savage also ran with the leaders until his engine exploded on the eighth lap. Chunks of metal went flying, and, seconds after Swede had made a hurried exit, the orange Camaro caught fire. "That Yunick," someone said, "sure builds one hot car!"

While playing catch-up, George Follmer recorded a 111.769 mph lap, the day's fastest, which helped him regain first place. Then George picked up a piece of metal and made an unscheduled pit stop and was obliged to drive very hard to finish second.

Gregg's Mustang wound up in third, one lap off the pace. Elford's Javelin was still a lap farther back. Maurice Carter's Camaro was fifth, Jerry Thompson's Mustang sixth. Seventeen of the thirty-one starters went the distance.

Following the Glen, which was Trans-Am

Follmer in Parnelli's old car at Road America in 1971. George overcame severe tire problems to finish a strong second to Donohue's Javelin. Jim Drago/Road America

number eight, AMC had fifty-two points to Ford's forty-three.

The Glen's 2.5 Challenge saw Kwech's Alfa beat Morton's Datsun when the 510 ran out of fuel on number forty-six of the fifty-one laps. Kwech, who had made a quick last-minute gas stop, finished more than a minute over Peter Schuster's BMW and Mike Downs' BRE Datsun.

Everett, who was running a new Herb Wetson Alfa for the first time, ran a 110.411 mph lap for the day's fastest. Then Bert lost a wheel while leading the race. The GTA was badly damaged when it crashed into a guardrail but Bert was unhurt.

The three-week layoff between Watkins Glen and the September 6 Michigan Trans-Am was a busy time for the series stars. At Road America, Revson had come from last on the grid to win his third CanAm for Team McLaren. Donohue had won the pole and ran the fastest race lap at Ontario. But Mark was to drop a valve while Peter came in seventh.

It was Mark's September 6 win at Michigan that clinched the 1971 Trans-Am Championship for American Motors. Remarkably, Donohue had won seven of his nine starts. Perhaps even more remarkable was that Roger Penske had won the championship with a single-car team.

At MIS, Follmer and Donohue again shared the front row. And, once more, George trailed Mark over the line by thirty seconds.

Perhaps George's bitching had done some good. For the first time in ages, Firestone had a service van at a race. This gave Bud Moore some help at Michigan. Even though it didn't change the results, it had been good for the Moore Team's morale.

Starting and finishing third and fourth were the Revson and Minter RWR Javelins. The first four cars starting and finishing in the same position. But the coincidence ended

Donohue exiting the bridge where Jerry Titus crashed during practice the prior year. Mark went on to win the 1971 Road America Trans-Am. S. P. Clark/Road America

there, as Peter Gregg and Jerry Thompson, who had qualified fifth and sixth, wound up DNF and thirteenth.

Following a race-long duel with Mo Carter, Bob Tullius picked up two more points for Pontiac by coming in fifth to the Camaro's sixth.

Appropriately, the forty-car Michigan field was the season's largest. Appropriately, because Michigan was to be the final Trans-Am for Mark Donohue and Peter Revson, two of racing's best drivers and nicest guys.

One week after Michigan, Seattle canceled the September 19 Kent Trans-Am and 2.5 Challenge. Only seventeen entries had been received by the track's deadline. And it was mentioned by the track management that the major teams were either skipping Seattle or sending substitute drivers.

Hank Loudenback, who had succeeded Jim Kaser as the SCCA director of professional racing, moved the 2.5 Challenge to Laguna Seca on October 17. With the series championship still a toss-up between Dat-sun and Alfa, holding the final race was imperative.

The Seattle Trans-Am was not rescheduled. The final 1971 Trans-Am ran at Riverside on October 3.

The old cliché "a race driver is a race driver is a race driver" was evident at Riverside where George Follmer drove a Roy Woods Javelin. Before switching to the Goodyear-shod car, Follmer first had to get a release from Firestone. Getting permission to drive the Javelin had not been a problem, George said, as no suitable Firestone entry was available.

The Riverside Trans-Am was all Follmer. He earned the pole with a 103.70 lap, sharing the front row with new teammate, Vic Elford. The Robbins Camaro and Thompson Mustang filled row two, with Mark Waco's Camaro and the DeLorenzo Mustang fifth and sixth on the grid.

If Roger Penske's plan to have Donnie Allison drive Mark's Javelin had gone through, undoubtedly Follmer would have had to

Winner Donohue rolling to a win in the 1971 Road America Trans-Am. Roger Penske collection

work harder. But the stock car ace broke his hand in a freak accident during practice when a bump sent the steering wheel spinning out of his hand.

With Donohue still tied-up in a postponed USAC race at Trenton, the Brit, Jackie Oliver, who had moved his CanAm Shadow race shop to southern California, got the ride. Still another Riverside Trans-Am newcomer was NASCAR's Dick Brooks, who qualified a Dodge Challenger eighteenth. Oliver, who was driving a Trans-Am sedan for the first time, was a cautious twelfth in the thirty-one-car field.

Except for Elford getting into first for four laps during Follmer's first pit stop, George led for seventy-five of the seventy-nine laps. Earning $6,700 in prize money, Follmer finished with a 98.3 race average.

Elford brought in the second RWR Javelin forty-two seconds behind Follmer, and Jackie Oliver made Riverside American Motors' finest hour by slipping Mark's big

number 6 into third place, on the same lap as the leaders. Thompson's Mustang, Robbins' Camaro and Carter's Camaro filled the next three places with twenty-three of the thirty-one starters seeing the checker.

Looking back on what was to be the final real McCoy Trans-Am shoot-out, only two drivers made the winners circle during the entire 1971 series. With seven wins, Mark had owned the series. George Follmer collected three firsts, two with Mustang and one for Javelin—an outstanding job when you consider the handicaps he worked under.

Even though Roy Woods had a working relationship with Penske, his Javelins seemed to suffer from more than their share of mechanical misfortune. RWR had a good team, but it wasn't in a class with Penske's.

Figured on the basis of eight best finishes out of ten races, Javelin completed 1971 with seventy-two points, Mustang fifty-four, Camaro seventeen and Pontiac seven.

Donohue's Javelin taking the checker, 1971 Road America. S. P. Clark/Road America

When John Morton won the 2.5 Challenge at Riverside, he set the stage for a dramatic but disputatious climax at Laguna Seca two weeks later. In addition to BRE's regular 1622 cc 510s, Pete Brock brought an 1800 cc (no one ever had anything near 2500 cc) for Mike Downs.

Alfa Romeo stayed with its aces, Kwech and Everett, as twenty-seven entries, the season's largest 2.5 field, started at Riverside. Downs sat on the pole, but Morton led most of the laps. Following a race-long tussle, Bert Everett's Alfa finished two seconds ahead of Downs, with Kwech finishing a distant tenth.

Race stewards for the October 17 Laguna Seca CanAm and 2.5 Challenge double bill had an unusually trying weekend. To start with, officials tried to rob Peter Revson of his fifth 1971 CanAm win by black-flagging his smoking McLaren with less than two laps to go. As he was driving into a brilliant setting

Donohue starts lap of honor after winning 1971 Road America Trans-Am. Jack Salika/Road America

sun, Peter's explanation was that he had not seen the black flag.

The owner of second-place Jackie Stewart's car, Carl Haas, did yowl. But Revson's failure to stop on the next-to-last lap and hand the win to Stewart was understandable. None of the course marshalls had shown Peter the oil flag while McLaren was smoking. It's said that fact influenced the official's final judgement. A $250 fine was Peter's punishment.

Neither Horst Kwech, car owner Herb Wetson nor Alfa Romeo was to enjoy so happy an ending. With all the 2.5 marbles going to the Monterey winner, both Datsun and Alfa mounted a maximum effort.

By coincidence, both teams lost strong contenders when Downs and Everett retired on the twenty-third of fifty-eight laps. Never more than a few feet apart, Kwech and Morton pushed on, seemingly prepared to gamble on going the distance without a fuel stop.

Then, just eleven laps from the finish, Pete Brock brought Morton in for a hurried splash of gas. John made up most of the fourteen seconds he had lost, but Kwech finished first. Just how chancey the gamble had been became evident when the Alfa ran out of gas on the first turn of its victory lap.

So Alfa won the 2.5 Challenge. At least that was the way it looked to those who may not have spent all night at the circuit.

During the mandatory post-race inspection, John Timanus found the Alfa's fuel tank to be oversized. Explanations and deliberations lasted until the next morning. Admirably the stewards stuck to their guns. Kwech was disqualified. John Morton won.

The best eight out of ten formula showed Alfa and Datsun to be tied with sixty points. But the 2.5 Challenge Cup belonged to Datsun, as it had the greatest number of wins.

Chapter 12

"... one long chicane"

During the winter of 1972 the SCCA released a tentative twelve-race Trans-Am schedule. Seattle then gave some indication of what the club was to face when it dropped its Trans-Am date before the season opened.

Roy Woods Racing inherited Team Penske's arrangement with American Motors as well as two of Penske's Javelins. RWR did not, however, get Donohue's car. Number 6 was sold to Bill Collins, the son of one of Roger's

John Morton and Mike Downs Datsun 510S led the 1972 2.5 Challenge through Road America's turn five. John and Roger Schreiber/Road America

friends, who also happened to be a Chevy dealer. No one was surprised when RWR also hired George Follmer who had run, and won, the final 1971 Trans-Am for Woods.

Many team owners, including Bud Moore, spent a largely fruitless winter looking for sponsors.

Early reports indicated that the defending 2.5 title holders, the BRE Datsuns, would mount a strong defense. Long Island hamburger king Herb Wetson talked of bringing a team of Alfa Romeos, but on a reduced basis. Bert Everett said that he would go it alone in his seven-year-old GTA.

Rumbles of discontent over Trans-Am and 2.5 purses finally reached SCCA headquarters. But the club's new director of competition, Watkins Glen founder, Cam Argetsinger, flatly stated that they could not afford an increase in either the Trans-Am or 2.5 prize money.

By the spring of 1972 the Trans-Am and 2.5 payoffs were conspicuously small, even by the SCCA's modest standards. For example, the first three places in the SCCA's F/5000 Continental, which was an indifferent success at its best, paid $13,800, $8,300 and $6,500. The same weekend, the first three Trans-Am places were awarded $4,000,

$3,000 and $2,500, while the 2.5 front-runners received $2,000, $1,300 and $900.

For the first time, the 1972 Trans-Am included a driver's championship. Manufacturer's points stayed at 9-6-4-3-2-1. Driver's points were allocated on a 20-15-12-10-8-6-4-3-2-1 basis to the top ten.

The May 6 Lime Rock opened the 1972 season. On May 5 Follmer qualified third in the Laguna Seca F/5000. George flew East that night and stuck Roy Woods' Javelin on the pole the morning of race day. Three hours later, after winning the Trans-Am by better than two laps and collecting his $4,000, he headed back to California. On Sunday May 7, Follmer finished third in the Continental.

Warren Tope, in a former Bud Moore Mustang, sat next to George. Carter's Camaro and Roy Woods' Javelin shared the second row.

The finish saw Warren Agor's Camaro second, Tony DeLorenzo's 1972 Firebird third, Roy Woods driving his own RWR Javelin home fourth, Warren Tope's Mustang fifth and Paul Nichter's Camaro sixth. Bill Collins, the rookie who had Donohue's

Second-place finisher Mike Downs in the 1972 2.5 Challenge at Road America. Jim Drago/ Road America

2.5 Challenge champion John Morton winning the 1972 Road America. Jim Drago/Road America

Sam Posey's BRE Datsun failed to finish the 1972 2.5 Challenge at Road America. Jim Drago/ Road America

1971 number 6 Javelin, was in seventh place, five laps behind Follmer.

The 1972 Trans-Am continued to pull good fields of thirty or more pony cars. But the series had a quality problem that was accented by its miserable purses.

When Lime Rock's "still running" tenth-place Mustang finished eleven laps behind the winner, it drew attention to a talent gap that was to become critical. Later that year one Trans-Am veteran remarked, "Running the '72 Trans-Am has been like driving one long chicane."

The Datsun 510s began the year with a 1-2-3 finish at Lime Rock. Bob Sharp, a six-time national champion, drove his BRE 510 to an easy win over Mike Downs. 2.5 champion John Morton broke early. (But the word was that he would have been disqualified for having received a push start.) Bert Everett's ancient GTA and John Buffum's new Ford Escort ran with the leaders until they faltered, and the three 510s ran away from the twenty-seven-car field. Ominously, although both races had large fields, the gate was way down.

On May 29 Follmer and Morton cleaned-up at Bryar before another sparse crowd. Two days before Bryar, spectators had seen Donohue and Revson share the front row at Indy before Mark went on to win the 500 in a record-shattering time that was to stand for twelve years.

Although Follmer earned the pole at Bryar, he gridded last. After failing to start for the warm-up lap, Roy Woods switched cars with George, who went to the back as he had not qualified Woods' car. A post-race check showed that the battery in Follmer's Javelin had exploded.

Seven laps after the start George had cut through the entire thirty-one-car field to grab, and hold, the lead. "We were watching him the entire race," said the Bryar race steward, "but he didn't bang into a single car."

Follmer's 200 mile run took 2:01:02. Milt Minter drove Herb Adams' 1972 Pontiac to a one-lap-down second place. Warren Agor's 1971 Camaro was third, Paul Nichter's 1968 Camaro fourth, Marshall Robbins' 1970

John Morton on 2.5 Challenge lap of honor, Road America 1972. Road America

Mustang fifth and the Tom Dutton/Lou Statzer 1969 Camaro finished sixth.

John Morton and Bob Sharp were 1-2 in Bryar's 2.5 Challenge, with John Buffum's Escort one lap down. After leading briefly, pole-sitter Kwech retired on lap thirteen with a broken gearbox. Everett's GTA finished fourth as thirteen of the nineteen starters completed 112 miles. Of the six 510s in the field, only winner Morton had the 1800 cc engine.

The script varied at Mid-Ohio where Milt Minter drove Herb Adams' Pontiac to a wire-to-wire win. Once again George tried to charge through the field from last on the grid. But this time, after suffering from two flat tires and a bent front end, second place was the best he could manage. Holding the lead for the entire 180 miles resulted in Pontiac pulling to within five points of Javelin— twenty-four to nineteen.

Agor's Camaro was third, Collins gave Mark's old car a look at fourth, Roy Woods' Javelin made fifth and Kent Fellows' 1969 Camaro took sixth. In averaging 78.99 mph, and winning $4,000, Minter put some new life in the fading series.

Peter Gregg and Mike Downs drove BRE 510s to a 1-2 win over John Morton's overheating 1800 cc 510. Alfas driven by Everett and Kwech were third and fourth.

After taking-off from the pole, Morton had everything his own way until lap twenty-nine when he pulled in with a steaming engine. Winner Gregg averaged 78.64 mph for 120 miles as twelve of twenty-three starters completed fifty of Mid-Ohio's 2.4 mile laps.

The June 17 Watkins Glen 2-Hours started with Follmer's Javelin feeling pressure from the Thompson and Tope Mustangs, and with Minter's Firebird lurking in the wings. But Tope and Minter retired early and Follmer motored on to a 1:41 win over Jerry Thompson's pony car. Woods' Javelin was third, Paul Nichter's Camaro, John Gimbel's Mustang and Dick Brown's Camaro filling the next three places.

Warren Tope's 98.272 qualifying time, Follmer's 98.479 fastest race lap and his 94.887 average speed for the 192.5 miles, all were Trans-Am records for Watkins Glen.

After four rounds, the 1972 Driver's Championship had Follmer with seventy-five points, Agor thirty-nine, Minter thirty-five, Woods thirty, Nichter twenty-six and Tope sixteen. Maker's points showed American Motors thirty-three, Pontiac nineteen, Camaro seventeen and Ford ten.

Following a full card of club racing on Sunday July 2, Donnybrooke staged the 2.5 Challenge as the day's feature race.

Datsun's invincibility was shattered when the Alfas of Horst Kwech and Bert Everett finished 1-2. Jerry Thompson's third prevented Datsun from being skunked as Ed Wach's Alfa made fourth, Richard Hall's 1600 cc Toyota fifth and a VW-44 sixth.

Morton had won the pole only to have his 510 wiped out on lap twenty-two in a minor shunt with Ken Schley's Alfa. Then, on lap thirty-seven of the fifty, Peter Gregg's 510 retired with a lack of oil pressure.

The July 4 210-miler at Donnybrooke saw George Follmer and Javelin win driver's and manufacturer's 1972 championships.

Pete Brock's Simoniz/Bre Datsuns led the charge for reigning champion Datsun in the fifth round of the 1972 2.5 Challenge series at the July 2 Donnybrooke Raceway in Brainerd, Minnesota. Bob Thomas Association

After starting on the pole, Follmer overcame a balky engine, broken suspension, malfunctioning transmission and two extra tire stops to finish twenty-eight seconds in front of Jerry Thompson's Mustang.

Twenty-six of the thirty-six starters were still running when the winning Javelin completed seventy laps with a 98.653 race average. Roy Woods brought his Javelin home third, Minter's Firebird was fourth, Steve Bradley's Camaro fifth and Warren Agor, whose Mustang had shared the front row with Follmer's Javelin, was sixth.

Five days after Donnybrooke, Roger Penske asked George to come down to Road Atlanta to pinch-hit for Mark Donohue, who had been injured while testing Penske's new Porsche 917K. Substitute Follmer won the Road Atlanta CanAm in record time.

July 15 saw Datsun return to its winning ways when eighteen 2.5 Challengers ran twenty-seven laps, 108 miles, over Road America's gentle hills.

There were six Datsun 510s, of which three were BRE works cars for newly recruited Sam Posey and regulars John Morton and Mike Downs. Kwech and Everett also led a six-car entry of Alfas with two Toyotas, one each VW Beetle, Austin-Cooper, BMW and Volvo filling the field.

Neither Kwech nor Everett ran the distance. Although Kwech lasted long enough to be classified in fifth place. Posey's engine went sour, but Morton and Downs came in 1-2 with Richard Hull's Toyota third.

The Road America Trans-Am that followed the 2.5 race gridded forty-two cars,

---

VOLVO 122S

Engine: ohv inline 4, 109 ci (1800 cc), 115 hp, dual 1-barrel SU carb
Transmission: 4-speed
Brakes: front, disc; rear, drum
Suspension: front, upper and lower wishbone, coil springs; rear, live axle, coil springs
Chassis: front engine, rear-wheel drive
Weight: 2300 lb
Notes: Street car had 1800 cc, 100 hp, 2400 lb.

John Buffum, who was to gain fame as an international rally driver, running the 2.5 Challenge in a Bobcor Alfa at Bryar. Bruce Czaja/Road America

Pre-race hustle at the 1972 Road America Trans-Am. Gordon Means/Road America

the season's largest field. Follmer sat on the pole and his Javelin recorded the 93.609 fastest race lap. But, for the second time that year, he failed to win, a sick engine putting him out eleven laps short of the fifty-lap distance.

Warren Tope, who had shared the front row, won a thriller from Milt Minter's Firebird. The Michigan driver beat the Californian by 1.5 seconds to win $4,000 in prize money plus $1,650 in accessory awards.

Bill Collins brought Donohue's old number 6 Javelin home third, with the Gene Harrington, Dick Brown and Paul Nichter Camaros filling the next three places. Tope averaged 89.824 mph for fifty laps around the four-mile course to join Minter in the "I beat Follmer" club.

When questioned about his plans, George Follmer replied, "I think I'm seeing my last Trans-Am." There had been some tight racing, but the 1972 crowds were way down. Trans-Am promoters were hurt and hollering. By this time Edmonton, Summit Point and Riverside had followed Seattle in canceling their Trans-Am dates.

In late July, SCCA announced that ten Trans-Ams were scheduled for 1973. It actually held six in 1973 and three in 1974. The 2.5 series also was in jeopardy. Promoters rejected it for its failure to attract a following and for the club's failure to promote it. Then the SCCA confused the big-car Trans-Am picture by saying it was considering the use of 366 cid, 6000 cc engines.

Pete Brock's Datsuns passed-up the July 29 Sanair when Nissan of Canada lost interest in supporting BRE's over-the-border venture. When Kwech decided to run the Donnybrooke F/5000, it left Bert Everett in charge, his seven-year-old GTA finishing a full lap up on the Schley and Theodorpopulous Alfas.

With three 2.5 races to go, Datsun had fifty-two points to Alfa's thirty-five.

The July 30 Trans-Am was an ignominious climax to what had been a bright chapter in American road racing. Held at St. Pie, Quebec, on Sanair's 1.3 mile drag strip cum

Bill Collins brought Donohue's 1971 Javelin home third in the 1972 Road America Trans-Am. Gulf Oil gave number 6 partial support. Road America

racetrack, it witnessed the withdrawal of the series champion to be.

Roy Woods had trucked his two Javelins from California. He had hired Baja winner, Bob Ferro, to drive in Follmer's place. He had already qualified his car on the front row next to pole-sitter Warren Tope. And the Ferro Javelin was safely in the field in the fifth row.

But Woods decided that Sanair's rough surface and battered Armco barriers made the track unsafe. Pulling-out under these circumstances was an especially courageous act.

The race was a demolition derby. Officially, accidents took out six cars, including that of the local favorite, Maurice Carter, who had qualified in the second row, only to be the victim of an accident on the second lap.

Tope's former Bud Moore Mustang won. St. Paul's Bill Collins stuck Donohue's old

Pole-sitter George Follmer in the number 1 Javelin and winner Warren Tope, number 31 Mustang, led 1972's 42 car field through Road America's first turn. Follmer made fastest lap, 93.609 mph, but fell out with engine failure on lap 39 of the 50 lap race. John and Roger Schreiber/Road America

Javelin into second, twenty-one seconds behind Tope. The third-place Nichter Camaro was two laps behind the leaders. Fourth-place Carl Shafer ran 124 laps, six behind. And the fifth- and sixth-placed cars of Dick Hoffman and Warren Agor made 121 laps, which was nine laps off the pace.

Only seven of the twenty-seven starters saw the checker. After the race, it was said someone asked Roy Woods where he bought his crystal ball.

Based on the best six of seven finishes, the 1972 Trans-Am final count showed Javelin with forty-eight points, Mustang thirty-four, Firebird twenty-eight and Camaro twenty-four.

But the 2.5 lived on. John Morton averaged 89.05 for fifty laps (126 miles) to give Datsun the 1972 championship with 510s finishing 1-2-3-5 in the August 19 Road Atlanta.

Sam Posey, a last-minute substitute for ailing Mike Downs, was second, Dave Madison third and Corky Bell's private 510 fifth.

Jim Fitzgerald's BRE 510, which had shared the front row of the thin, sixteen-car grid, broke its engine on lap ten. Neither the Kwech nor Everett Alfas went the distance, but Ken Schley's Alfa made fourth to keep Milano from getting skunked.

The September 17 Portland 2.5 got a much needed shot of publicity when BRE gave popular Hershel McGriff, NASCAR's Western champion, a ride.

McGriff shared the front row of the twenty-car grid with John Morton. The stock car veteran went on to come in second to Morton in the 105 mile main event.

The cast changed at Laguna Seca, but the idea remained when Bobby Allison was given the BRE guest shot.

Allison was winding-up one of his best years—he had won ten of NASCAR's thirty-one Grand Nationals and had been named stock car racing's Driver Of The Year. He started by driving the Datsun cautiously,

especially while it rained. But the man from Alabama soon took off after the leaders, Morton and Kwech, to set the day's fastest lap and finish third in the twenty-eight-car field.

That Laguna October weekend also saw a potentially stirring CanAm finish between teammates Donohue and Follmer turn into an orderly procession. As related by Mark in *the unfair advantage*, he was crushed when Penske signaled him to let Follmer, who had already earned the 1972 CanAm title, get by. In the "what it might have been and where it was" department, four of the first five finishers in the Laguna Seca CanAm—Follmer, Donohue, Minter and Posey—had been Trans-Am regulars.

Two incidents, one funny and one sad, livened the 2.5's last days.

Bob Cozza, the up-state New York Alfa wizard who kept Bert Everett's ancient hulk in one piece, became annoyed at the SCCA for not allowing the new Alfa two-liter GTAM sedan in the 2.5 Challenge. It also frustrated Cozza to see Pete Brock getting substantial support from Datsun, while he got the short end of the stick from his friends in Milano.

Near the close of the 1972 season, Bob Cozza wrote an open letter to *Competition Press*, in which he challenged Pete Brock to a duel. John Morton was to drive a BRE 510, Bert Everett would be in the Alfa GTAM. Head to head, may the best man win, just the two of them.

Brock accepted Cozza's challenge—with provisions. Cozza was to find a promoter willing to pay travel expenses, starting money and a sanction fee. Brock demanded that BRE's 510 be allowed to run on ten-inch wheels, the same as on the new Alfa, and that the 510 engine be bored-out to 2000 cc, the displacement of Alfa's GTAM.

Then Brock also decided that while Cozza would be allowed to pick the race distance, he would select the circuit. Finally, Brock said that the winner should keep the loser's car.

As with most editorial-page battles, not a shot was fired.

Incident number two took place following the final 2.5 Challenge at Riverside on

George Follmer's number 1 and Roy Woods'
number 2 1972 Javelins. American Motors

October 29. After sharing the front row with Kwech, pole-sitter Morton went on to win over Peter Gregg's 510, scattering the thirty-two-car field with a record 93.279 mph race average. Everett's Alfa was third, but Kwech's DNF'd with a blown engine, as did Allison's BRE Datsun.

As at Laguna two weeks earlier, race day at Riverside included a CanAm as well as the 2.5 Challenge. Consequently, when Morton pulled the Datsun into victory lane, an unusually large number of photographers crowded around to record the championship award ceremony.

Pete Brock rushed out to pump John's hand. BRE and Nissan personnel cheered. Then everyone stood around looking at the cameras with egg on their faces. When the embarrassment became acute, someone rushed off to explain the situation to race steward Joe Henderson.

A good guy, Henderson hurried to victory lane and had his picture taken shaking hands with John Morton. But there wasn't any trophy until someone suggested that Henderson present the new champion with the beat-up old fishing hat that was his trademark.

A few pictures of Henderson giving Morton his hat, and a couple of mildly negative comments about the lack of a trophy appeared in the racing press. But what blew the oversight into a *cause célèbre* was Tracy Bird's open letter to *Competition Press*. In substance, what Bird wrote was that the SCCA was not responsible for driver awards made at racetracks. And that the club handled such matters at its annual meetings.

Okay. But what Executive Director Tracy Bird's letter did reveal was that the SCCA's then-number-one man had been nearby during the fiasco, but that he had not bothered to come forward and offer the new champion his best wishes.

In the meantime, as an indication of what lay ahead for the SCCA, John Bishop's fledgling IMSA announced that its November 1972 Camel GT had pulled over 120 entries.

Winner Warren Tope Mustang keeps in touch with George Follmer's Javelin during running of 1972 Road America Trans-Am. William Schultz/ Road America

Chapter 13

Number 14

Road racing enthusiasts realize that Sports Car Club of America race drivers are a varied lot. Lawyers and doctors, teachers and their students, not to mention mail carriers, astronauts, pensioners, jet setters and most everyone between, are among the SCCA's 6,000-plus licensed drivers.

Bert Everett, quiet, average-sized, middle-aged, cigar-smoking, stands out. It isn't because he is comfortably fixed. One look at his Tara-like home or, more to the point, at some of the cars in his barn—a 633 BMW, GTS Ferrari, new Rolls-Royce Corniche or the immaculately restored Austin-Healey and the Porsche 914 with a 2.5 engine—only sends a part of the message.

Unlike the many World War II Navy pilots who turned to flying as a career, Bert is a businessman who made a go of several chemical processing plants. What really distinguishes Bert are his courtesy and that intangible aura of authority that so often surrounds a successful businessman.

Bert was in the same class as Mark Donohue and Peter Revson when he attended driver's school in 1960 at Lime Rock and Vineland. He quickly became an active regional racer and went on to win the Northeast E-production title in his Porsche Speedster.

Bert did not run in his first Trans-Am until he was forty-six. "In fact," he told me, "until I met Steve Smith I'd not even thought about the Trans-Am. Steve, who was an editor at *Car and Driver* at the time, really was the one who got me interested in running the Trans-Am.

"Steve was coming down to Bucks County to see a girl and we met at a couple of parties. Naturally, we talked about racing. Steve didn't drive but he suggested that we pool our resources and buy a new 911 for the under-2 series.

"We each put up $4,000 and had the car shipped over by air freight. I believe that the 911 cost us $6,200 and that shipping ran another thousand. So we had enough left over to buy two NASCAR fueling cans and eight mag wheels.

"Our first race was St. Jovite. On the way we stopped somewhere on New York's East Side for lunch. I remember that it was a French restaurant and that we left the race

Sebring Governor's Cup winner 1968. One happy fella! Dennis Koelmel/Bert Everett collection

car out front and asked the owner to keep an eye on it.

"The plan was that Steve would run the pits and I'd drive. But we soon disagreed over our responsibilities. Steve thought that he should plan my driving tactics and direct the team. I was to confine myself solely to driving. Pretty soon Steve was walking around the pits acting like Neubauer. All I wanted was good pit work and for someone to hold up a board every once in a while so that I knew where I stood in the race.

"Actually," Everett continued, "we didn't spend all the $8,000. Even though the under-2 prize money was bad, we made money, as I'd started to win a few races. Firestone started to give us a little help and later on we worked with Goodyear.

"When Steve left the team after Mid-Ohio we had a couple of thousand dollars profit. But Steve would not take a penny more than he had put into it. We had a joint bank account that I wanted to split with him. But he insisted that all he wanted was his origi-

nal investment. At that point we were about $6,000 ahead.

"We're still friends. In fact, Ginny and I spent a recent weekend at his place in Southampton.

"Why number 14? I suppose it was because I had the car serviced at Bob Holbert's. Bob had retired from racing in 1964 and that was his old racing number. As his shop maintained the car, it just seemed like the natural thing to do.

"I dropped number 14 and started to use number 25 when I switched to Alfas. Young Al Holbert was just getting started about that time so, of course, he began to use his dad's number.

"But the 911 didn't need much work. I recall a funny incident one time when I came back from a race with a nonfunctioning oil temperature gauge. I wasn't getting any reading so I asked them to fix it before the next race.

"But Bob Holbert told me to forget it. 'Obviously,' Bob said, 'your oil temperature and pressure are okay or you wouldn't have been able to run.' But I still asked them to fix it because looking at that zero oil temperature reading made me nervous. 'Okay,' Bob told me, 'we'll fix it so you won't get nervous.' So when I picked the car up for the next race

Watkins Glen, 1968. Bert Everett's Porsche 911 was sixth overall and second under-2 liters. Bert Everett collection

Kwech Capri leading Ford Escort.

they had covered the gauge with masking tape!

"Another incident I enjoyed happened early in the series when things were still pretty disorganized. You couldn't bring your car in underweight. But lots of Porsche drivers were rearranging the weight distribution because the 911 was so heavy in the back and too light in front. One car I recall had about forty pounds of lead in his front bumper. This was when the SCCA's Jim Patterson looked my car over and then told me, 'I can tell that your car is okay, Everett, because it still has the cigarette lighter in the dash.'

"After the Porsche was ruled out, I started using number 25 because that was the number Gus Andrey had used on his Alfa. Gus ran the Alfa for the first two races in 1970. Then I picked it up starting with Mid-Ohio. But Gus had busted the engine. So Andrey's mechanic, Oskar Feldman, and I drove all night. Like Gus, Feldman was a Swiss, and a really wonderful guy. We worked around the clock and got the engine in and I won Mid-Ohio.

Bert also told me, "I'd never driven an Alfa before and it took some time for me to get used to not seeing the horizon when I looked out the window on hard turns. Then some-

Corvette driver/owner John Greenwood, center, driver/journalist Ron Grable, right, and engine builder, Skip McCarthy, work on a Greenwood engine. Six Trans-Am races were held in 1973. In 1974 the series fell to three, but went up to seven in 1975. As SCCA's regulations favored A-B-C production and class A sedans, six of the seven 1975 Trans-Ams were won by 427 and 454 Corvettes. Road & Track

one came up to me in the pits and said that I was on two wheels most of the time.

"I knew that Alfas normally leaned a lot and that this one was especially bad because it had both driver's weight and the gas tank on the right. But I still didn't really believe I was on two wheels until I went out and charged at a line of pipes that ran crossways lining one of the fast turns. When I didn't feel a thing, no jolts, no bounces, I figured I must be lifting both wheels.

"I'd bought two Alfas from Gus Andrey and I met Bob Cozza when I advertized the second one in *Comp Press.* Bob had a good mail-order business on high-performance Alfa parts. We got to know each other and Bob became my car owner, first with the Alfa . . . then with the Escort.

"The Ford Cosworth Escort I drove in 1973 was Cozza's. John Buffum and I won nineteenth.] That Escort was a better race ished fifth overall. [The next under-2 was nineteenth.] That Escort was a better race car than either the Alfa or the 911. Two weeks after Road Atlanta I won Lime Rock's under-2 and we made a couple of thousand dollars.

"Cozza had two Escorts at the Glen the next month. I was first under-2, but Buffum's broke. I got a kick out of that Watkins Glen when I finished on the same lap with Mark Donohue and Al Holbert's Porsche Carrera RS.

"John Buffum and I teamed-up again at the '73 Sanair in the Escort. We won the under-2, or 2.5, or whatever they called it. I remember that we finished seventh overall and were just surrounded by Corvettes and Camaros.

"Then Bob got the idea of racing a [Alfa Romeo] Montreal. We went to the factory in Milan and the Alfa people were going to loan us one of their racing mechanics and give us lots of help. Absolutely nothing happened. . . . That three-liter Montreal was a real pig. Unlike other Alfas I've raced, it was a piece to handle.

"We never did get the Montreal running right during 1973. John Morton and I ran it in the combined World Championship and Trans-Am at Watkins Glen in 1974. But the engine broke after six laps.

"In 1975 I only raced once. Bob Cozza had opened an Alfa dealership on the Jersey

Greenwood Corvette at practice, Sebring, June 1973. Road & Track

shore and he entered the Alfetta at the Glen. But the engine went sour after ten laps."

Everett continued, "I think that the race I remember the best is one that I didn't win. It was 1971 at Riverside where I came in second.

"We had stopped off in Denver to visit Del Taylor, a friend who I think may still be racing. The four of us went to a combination night club and restaurant. When we were leaving I tripped and fell down a couple of stairs.

"I didn't see the doctor until the next morning. Then Del and his girl decided to fly out to Riverside with us, as I needed someone to help me work the Navion's brakes."

"The doctor put me in a cast and said I should stay off my feet for six weeks. But I figured that I might still be able to drive so I had the cast made smaller so that it just covered the lower part of my leg.

"But you should have seen the way that I had to twist around to get at the gearbox and peddles. The race stewards at Riverside didn't like the idea of my racing at all. They watched me real close in practice. And they tried to talk me out of it several times. But I made it. Like I said, I came in second.

"But the biggest kick I ever got out of any Trans-Am was at Green Valley when I was able to stay with Parnelli going through those little squiggles near the pits. We came into them side by side a couple of times and he'd get mad because he couldn't pass me.

"Of course Parnelli could blow me off almost anywhere else, but he couldn't catch me going through those little corners. He'd get real mad, and once, at Michigan in 1968, he did bounce me. But he came right up afterward and apologized. I remember that I told him that his bump had cost me two thousand bucks.

John Greenwood Vette displays the latest in paint jobs and ornaments at 1974 auto show.
Road & Track

Peter Gregg's Porsche RSR winning 1974 Road America Trans-Am. Bill Jennaro/Road America

"There were many fine drivers in the big cars. But Parnelli was the best. He just did everything right," Everett concluded.

Bob Holbert can't recall when he first used number 14. "All that I know is that it was on one of my early MGs. I sort of stayed with it. Then number 14 became a trademark for my cars," Holbert said.

Bert Everett no longer used number 14 in 1971 when it graced Al Holbert's Porsche 914-6, his first race car. To no one's surprise, number 14 has remained Al's number at least as late as 1986, where it's on the big Porsche 965 that Al and Derek Bell drove to many wins during the 1986 Camel GT series. However, as A. J. Foyt adopted number 14 years ago, Al's 1984 Indy car displayed number 21.

As Al Holbert related, "My first Trans-Am was the 1973 Road Atlanta. And it also was my first professional race. Roger Penske had arranged for me to have the factory sell me the same Porsche that they had used at Daytona.

"It was pretty exciting. I remember getting a big charge out of qualifying faster than Peter Gregg. Peter was very important. But he beat me in the race by about ten seconds."

As the SCCA's 1973 and 1974 regulations permitted a wild assortment of much-modified Camaros and Corvettes, I asked Al if running close to the, at least in theory, less agile Detroit iron, had made him uneasy.

"Well," Al replied, "the Corvettes did use a lot more room, and you never knew where some of them were going to end up. But then there were guys like Mo Carter, DeLorenzo and Greenwood who were a real challenge. The most difficult thing about those '73 races was that most of them were for 500 kilometers. I usually drove them alone and they could be pretty tiring."

That year's Watkins Glen was where Penske suggested that Al and Mark Donohue team up for the Trans-Am. Holbert said, "Mark was at the Glen for the CanAm in Penske's 917. But he hadn't qualified for the Trans-Am, so we started last. I got up to

Al Holbert number 14, leading third-place-finisher George Follmer number 16, as Hurley Haywood, who would beat Holbert by one second, is on far right. All three Porsche 934s were fresh out of the box for the 1976 Pocono Trans-Am. R. N. Masser, Jr./Al Holbert collection

Al Holbert's new 934 at 1976 Pocono Trans-Am.
Images by Fischer/Al Holbert collection

Carl Shafer's category II Camaro was overall
winner of the 1976 Road America Trans-Am. D.
R. Boyd/Road America

Ludwig Heimrath's Porsche was declared the overall winner of the 1977 Seattle Trans-Am when Peter Gregg's Porsche was disqualified following Heimrath's protest. On the right of the race queen is Bob Tullius, who brought Jaguar's XJS its first Trans-Am points by finishing fourth overall and winning category I. Mark Mooney/ Road & Track

second place when it started to rain. But I didn't have the sense to come in for rain tires and I crashed into the guardrail on the next of the last corner before you come into the pits.

"I limped back in and we replaced a part of the front suspension. We worked our way back up to eighth place, but the fog became so heavy that the race was red-flagged with twenty laps to go. Mo Carter's Camaro won and Peter was second. . . . Driving with Mark had been a real thrill."

The Trans-Am came close to going belly-up in 1974. Entries had remained fairly strong but attendance dropped below the break-even point.

Only three Trans-Ams were run during all of 1974. One of them was combined with the FIA 6-Hour World Championship of Makes, an event that Al Holbert will never forget.

Holbert opened the Trans-Am's ninth sea-

Start of 1977 Seattle saw Gregg Pickett's Monza take out Peter Gregg's Porsche, number 59, as George Follmer's Porsche, number 16, slips by. Ronald Miller/Road & Track

son by winning the Lime Rock 200-miler. Running a record 94.426 mph, the Bucks County, Pennsylvania, Porsche dealer finished nearly a full lap in front of Ludwig Heimrath. Coupled with Al's winning his first Camel GT, May was a very merry month indeed.

Sharing a Ford Escort with Tom Ciccone, P. L. Newman made his professional debut by retiring with engine failure after ninety-one laps.

Holbert's 1974 Glen Trans-Am was a memorable one. Soon after he qualified, he got a phone call that made him hurry home to attend the birth of his son Todd. Al's Glen partner, Elliott Forbes-Robinson, hitched a ride with the Posey/Hobbs Carrera.

The Beltoise and Jarrier Matra made mincemeat of the opposition. Finishing nine laps in front of the Hans Mueller/Gijs van Lennep works Porsche, the French pair was seventeen laps ahead of Trans-Am winners Peter Gregg and Hurley Haywood, who drove a Porsche Carrera.

Road America, the final 1974 Trans-Am, went to Gregg's Porsche over Warren Agor's Camaro by less than one second, with third-place Holbert and fourth-place Haywood all pushing the leader.

George Follmer's Porsche leading Greg Pickett's Corvette during the 1978 Sears Point Trans-Am. Joe Rusz/Road & Track

For 1975 the SCCA adopted a completely new set of regulations. Using the SCCA A-B-C production and A-sedan specs, as well as shortening the events to 100 mile sprints, turned out to be far from a solution.

Six of 1975's seven events went to 427 and 454 Corvettes driven by John Greenwood (3), Jerry Hansen (2) and Babe Headley/Paul Misurielo (1). Winners of the Trans-Am class at the Glen, the Headley/Misurielo Corvette, came in ninth overall. The Datsun 280Zs of Walt Maas (1) and Bob Sharp were the only non-Vettes to figure in the standings. The 1975 Trans-Am champion, John Greenwood, took home a total of $9,075 for his season-long prize and accessory awards.

The situation may not have improved from 1976 through 1979, when the SCCA introduced a set of regulations that even those who participated had difficulty understanding. However, confusion aside, it was agreed that the new rules had been different enough to add interest.

Category II cars, those prepared to specifications for FIA Group I through IV, plus "specially authorized cars," would produce the overall winners. Category I consisted of "cars prepared to SCCA production and sedan specifications."

Porsche 934s and 935s, hairy Corvettes and Chevy Monzas were in Category II. Category I, the slower class, included the Jaguar XJ-S, TR8s, Javelins, Camaros and those Corvettes that weighed less than 2,951 pounds and used ten-inch rims.

The SCCA sanctioned two categories of Trans-Am racing from 1976 through 1979. Category I covered SCCA classes previously approved—Camaros, Mustangs and Corvettes weighing less than 2,951 pounds that used 10-inch rims, the Jaguar XJS, Javelins and so on. Category II included hairy Corvettes, special Chevy Monzas, modified Camaros, FIA groups 1 through 4, plus those cars "specially authorized by the SCCA."

The Whittington Brothers number 95, and John Paul number 18 (both Al Holbert Porsches) crest the hill early in the 1979 Watkins Glen Trans-Am. Paul and Holbert were second in Category II, the 6-Hours overall win going to the Rob

McFarlin/Bob Akin/Roy Woods Porsche 935 while Category I was captured by the Tullius/Fuerstenau TR-8. Images by Fischer/Road & Track

The eight-race 1976 Trans-Am opened at Pocono with fresh out-of-the-box turbo-charged Porsche 934s filling the first three places. Hurley Haywood beat Al Holbert by less than a single second in Category II, with Jocko Maggiacomo's Javelin winning Category I.

All three of the front-running Porsches were in their first events. Third-place Follmer's and winner Haywood's white coupes were owned by California dealer, Vasek Polack. Holbert owned his car, which he had tested briefly at Weissach.

While Al was in Germany the works had agreed to paint his 934 the characteristic Sunoco blue used by Holbert Racing, and to affix its number 14. Al recalled that the special pleasure he had in having his first new race car was somewhat clouded by the troubles caused by the special paint job.

"Somehow," said Al, shaking his head in bewilderment, "some of the blue paint found its way into the oil line." Then Al recounted how paint chips had not only clogged the oil filter, but how extremely cold weather at Pocono that May had partially blocked the line and caused it to explode!

Round two saw Follmer and Haywood run 1-2 at Nelson Ledges with sixth-place Jocko's Javelin again taking Category I.

At Portland, broken turbo seals sidelined Follmer and Haywood, with Monte Shelton's Carrera finishing almost two laps in front of Joe Chamberlain's Category II-winning Camaro.

Round four traveled to Watkins Glen where the Trans-Am was again staged as a part of the six-hour, 575 mile World Championship for makes. Driven by Gregg/Haywood, a BMW CSL finished fourth overall to win Category II. The John Bauer/Walt Maas Porsche 911 finished tenth to win Category I.

Number 14, piloted by Jim Busby and owner Holbert, had its fuel line split and

John Paul's Porsche during 1979 Watkins Glen 6-Hours. Al Holbert (helmeted figure over crewman holding tire) made his only Trans-Am appearance during 1979 here. Ken Zepp/Al Holbert collection

wound up sixteenth. Al explained, "The fuel line was located under the gas tank. It took forever to repair."

Road America went to Carl Shafer's Category II 454 Camaro. Follmer's Porsche was second, another 454 Camaro driven by Greg Pickett was third and Al Holbert fourth. Sixth-place Don Hager's Corvette won Category I.

Brainerd, another horsepower circuit, saw Carl Shafer's Camaro finish less than two seconds in front of Follmer's Porsche. Category I honors were taken by Ron Weaver's Corvette.

Number 14 lost to the Canadian veteran, Ludwig Heimrath, at Mosport, where Porsche turbos filled the first three places. Sixth overall and first in Category I was John Huber's Corvette. Al Holbert held the lead at Mosport until a flat forced him in for a tire change three laps from the finish. "Making matters more complicated," Al told me, "was that we discovered that our tire gauge was off by seven or eight pounds. Now we carry at least two tire gauges."

"George really gave me a driving lesson at Three Rivers," Al mused. "Both Mark and George were racing in the Trans-Am for Penske when I worked at Roger's garage in Newtown Square. I remember that Follmer would always finish with broken gearboxes,

but that Mark would always wear out his brakes. When Mark came in, there were absolutely no pads left.

"Now I was really having a tremendously exciting race with George at Three Rivers. George had qualified fastest and he'd set a lap record during the race. It was great. The results show him beating me by 1.8 seconds. But I think it was even closer."

Chevrolet earned Category I honors for 1976 with Porsche winning Category II. George Follmer, Hurley Haywood and Jock Maggiacomo headed the final driver standings.

Three races of the eleven-race 1977 Trans-Am series were held at Westwood, Mosport and St. Jovite. Two others, each for eighty laps, were run on consecutive September days at Road America. As had become customary, Watkins Glen held a Trans-Am in conjunction with its FIA Makes Championship. The remaining five were held at Seattle, Portland, Nelson Ledges, Hallett and Brainerd. Overall, an odd mix of circuits.

Porsche 934 Turbos, with Peter Gregg (185 points), Ludwig Heimrath (162) and Monte Shelton (97) leading the way, easily won Category II—117 points to Chevrolet's thirty-three. Missing from the Trans-Am in 1977 was number 14, as Al Holbert was successfully defending his Camel GT title, running Le Mans and appearing on TV's IROC.

Category I in 1977 was a down-to-the-wire battle between the Tullius Group 44 XJS Jaguar and an army of Porsche 911s. Bob took the driver's title, 170 points to John Bauer's 162. But Porsche nosed-out BMC for the maker's crown, seventy-six to seventy-four.

The Watkins Glen Trans-Am had pulled a good number of celebrity racers. The 1976 Indy winner, Johnny Rutherford, shared the fourth overall, second in Trans-Am, Porsche with Dick Barbour. One place back was the Danny Ongais/Ted Field Porsche 934. The Dickie Smothers/John Greenwood Vette was sidelined when it lost an engine, the same fate that hit the BMW driven by the unusual duo of Formula One's Hans Stuck and NASCAR's Benny Parsons.

G. W. Dickinson, one of Al Holbert's early backers, and Al's father, Bob (in cap), who was the first US Road Racing Champion. Images by Fischer/Al Holbert collection

Mexico City joined Sears Point, Laguna Seca, Brainerd, Road America, Portland, Watkins Glen and three Canadian circuits—Westwood, St. Jovite and Mosport—in running ten 1978 Trans-Ams.

Corvette 427s and Porsche Turbos each won four times. Chevy Monzas driven by Jerry Hansen and Tuck Thomas entered Category II's winners circle for the first time.

Porsche wins were registered by Heimrath (2), Monte Shelton (2) and Hal Shaw who shared Shelton's win in the Glen 6-Hours.

The four victories that Greg Pickett earned in his 427 Corvette saw him finish with 132.5 points to 114.5 for Tuck Thomas, whose Monza was a consistently high finisher.

Chevrolet won the Category II manufacturer's crown with seventy-four points, to sixty-five for Porsche.

Bob Tullius skewered the field in Category I. In winning seven of the ten races, Bob took the 1978 crown with 189 points to Babe Headley's 98.5. However, Jaguar's points were barely enough to take the maker's title, seventy-three to Chevrolet's sixty-nine.

When the nine-race 1979 season opened in Mexico City, it was the Camaro of Miguel Muny and the Porsche 935 of John Paul, Sr., that entered victory lane.

One month later John Paul repeated his south-of-the-border caper with a win at western Canada's Westwood. Taking the less-exotic-car honors was Gary Carlen's Corvette.

Portland saw both Gene Bothwell's Corvette and John Paul's 935 lead the entire race. The Corvette went forty-seven laps, to the Porsche fifty.

The Rob McFarlin/Bob Akin/Roy Woods 935 won Category II at Watkins Glen with

*Bob Tullius winning the 1978 Trans-Am season final in Mexico City to earn his second Drivers title, as well as giving the Category I Manufac-*turer's Championship to Jaguar's XJS. Road & Track

Category I going to the Tullius/Fuerstenau TR-8. John Paul and co-driver, Al Holbert, who was making his only 1979 Trans-Am, were second in Category II. The Feinstein/Oleyar/Engels 454 Corvette finished second in Category I.

Road America fell to Gene Bothwell's Corvette and John Paul's 935, the Category I winner earning $3,800 while Paul took home $6,050.

Four weeks after it held a Trans-Am in conjunction with the Makes Championship, the Glen staged a 100 mile Trans-Am. The Tullius TR-8 again took Category I honors as John Paul copped Category II. Both winners earned the pole in their classes. Then Tullius led his race for twenty-five of its twenty-nine laps, with John Paul staying out front in Category II.

Round seven at Mosport was winners circle time for both Gene Bothwell's Corvette and John Paul's 935, which continued to dominate the faster class.

Except for a single Mach 1 Mustang, two old 914 Porsches, and one Monza, the entire nineteen-car Mosport entry consisted of Camaros and Corvettes.

Honors at Three Rivers, Quebec, round eight in the fading 1979 series, were shared again by Gene Bothwell's Corvette and John Paul's Porsche. Once more the winners led every lap of their respective classes. And this time it enabled them to sew-up their annual championships.

Laguna Seca, the final 1979 event, celebrated the end of the two-tier Trans-Am. Here too, both winners, Bob Tullius and Peter Gregg, led their events from start to finish, as well as having sat on the pole and having run the fastest lap in their category.

Race purses showed modest improvement. John Paul, who had scored 169 points to runner-up Tuck Thomas' seventy-one, earned $69,700.

Gene Bothello, who finished with 115 points to seventy-six for Bob Tullius, pocketed $37,357 for the year's work.

Chapter 14

House racer

Detroit has had its share of distinguished house racers. Beginning in the fifties, you weren't in the automobile business if you didn't race—the great Belgian-born Zora Arkus-Duntov worked for Chevrolet for a quarter-century. Contrary to popular belief,

he did not conceive the Corvette; Zora did, however, influence GM's performance posture.

Ronnie Householder, who ruled the early midget scene and regularly raced at Indy, directed Chrysler's many racing ventures

Ford Cougar paddock, Marlboro 1967. Shown here is Bud Moore, extreme left and Fran Hernandez, in dark glasses, center, next to driver Ed Leslie. Lincoln-Mercury PR man Monty Roberts, *wearing a tie, stands next to Leslie. Dan Gurney is in helmet on right. Timer/scorer Judy Stropus, sitting in truck, is about to work her first professional race. Pete Luongo/Judy Stropus collection*

during the fifties and sixties. Scott Harvey, Plymouth's long-time rallyist in residence, now heads a Chrysler performance operation in Los Angeles.

Currently, with racing "respectable" again, Detroit abounds in house racers, several of whom have Teutonic accents. Ford's Fran Hernandez, whose credentials tower over the present lot, sits on the sidelines.

Everyone who has watched our space shuttles make one of their amazingly precise landings at Edwards Air Force Base has been looking at the place where Fran learned his trade. Until World War II, Edwards was known as Muroc Dry Lake.

Lying 100 miles northeast of Los Angeles in the Sierra high desert country, Muroc is where hot rodding, and much that is innovative about American oval track and road racing, had its beginnings. Except during

The late Ronnie Householder ran Chrysler racing programs with a firm hand. An experienced race driver, Householder finished twelfth in the 1937 Indy.

brief autumn rains, Muroc's ten-by-twenty-two-mile desert floor is packed hard and smooth. Here is where drag racing czar Wally Parks, the legendary Ed Winfield, journalist Dean Batchelor, Shelby's Phil Remington and a host of future automobile racing greats, including a skinny Mexican kid called Fran, got their start.

Hernandez's card reads: Ford/F. A. Hernandez/Section Supervisor/Advanced Vehicle Development/Engineering Department/Car Product Development. Fran still seems to be the same "Let's get the job done" sort of man who first directed the Cougar, then the Mustang, Trans-Am programs.

"Directed" does not mean that Fran outranked Ford's overall racing boss, Jacque Passino. But Fran, who had long looked after both the Ford and Lincoln-Mercury stock car activities, was Ford's Trans-Am field boss.

Fran had worked for Fred Offenhauser and cam specialist Vic Edelbrook before going with Ford. Following assignments with Ford on a freelance basis, Fran became a Ford employee in 1957.

This was the time of NASCAR's flowering. Bill France's rules didn't allow any one make or model to dominate his Grand National series. One manufacturer might enjoy a temporary advantage, but before the season ended you could be certain that Big Bill would write new regulations that equalized the competition.

To a large degree it was up to the Richard Pettys, Bud Moores, Junior Johnsons and Smokey Yunicks to get the most out of what Detroit produced. Equally important, it was up to each maker to supply the car builders and engine men with an automobile that had the potential to run out front. The fact that Fran Hernandez was the liaison for a company whose founder once held the Land Speed Record was a questionable advantage.

Dearborn is like a huge college campus that lacks a basic design. Dozens of large buildings, most of which are pleasant glass shoeboxes, occupy their own carefully tended grounds. Overwhelming the greenery and buildings themselves are each unit's gargantuan parking lot.

If Ford's Dearborn has a center, it would

be the Henry Ford Museum/Greenfield Village/Dearborn Inn complex on Oakwood Boulevard. Another possible Dearborn hub may be Ford's huge World Headquarters, which is located about one mile from the Dearborn Inn, as the crow flies. By car, however, it is an overnight journey. Exaggerations aside, it is about a four-mile drive and there's no way to walk.

I was expected at Ford's Photo Archives, which is housed in the sub-basement of the World Headquarters Building. As it was a nice autumn day, I told the desk clerk at the Dearborn Inn that if she would give me directions to World Headquarters I'd leave my car in the lot and walk.

"We don't recommend that," she replied. "There's just no way to walk there and get around the freeways unless you walked miles. And some of the roads you'd have to cross are fenced in. We don't even think it's a good idea for our guests to walk to the Greenfield Village and the museum. And they are only a quarter-mile right up Oakland."

When I told Paul Preuss, Ford's race-wise PR man, about not being able to walk to the World Headquarters appointment he had arranged, he said, "If it's exercise you want, go jogging."

Fran Hernandez told me that he started in the Trans-Am late in 1966 after Lincoln-Mercury announced it would have a team the following year. "We had Parnelli Jones, Dan Gurney and Ed Leslie. I'd been concentrating on NASCAR where we had such great stock car drivers as Joe Weatherby, Curtis Turner, David Pearson and guys like that.

"When you grow up in this business, like I did, you depend an awful lot on friendship. It's very important in racing. I wanted to go with a group that I had access to. Bud

Lincoln-Mercury's Leo Beebe, who was to encourage fielding a strong Cougar entry for the Trans-Am, is seen here with Ford "whiz kid,"

Ray Geddes, in the Ford garage at the 1965 Le Mans.

Moore's shop in Spartanburg was a good one for the Trans-Am Cougars. Besides," said Fran grinning, "it belonged to Ford."

"You know that Carroll Shelby at that time," Fran went on to say, "had a lot going on. He was mixed-up in Le Mans and all that stuff."

I mentioned that just before Dan Gurney went to Chrysler, he had been somewhat critical of the politics between the Shelby and Bud Moore teams. Fran's reply was, "Dan liked to be on his own. He was always trying to get something started for himself. He was used to running his own shop over here and in Europe. We just weren't set up that way."

Fran, Paul Preuss and I got talking about the Trans-Am drivers. With a few teams fielding so few cars, we agreed that the pressure to get the best drivers was unprecedented. Inevitably, I asked Fran who he considered to be the best of all race drivers.

"Parnelli Jones. Unquestionably," Hernandez replied. "Not only was Parnelli the best in the Trans-Am, he was the best race driver I've ever seen in any type of racing. People may not realize it, but Parnelli had a good deal of experience in road racing before he drove the Cougars and Mustangs.

"Of course he had his own style and he had gotten used to downshifting on turns and I

A. J. Foyt, in helmet, takes over from Dan Gurney during the 1967 Le Mans. Carroll Shelby's Al Dowd is on the fuel pump. Shelby's Phil Remington stands on pit counter. Goodyear's Mike Babich is with air hose on right. Team McLaren's Teddy Mayer, with headset and clipboard, on pit counter at extreme left. Homer Perry, with necktie, who was to act as Ford Motor Company's fiscal liaison between Dearborn and its Trans-Am teams, is next to Foyt behind the wall. Photo Actualities/ACO

had a hard time trying to get him to use the brakes. I just wanted him to stop the downshifting and use the brakes because it's much faster.

"'You don't realize it,' I told Parnelli, 'but you'll make better time if you get on the brakes and stay away from that gearbox.' What finally convinced Parnelli was when I showed him his times. Parnelli could hardly believe it. But I had the times right there. After that he used the brakes more."

Then I asked Fran about the problem Ford was reported to have had in getting the SCCA to allow a new carb setup for the Boss 302. "Well," Fran replied, "we were planning to use the inline four-barrel carb. But we simply couldn't satisfy the SCCA that we had gone into production on it." When I asked if they *really* had, Fran smiled and said, "Sure, sort of."

We got talking about Jerry Titus and I commented on how surprised I'd been when he left Carroll Shelby. "The reason for that," said Fran, "wasn't because of any problems Jerry had with Carroll. What people didn't realize is that Jerry considered himself a number-one chassis man. This was hard on Jerry because we just wouldn't build the cars the way that Jerry wanted them. When that Canadian guy came along with that deal on the Pontiacs, it gave Jerry a chance to run his own show."

Then both Fran and Paul told me a story that they believe reveals how Jerry really felt about Ford: In August 1984, a month before my meetings in Dearborn, Jerry's son Rick, who is with *Sports Car Graphic*, had addressed the Shelby-American convention in Anaheim, California. During his talk, Paul Preuss recalled Rick Titus saying, "Although he died in a Pontiac, my father always was a Ford Man."

Turning to Fran, I said that I hoped the story I was about to tell would not get his nose out of joint, but that I'd dearly like to know if it was true. It was said to have happened at the 1968 Riverside where Horst Kwech had been hired to drive an extra Mustang.

Kwech, I heard, had pulled into the pits after registering some so-so practice times. Then Fran was supposed to have walked over to Kwech and to have pointed to the Armco barriers that lined the long, fast, sweeping curve through Riverside's turn nine.

"Kwech," I understand Fran said, "The next time you come back in, I want to see yellow paint on these barriers and the marks of those barriers all along the left side of your car."

"The story is absolutely right." Fran replied. "That's just about what I said. But what you don't know is that the next time Horst went out he took two seconds off the lap record." (The following day Horst Kwech won his only over-2 Trans-Am.)

We got talking about American Motors and its track-side dealer tents and of how aggressively it had pushed Javelin's two championships. Even Chevrolet, we agreed, had capitalized on the Camaro's Trans-Am success in its advertising, particularly in the enthusiast press.

"Ford had a different philosophy about advertising racing," said Paul Pruess. "We looked on racing to generate its own coverage. We never had a separate racing budget. In fact, even though we had muscle cars

*Bud Moore, left, and Fran Hernandez flank the SCCA's John Timanus during the 1970 Trans-Am at Laguna Seca. Cam Warren/*Road & Track

from the very beginning, we never promoted them as aggressively as the others.

"We were doing well in all forms of racing. Ford covered everything at that time. And we won everything in sight: Indy, Le Mans, NASCAR Championships, Formula One. What really was unbelievable was the publicity we got after Ford won its first Indy with Jim Clark in 1965. The worldwide coverage that came from that one race was simply incredible."

After talking about the present Trans-Am series, in which, not incidentally, Ford is doing very well, Fran Hernandez made the following comment: "I know that the Trans-Am is finally coming back. They've got some good cars again, and some good drivers.

"But what's being raced in the Trans-Am today are out-and-out race cars. From '66 through '70 we had the best drivers anybody could find. And we had them driving those nearly stock production cars.

"As far as I'm concerned," Fran concluded, "The old Trans-Am was probably the best race series ever run in the United States."

Chapter 15

Performance was no handicap

The foundation for the Trans-Am regulations that started in 1980 (and have continued through 1986, at least) is "performance handicapping by a weight/displacement table." Depending largely on the Category I 1976 through 1979 cars, the series consisted of domestic and imported production cars. According to the SCCA,

"The cornerstone of the formula is five liter machines at 2600 pounds and all cars have a maximum 10-inch wheel width and 110-inch wheelbase maximum."

The fact that the SCCA also used the term "stock-appearing" in describing the current Trans-Am car has had a lot to do with the marked improvement in the series' health. Rules are adjusted as years pass. But the power/weight principle, plus intuition, remains in force.

With firsts at Hallett, Watkins Glen, Donnybrooke and Westwood, John Bauer and his 911SC Porsche won the 1980 championship with 127 points to 76 for Greg Pickett's Corvette. Road & Track

Although the field was dominated by Corvettes, the nine-race 1980 Trans-Am championship went to John Bauer's Porsche 911SC. First-place finishes at Hallett, Watkins Glen, Brainerd and Westwood, backed by a second at Portland and a fourth at Road America, brought the San Luis Obispo driver 127 points, the annual title and $37,357.

Late series starter Greg Pickett acquired seventy-six points and the runner-up spot by knocking off second-place finishes at Brainerd and Three Rivers before his Corvette won the season's last two events at Laguna Seca and Riverside.

Monte Shelton's 911SC ended the year in third place, Roy Woods' Camaro was fourth and Mark Pielsticker's Chevy Monza was fifth.

In 1980 the Trans Am returned to single class racing with a driver's as well as manufacturer's championship. The key to the SCCA's new regulations, "Performance handicapping by a weight/displacement table," remains in force. New regulations allowed tube-frame chassis. As noted by John Timanus, the club's technical director of professional racing, "By 1982 the new construction principle had really come alive and the Trans-Am championship was won by the Huffaker Pontiacs. The tube-frame chassis being developed was along the lines of NASCAR Winston West short-track chassis, but with stricter control over the body shape." Rules have been changed as conditions change. But the power-to-weight principle, *plus intuition,* remains.

Canadian veteran Eppie Wietzes' Corvette opened the nine-race 1981 season by win-

WILLY T. RIBBS   DAVID HOBBS   FRANK LEARY   LYN ST. JAMES

GEORGE FOLLMER   ROB McFARLIN   VERN SMITH   ELLIOTT FORBES-ROBINSON

Ribbs, Hobbs, Leary, St. James, Follmer, McFarlin, Smith and Forbes-Robinson.

ning the first-ever Trans-Am to run on the banks of Charlotte Motor Speedway.

Averaging 101.25 mph for 101 miles, Wietzes finished six seconds up on the Bob Tullius XJ-S Jaguar. Driving a 924 Turbo, which VW of America had helped Holbert's race shop prepare, Doc Bundy came in third.

Fourth-place-finisher George Follmer had an interesting return to the Trans-Am wars. His Cooke/Woods Camaro led for twenty-seven of the forty-five laps, and George recorded the day's fastest race lap. But Follmer finished fourth after being penalized fifteen seconds for jumping a yellow-light restart.

Having run NASCAR sedans through much of 1978, Al Holbert was no stranger to the high banks of Charlotte. It was around this time that Al got his own plane. Running stock cars, in addition to a heavy CanAm and IMSA program—he won Camel titles in 1977 and 1978, plus winning Sebring and becoming one of the few American road racers to appear on TV's IROC—didn't allow much time between events. But a broken turbo resulted in number 14 being DNF at Charlotte.

Three former Trans-Am champions—Bob Tullius, Eppie Wietzes and John Bauer—led the forty-nine-car Portland entry where Group 44's Jaguar nosed-out the Wietzes Corvette and the Bauer 911 by split seconds. Follmer's Camaro, which had qualified second, wound-up an ignominious ninth and Doc Bundy crashed his 924.

After failing to remain healthy at Charlotte and Portland, Greg Pickett's Corvette

TOM GLOY   GREG PICKETT   PAUL NEWMAN   DOC BUNDY

HURLEY HAYWOOD   PHIL CURRIN   BRAD MURHPEY   BOB BERGSTROM

Gloy, Pickett, Newman, Bundy, Haywood, Currin, Murphey and Bergstrom.

led for sixty-three of the sixty-six laps to win Lime Rock by a half minute over the Holbert and Bundy 924 Turbos. Lime Rock pole-sitter, Brian Redman, led for the first two laps, but crashed the Cooke-Woods Camaro on lap twenty-one.

Monte Shelton became the fourth different winner in the first four 1981 Trans-Ams. Having switched from a 911SC, Shelton's new Porsche 930 took the pole and led for all twenty-five laps of the Road America 100-miler. Second and third fell to Wietzes' Corvette and John Bauer's Porsche as thirty of the forty-nine starters went the distance.

Brainerd saw Tullius become the 1981 season's first repeat winner. Wietzes' Corvette finished four seconds behind the XJ-S Jaguar, with Roy Woods' Camaro coming in third.

After qualifying third at Quebec's Three Rivers, Eppie Wietzes' Corvette led for twenty-eight of the thirty-five laps to earn a fifty-eight-second win over the Woods Camaro. Bringing his Mustang home third was Lafayette, California's Tom Gloy.

Mosport, round seven, saw Bob Tullius return to the winners circle for the third time in 1981. Doc Bundy's 924 and Mo Carter's Camaro filled the next two places as Eppie Wietzes tightened the point chase when he retired early with a broken engine.

Laguna Seca saw George Follmer win his thirteenth Trans-Am (his first since 1977), the year that he only ran two Trans-Ams and turned to other fields. After sticking the Cooke-Woods Camaro on the pole, Follmer proceeded to run at the head of the pack for all fifty-two laps. Gordon Smiley's Camaro was second, Wietzes' Corvette third.

Tom Gloy, the 1979 Formula Atlantic title holder, won his first-ever Trans-Am in the season finale at California's hilly Sears Point. Gloy's Mustang earned the pole with a record 88.672 lap and won the 100-miler with a record 84.547 average speed. Completing the record-breaking weekend was stock car's Jimmy Insolo, who ran a record 87.276 race lap. Pickett's Corvette was fourteen seconds off the pace and Wietzes' Corvette again finished third.

Final 1981 standings showed Wietzes with 179 points, followed by Bob Tullius at 126. Steady Phil Currin, whose Corvette registered three fourths, one fifth and two sixths, gathered ninety-one points, which earned him third place.

Earning points from both Camaro and Corvette helped Chevrolet take the make's title with sixty-four points. Porsche finished with thirty-six, Jaguar thirty-five and Ford thirteen. Considering that Chevrolet's points came from four drivers, and that Porsche's were scored by six, the feat of bringing the Jaguar within a single point of Porsche is a tribute to Bob Tullius.

Performance handicapping remained the foundation for 1982 rules. It didn't much matter that 5100 cc Corvettes and Camaros

Winning the 1982 Donnybrooke in Bob Sharp's 280 ZX brought the veteran actor Paul Newman long overdue recognition as a race driver.

Greg Pickett, one of the winningest drivers in recent Trans-Am racing, lifts a wheel in his Corvette while leading David Hobbs' DeAtley Camaro.

During 1982, Doc Bundy drove the Holbert 924 Turbo to wins at Sears Point and Portland. Al Holbert collection

ran against 2000 cc Porsche Turbos, or that a 1,600 pound, 2700 cc Pontiac Firebird mixed it up with a 2,464 pound, 5100 cc Mustang, as most of the match-ups worked.

Race purses again inched upward, now paying $7,500, $5,000 and $3,500, plus pole and accessory awards. Prize money went to the first twenty finishers; although once you dropped beyond the first ten, the payoffs fell to $200 for the backmarkers.

In 1982, ten 100-mile sprints were held at nine courses: four on the West Coast (Sears Point with two, Portland, Seattle and Laguna Seca), three from the Midwest (Mid-Ohio, Road America and Brainerd), and one each in the South and Canada (Road Atlanta and Three Rivers). New cars, such as Pontiac's Trans-Am, and new drivers, especially Paul Newman, added interest to the series.

Veteran Jerry Hansen's Corvette took the opener at Road Atlanta, and won round seven at Road America. Nine of the first ten finishers at Road Atlanta were Corvettes, Camaros and Trans Ams. The exception was Rob McFarlin's ninth-place Mustang.

1982 Trans-Am champion Elliott Forbes-Robinson. Hal Crocker/Road & Track

Doc Bundy, whose Holbert Porsche had been dead-last at Road Atlanta, charged to first-place finishes at the next two events, Sears Point and Portland. (Doc had explained his Road Atlanta crash to Al Holbert by saying, "I forgot to pump the brakes.")

After being the runner-up at Sears Point and Portland, Elliott Forbes-Robinson won a close one over Phil Currin and Tom Gloy at Laguna Seca. Behind Currin's Corvette and Gloy's Mustang was Milt Minter's Trans Am and Frank Leary's Datsun 280 Turbo.

On a roll with the Joe Huffaker-prepared Trans Am, Forbes-Robinson won the pole at Seattle and went on to beat Tony Brassfield's Trans Am and Doc Bundy's 924.

After leading for forty-two of Mid-Ohio's fifty-two laps, Elliott Forbes-Robinson finished four seconds up on Roy Woods' Camaro. Except for Tom Gloy's qualifying record (he dropped out early and finished thirty-fifth), Mid-Ohio was all Forbes-Robinson.

Jerry Hansen's home course, Road America, gave him a fifty-four-second wire-to-wire win over Carl Shafer's Trans Am and Phil Currin's Corvette.

Brainerd saw Paul Newman set the racing world on its ear when he qualified Sharp's 280ZX on the pole and led all thirty-three laps to win with a record 102.589 race average. Tom Gloy's Mustang was 7.45 seconds behind the Datsun with Tim Evans' Trans Am in third.

At Three Rivers Elliott Forbes-Robinson took his fourth 1982 feature with a four-second win over his Huffaker-mounted teammate, Eppie Wietzes. Paul Miller's third-place Porsche 924 broke up a solid, eight out of ten, GM finish.

Tom Gloy's Mustang saw victory lane for the first time in 1982 at Sears Point. Forbes-Robinson had earned the pole, but Gloy got by to finish seven seconds up on Doc Bundy and Forbes-Robinson. Finishing seventh, on the same lap as the leaders, was the Loren St. Lawrence-driven DeAtley 380 SL.

After piling-up four wins, two seconds, one third and a fifth, Elliott Forbes-Robinson finished the 1982 season with 147 points. Doc Bundy and Phil Currin were tied at ninety-two. As Doc Bundy had the higher finishing record, the Porsche driver took second-place money.

Manufacturer's laurels for 1982 went to Pontiac with sixty-five points. Chevrolet had forty-two, Porsche thirty-seven, Ford twenty-two and Mercedes-Benz one.

The DeAtley name first appeared in Trans-Am results in the June 1981 Portland race where Loren St. Lawrence, an experienced club racer, qualified the DeAtley Mercedes 450 SL forty-sixth and retired with brakeline problems after one lap.

Road America saw the 450 SL start twenty-fifth and finish thirty-eighth. The same driver/owner/car combination qualified nineteenth at Brainerd and finished thirteenth, on the same lap as the winner. At Three Rivers, it was fifteenth on the grid, eighth at the finish, and $1,000 richer. After suffering gearbox problems in practice, the DeAtley team failed to start Mosport. Now known as the Michelob Mercedes, the 450SL

qualified twenty-eighth at Laguna before dropping out with bad brakes on lap twenty-three. Sears Point had them qualify twenty-first and finish tenth.

Neil DeAtley, the man behind this Don Quixote-like campaign, owned a Mercedes store in Portland and had mining and construction interests. During the 1982 Trans-Am, a $500 pole-position award was arranged by DeAtley.

Following a series of indifferent finishes in 1982, highlighted by a tenth at Monterey, sixth at Road America and seventh at Sears Point—in a new alloy version of the 380's engine—DeAtley apparently decided to go for winners.

The result of Neil DeAtley's decision to support a first-class team was to propel the Trans-Am back into big-time racing. The 1983 and 1984 Trans-Am didn't match those

Willy T. Ribbs winning 1983 Mid-Ohio Trans-Am in the DeAtley Camaro. Sport Graphics/ Road & Track

halcyon years when Detroit poured millions into its struggle for pony car supremacy. But exciting new drivers, new cars and big-buck sponsorship from Budweiser added-up to the best racing since the Trans-Am's glory days.

Georgia veteran Gene Felton, who has raced everything on wheels, and had won four Kelly Girl IMSA Championships, won the 1983 twelve-race opener at Moroso Park in West Palm Beach. It was a typical Felton race. David Hobbs, Willy T. Ribbs and Tom Gloy had taken turns as the race leader before Felton arranged to stick the nose of his Trans Am out front for the first time on the last lap.

Driving a John Dick-prepared DeAtley Camaro, Hobbs was less than one second behind Felton. Pickett's Corvette, Leary's Trans Am and the second DeAtley Camaro driven by Ribbs rounded-out the first five.

Summit Point, West Virginia, round two, saw Ribbs earn the pole, run the fastest lap and crash on lap thirty-four of fifty. But teammate Hobbs led all the way to bring DeAtley his first win. Second-place Tom Gloy's Capri was followed by Paul Newman's Datsun, Phil Currin's Corvette and Paul Miller's Turbo Porsche.

In 1959 twenty-year-old David Hobbs began racing cars fitted with his father's unusual (some accounts of it in David's native England referred to it as strange) Meccamatic automatic transmission. Finishing well in Meccamatic and other well-equipped Lotuses and Jaguars brought Hobbs works rides and a well-deserved reputation as one of the sport's leading drivers.

The other member of the DeAtley team was Willy T. Ribbs of San Diego. Following a brief fling at local racing, in 1977 Willy T. went to England to learn his trade by racing Formula Fords. He won six of eleven races and was named Rookie of the Year in this super-tough league—that says it all!

Fast, handsome and black, facts that appealed to the series sponsor, the Team DeAtley combination of cool David and firey Willy gave the SCCA and Budweiser the stuff promoters dream of. Some observers carp about Willy being too aggressive for his own good—Muhammad Ali is his idol—but automobile racing has always had its share of combative young men.

Sears Point was another DeAtley win with Hobbs leading for thirty-six of forty laps. Felton's Trans Am, Tom Gloy's Capri and the Forbes-Robinson Trans Am filled the next three places.

At Portland, the team's home base, Ribbs displayed exquisite timing by winning the first of his five 1983 triumphs. Greg Pickett, whose Corvette Willy had nosed-out by less than one second, was followed by a determined group led by Gloy, Hobbs and Felton.

Elliot Forbes-Robinson brought his Pontiac Trans Am home first at Seattle with a three-second win over Morristown, New Jersey's Paul Miller. Paul's Porsche had set a record 96.41 qualifying lap and Willy T. had run the fastest race lap. But Elliott was out front when it counted. The Tom Gloy and Lyn St. James Capris tooled home third and fourth with Leary's Trans Am fifth.

Both DeAtley machines dropped out early with mechanical troubles. However, for the remainder of the 1983 season, the Hobbs and Ribbs cars were invincible.

Mid-Ohio had Willy Ribbs and David Hobbs running 1-2, with Willy beating David by twelve seconds as well as making the day's fastest lap. Tom Gloy's Capri, Darin Brassfield's Corvette and Forbes-Robinson's Trans Am ran third through fifth.

Road America was all Upper Boddington's David Hobbs. In dominating the fifty-four-car entry (largest of the year), Hobbs' Camaro earned the pole, led all 100 miles and set the fastest race lap. Elliott Forbes-Robinson, Tom Gloy, Ludwig Heimrath, Jr., and Jerry Hansen filled the next four places after Willy T. retired on lap two with engine failure.

Willy duplicated his teammate's Road America performance at Brainerd where he earned the pole, set the fastest race lap and led the entire race. Pushed by a healthy Hobbs to a less-than-two-second win, Ribbs earned $8,650 as Gloy's Capri, Forbes-Robinson's Trans Am and Paul DePerro's Camaro followed the leaders.

Filling in for Hobbs, who had a prior commitment, John Paul, Jr., won Three Rivers over Richard Spenard's Trans Am. Willy

Ribbs had sat on the pole and led the first seven laps before being slowed by a sick engine, and finishing twelfth. Elliott Forbes-Robinson, Dave Watson and Tom Gloy were in the next three places.

It was another Hobbs-and-Ribbs show at Sears Point, where the Englishman earned the pole, set the fastest race lap and led the first half of the forty laps. But David's motor broke on lap twenty-three and Willy went on to win with an 82.186 race average. Nine seconds back was Tom Gloy, who now led the 1983 standings with 129 points, to Hobbs' 124 and Ribbs' 109.

Riverside was a DeAtley sweep with David Hobbs on the pole. After leading all forty laps, Hobbs finished 11.6 seconds in front of Ribbs, with Paul Newman's Datsun Turbo third and the Trans Ams of Wally Dallen-

bach, Jr., and Frank Leary filling the fourth and fifth spots.

Caesars Palace, the Parking Lot Grand Prix, was all Ribbs, who led for eighty-nine laps over the 1.125 mile maze. Driving cautiously, so as to finish well enough to ensure his series lead, but still be on the same lap as the winner, Hobbs came in fourth with David Watson second, Tom Gloy third and Wally Dallenbach, Jr., fifth.

Complete 1983 twelve-race standings showed David Hobbs with 158 points (and $59,350), Willy T. Ribbs 148, Tom Gloy 143, Elliott Forbes-Robinson 102 and Frank Leary 79. Chevrolet finished the year with ninety-seven points, Pontiac had fifty-nine, Ford fifty-three, Porsche thirteen and Datsun eight.

*Willy T. Ribbs leads teammate David Hobbs at 1983 Mid-Ohio. But Hobbs went on to win the 1983 championship with 158 points to Ribbs' 148. Sport Graphics/*Road & Track

Chevrolet desired to have Neil DeAtley race its new, relatively untried Corvettes, rather than the race-tested DeAtley Camaros that had overpowered the 1983 series with ten wins out of twelve Trans-Ams. This may have been bad break number one. Having DeAtley driver Willy T. Ribbs lose his cool at Road Atlanta on the morning of the 1984 season's first race was misfortune number two. Whether number two was the result of the countless frustrations that go with getting new models ready to race is a moot point. But there isn't any question about how wrong it was for Willy to take a poke at Bob Lobenberg, especially while Lobenberg was strapped in his car.

Ribbs quit on the spot. Neil DeAtley issued the following statement: "Willy said he didn't want to drive anymore. So I accepted his resignation. That's the size of it. It's very unfortunate. He's a very talented driver." The SCCA hit Willy with a $1,000 fine.

Young Darin Brassfield's first win at Road Atlanta may have taken Neil DeAtley's mind off his problems. Following the winning Corvette were Lobenberg's Trans Am, David Hobbs in the second DeAtley Corvette, the Wally Dallenbach, Jr., Camaro and the veteran Eppie Wietzes' Firebird.

Summit Point saw Bob Lobenberg's Trans Am take the lead on lap forty-seven of the fifty-lap event. He won a close one over David Hobbs' Corvette and Tom Gloy's 7-Eleven Capri. Wietzes' Trans Am and Greg Pickett's Roush Protofab Capri filled fourth and fifth as Paul Newman blew the engine on Sharp's new 300 ZX Turbo.

Greg Pickett broke a three-year no-win jinx at Sears Point by bringing Jack Roush's Capri home in record time. Once again the race winner did not get out front until the closing laps. Gloy's Capri and the Brassfield Corvette, the duo that led for thirty-six of the forty laps, were second and third. Fourth and fifth were young Dallenbach's Trans Am and Paul Newman's Nissan 300ZC Turbo.

Round four, the June 16 Portland International Trans-Am, witnessed Greg Pickett displacing George Follmer as the all-time top money winner in the series history.

Collecting $10,400 when his Capri again led Tom Gloy and Darin Brassfield over the line, the Alamo, California, veteran's career earnings reached $127,607, compared to George Follmer's $124,366. Obviously, Follmer recorded more top placings, as his pile was made when Trans-Am pots were a fraction of current payoffs.

Held as a Saturday warm-up for the Detroit Grand Prix, round five made news on several fronts. Tom Gloy enjoyed his first win in two years, Willy T. Ribbs returned to the series, and Capris driven by Gloy, Ribbs and Pickett must have pleased Dearborn-on-Rhine by finishing 1-2-3.

Making a DeAtley guest shot was Michael Andretti, who retired ten laps after his car and Lobenberg's Trans Am made contact. Dallenbach's Camaro and Watson's Firebird were fourth and fifth after Bob Lobenberg made a 72.354 record race lap.

Willy T. Ribbs won the second heat of the July 3 Daytona Paul Revere Trans-Am by taking the first seventy-eight miler and coming in third in the encore. After second-place finishes in both heats, Tom Gloy led the season standings with eighty-three points to Pickett's seventy-three, Lobenberg's sixty-three and Darin Brassfield's sixty-two. At this point Ford led the manufacturers' point chase with forty, to Chevrolet's twenty-seven and Pontiac's twenty-four.

Willy T.'s Capri made it two straight at Brainerd when he took Lobenberg's Trans Am by three seconds. Leading all but one of the thirty-three laps, Willy set the fastest race lap to win with a 105.99 mph record race average. Second through fifth in the twenty-two-car field were Lobenberg's Trans Am, Gloy's and Pickett's Capris and Jim Miller's Trans Am.

Driving a DeAtley Corvette, Canadian Richard Spenard won his first pro race by taking the lead over Tom Gloy on the next to last lap. Road America pulled forty cars; Jim Miller's Trans Am, Paul Newman's Nissan and Wally Dallenbach's Camaro finished behind Spenard and Gloy. Held in conjunction with an Indy car race, Road America pulled one of the year's largest crowds.

The Capris bounced-back at Watkins Glen when Willy T. and Tom Gloy crossed the line eight seconds apart. David Hobbs gave the DeAtley Corvette a strong third with Dallenbach and Wietzes fourth and fifth. Bob Lobenberg set a qualifying record but Ribbs led for twenty-nine of the thirty laps, to win his third race in five starts.

Watkins Glen was the second-straight race that saw Bob Lobenberg become the victim of bad luck. At Road America he ran out of gas on the last lap while in the lead. And at the Glen he got a flat tire on the first lap.

Round ten at Three Rivers found Tom Gloy again feeling at home on a street course, as his Capri finished less than three seconds up on Pickett's Motorcraft Capri. Willy Ribbs had made the fastest race lap before falling back with tire trouble to finish eighth.

Phillippe Alliot, a French Formula One aspirant, earned the pole with a record 80.305 lap and led the race from laps ten through sixteen, only to retire his Trans Am after meeting the barrier. Wietzes' Firebird, Spenard's Corvette and Paul Miller's Porsche were third through fifth.

For the first time since Paul Newman's Datsun won the 1982 Brainerd, an import, Paul Miller's Porsche Turbo, won a Trans-Am. Willy T. had taken the Mosport pole in record time and had led for thirty-four of the forty laps. But the Morristown, New Jersey, Porsche dealer slipped past on lap thirty-five to finish in record time, his 99.227 mph average being six mph faster than the old mark. The Capris of Pickett, Ribbs and Gloy followed the Miller Carrera.

Almost fifteen years after they first tried, a thirty-seven-year-old former Corvette ace, Greg Pickett, gave Ford's Lincoln-Mercury Division its first Trans-Am title. Pushing his Roush Motorcraft Capri to a full-minute win over Tom Gloy's Capri, Pickett led for all forty-four laps at Seattle International Raceway.

Jim Miller's Trans Am, David Hobbs' DeAtley Corvette and Wally Dallenbach, Jr.'s, Camaro filled the next three places.

For the second time in 1984, Sears Point held a Trans-Am. And, as on June 3, the September 30 winner was Greg Pickett. Tom Gloy had taken the pole and had been the early race leader. But Pickett took over ten laps from the finish to win over Willy T. in just under five seconds.

It was Pickett's fourth 1984 win, and all four had come on West Coast tracks. Lobenberg's Trans Am, Paul Miller's Porsche and Gloy's Capri were third through fifth. Tucked away in thirteenth place was a businessman

After playing bridesmaid through much of 1983, steady Tom Gloy piled up 225 points to earn the 1984 Driver's Championship while bringing *Lincoln-Mercury the 1984 Manufacturer's title, 119 points to Chevrolet's 66.*

named Bondurant, who probably knows Sears Point better than most.

Darin Brassfield, whose DeAtley Corvette last won the Road Atlanta season opener, easily took Riverside after leading for thirty-nine of the forty laps. In contrast with 1983, when DeAtley Camaros won ten of the twelve Trans-Ams, this was only the third time a DeAtley car saw the checker in 1984.

Dallenbach's Camaro, the Ribbs and Gloy Capris, and Paul Miller's Porsche filled the next four places. Three great Trans-Am veterans, George Follmer, David Hobbs and Paul Newman, finished out of the first ten.

Green Valley, round fifteen in the 1984 season's endless summer, was an easy win for Ribbs as he led all sixty-three laps to finish with a record 91.733 race average.

In 1967, when Lincoln-Mercury last visited Green Valley, Dan Gurney's Cougar had barely nosed-out his teammate, Parnelli Jones. By bringing his Capri home second to Willy T. Ribbs seventeen years later, the Canadian John Jones enabled Lincoln-Mercury to replay the Gurney-and-Jones scenario.

One lap down was Jim Miller's Trans Am. And two laps behind him were John Brandt's Corvette and Del Taylor's Trans Am. Making news because he did *not* finish, was series leader, Tom Gloy.

Caesars Palace, a surprisingly fast 1.125 mile pretzel of a course (which looks like the Nürburgring next to the New Jersey Meadowlands) and even smaller parking lot circuit, closed-out the sixteen-race 1984 season on November 11 with Tom Gloy's third win. Young Dallenbach's Camaro, Hobb's Corvette, Pickett's Capri and Craig Carter's Camaro rounded-out the top five.

Wisconsin's Dave Watson, who had pushed his Camaro to a qualifying record and had led the first sixteen laps, broke his engine.

Gloy took the front spot from Dallenbach on lap thirty-one, the new champion went on to set a record race lap as well as a record 88.82 mph race average for eighty-nine laps.

Both DeAtley (with Hobbs, Jimmy Insolo and Darin Brassfield) and Lincoln-Mercury (with Gloy, Pickett and Ribbs) had three cars at Caesars Palace. One wonders what might have happened if DeAtley had stayed with his Camaros in 1984; or if Willy T. hadn't blown his top and missed the first four races; and, in view of the way DeAtley's Chevrolets dominated 1983, if Ford getting back in the Trans-Am wasn't inevitable.

As to the degree of Ford's 1984 involvement, here is how one highly placed SCCA staffer expressed it: "Jack Roush was not formally a Ford/Mercury team as their finance was not directly from Ford coffers. However, they were sponsored by Motorcraft, a Ford division. I would say it was as close to a manufacturer's official team as you could be without having the cars entered by Ford Motor Company. It would certainly relate to Bud Moore's efforts in the late sixties and early seventies."

Final 1984 standings

Driver	Points	Prize
Tom Gloy	225	$87,800
Greg Pickett	189	74,050
Willy T. Ribbs	155	62,750
Wally Dallenbach, Jr.	142	40,440
Bob Lobenberg	138	45,350
Darin Brassfield	120	46,400

Final 1984 standing

Manufacturer	Points
Lincoln-Mercury	119
Chevrolet	66
Pontiac	55
Porsche	18
Nissan	8

Chapter 16

Yesterday's heroes

If Trans-Am fans wonder how the world is treating yesterday's heroes—Dan Gurney, Parnelli Jones, George Follmer, Roger Penske and Team Mustang's first leader, Carroll Shelby—the answer is very well indeed.

Shelby's new place in Gardena, "Turn right onto Figueroa and stay on it until you see the big white building," houses just one of his many interests.

Also, Lee Iacocca and Shelby are working together again. Only this time it's on high-performance projects for Chrysler. In Texas, Shelby has his chili mix business and a world-renowned prize bull artificial insemination setup. His Goodyear race tire business is said to be the largest in the country. And the new building I was in, which is devoted almost entirely to making wheels, employs 400 people.

When I recited some of this one evening to my dinner companion she said, "Shit. That's nothing. Carroll owns half of Texas."

Officially, Lew Spencer's job title is Assistant to the President of Shelby-American Management Company. Calling him Shelby's Man Friday, however, expresses it better. One of Shelby's first Cobra drivers, a former national governor of the SCCA, Lew stopped racing in 1965 when he went to work for Carroll.

By the time Lew Spencer had shown me only half of Shelby's wheel plant, it had struck me as being an industrial war game. First impressions were of blistering heat, mind-boggling noise and floors completely covered with aluminum shavings, varying in size from razor-sharp slivers that cut into the soles of your shoes to large reclaimable chunks.

After feeding raw aluminum into one of three smelters, a relentlessly moving belt carries the rough, dirty-gray casting through endless millings, washings and polishings. By then both the men and machines are a blurr, so that coming upon neat snacks of gleaming wheels is a shock.

Well away from the noise, almost hidden in the back of the plant, were Carroll Shelby's and Lew Spencer's offices. Carroll was off somewhere and Lew and I settled down to talk about the Trans-Am. "Until the 1966 Riverside, which is where Ford was tied with Plymouth for that year's championship, we

Shelby's new Boss 302 provides background for team manager Lew Spencer flanked by drivers Horst Kwech, left, and Peter Revson. Ford Motor Company

had been busy with our 350GT program. Now," Lew continued, "Ford got after us to prepare a car for Riverside.

"Until that time, Ford's Trans-Am policy had been to help private Mustang owners. The program had been somewhat informal, but we had had good results. But everything changed after the '66 Riverside. From then on, the Trans-Am became a deadly serious venture.

"To compete you had to have the best cars and the best drivers in the country. It was extremely competitive and the racing was very hard.

"But it was very exciting too. The level of preparation was simply unbelievable. Ford had sent us two bright young guys, Ray Geddes and Peyton Cramer to work with us at Shelby American. Then they had Homer Perry, who would come to every race to act

as a sort of coordinator between the two teams and the factory.

"Yes, we saw a lot of Bud Moore and of Holman-Moody too. Some people won't accept this, but the level of preparation in the Trans-Am was better than in stock cars. Bud Moore never said much, but the rivalry between us was bitter and he took some of what he learned back to NASCAR.

"One thing that I'll never forget about the Trans-Am is the day we actually got Ford to shut down the line at River Rouge," Lew continued. "According to the rules that year, I think it was the Boss 302 in '68, we had to have 500 cars made by the time of the first race. But all we had been able to get was 300.

"Then Walt Hane came from the SCCA to verify the FIA homologation production figure. The Federal Government always had a man on duty at the end of the line. His job was to count cars and, somehow, we got his cooperation.

"What happened then was that after Walt Hane counted a batch of cars, we would drive them around the plant and stick them back on the line. The problem was that each

Jerry Titus with his wife Anne. Jerry, a motorcycle enthusiast, is shown on his Kawasaki prior to the 1968 Continental Divide Raceway Trans-Am where his Ford made the fastest race lap before falling out. Deke Houlgate collection

Roger Penske (right), driver of the "Telar" Special, with his Kimberly Cup and Marshall A. Stephens, antifreeze sales manager for the Du Pont Company. The award was given by the SCCA for being the "most improved driver of the 1961 racing year." Road & Track/Albert Bochroch photo

time we stopped the line all hell broke loose. Red lights would flash and gongs and sirens went off.

"But Walt Hane just kept on counting. Then he said that he wanted to see the cars in the lot. We had been expecting something like that so we had parked the 300 in such a way that they looked like more and made them hard to count. We got away with it. But it wasn't very long before we really exceeded the 500 figure.

"But we had a good time. I think it was at Bryar that we pulled the nitro bit. Jerry Titus came into the pits pretending that his eyes were watering. Picking a place where he would be overheard, Jerry said something like, 'I just had to stop following those Javelins. That nitro really has my eyes burning.'

"Another time we faked pouring something that looked like nitro into one of the Mustangs before practice. Someone told the crew to shake the car real well to mix it up. Sure enough, seconds later John Timanus came running up."

Lew and I then recalled the 1967 FIA Double-500 at Bridgehampton where Ken Miles had won and Cobras filled the first four spots. Shelby and Al Dowd were so pleased because Cobras were in contention for the World Championship. But minutes after the Bridge ended, while Carroll was still in the winners circle, he got word that Ferrari had won a hill climb, or maybe it was the Tour de France, and had got just enough points to win the World Championship. That was when Shelby said, "Next year Ferrari's ass is mine." And it was.

In 1971 the esteemed *Encyclopedia of Motor Sport* referred to Roger Penske as "America's Alfred Neubauer." By focusing on Roger's superlative organizing skills and meticulous attention to detail—what Mark Donohue called Team Penske's "unfair advantage"—the encyclopedia only revealed a part of the man.

Automobile racing has had its share of good salesmen. For example, Formula One's Bernie Ecclestone and NASCAR'S Bill France, Sr., are exceptionally persuasive. But Roger Penske is in a class by himself.

Two changes become apparent when seeing Roger in 1986. The boy wonder is pushing fifty. And his excellence as a race driver is in danger of being eclipsed by his startling success as a businessman.

Little wonder: For 1986 the Parsippany, New Jersey, based Penske Corporation expects to reach $700 million in annual sales. Penske/Hertz Truck Leasing, a major Detroit Allison Diesel distributorship and several large-volume car dealerships are only the most visible of activities handled by more than 3,400 workers in 186 Penske facilities located in thirty-two states. Yet, close to the heart of the company are Team Penske's Indy car program and Roger's ownership of Michigan International Speedway.

Roger Penske at the 1970 Road America Trans-Am. Gordon Means/Road America

Roger graduated from Lehigh University, where he majored in business administration, and the SCCA's Marlboro driving school, in 1958. Selling for Alcoa—Roger's Dad was a metals distributor in his native Cleveland—was Roger's first job. MGs, Jaguars and Corvettes were among his first cars. Good things happened in 1960 soon after Roger bought Bob Holbert's RSK. Together they won Sebring's Index of Performance and Roger earned SCCA national championships in 1961, 1962 and 1963.

A type 61 Birdcage Maserati and a Cooper-Monoco moved Roger onto the international scene. But it wasn't until he converted a wrecked Formula One Cooper Climax into the rule-bending Telar/Zerex Special sports car (Biggs Cunningham had sold Roger the bent tub and chassis for a song after Hansgen's Watkins Glen shunt) that Penske, with the help of DuPont dollars and publicity, really rolled.

After going from an independent to working for Jim Hall and John Mecom, 1965 saw Roger take off his driving gloves and join George McKean's Philadelphia Chevrolet agency, which he soon controlled.

Both Roger and his major sponsor, the Sun Oil Company, liked the Trans-Am. So too did Mark Donohue. Soon Roger's immaculate blue machines were giving Ford fits in the Trans-Am as well as running in the USRRC, the CanAm and Indy.

A founder and director of CART, whose current preoccupation with road courses was encouraged by Penske after he saw how well the Indy cars and drivers did at England's Silverstone (where Foyt broke the Formula One track record), Roger remains the only current Indy car owner with five

As both Mark Donohue and Roger Penske seemed to spend most of their time flying, whatever was up there must have been unusual. Road & Track

500 victories. (Danny Sullivan 1985, Rick Mears 1984, Bobby Unser 1981, Rick Mears 1979, Mark Donohue 1972.) Unquestionably looking on racing as the door-opening key to his success, Roger Penske continues to run the pits and direct his race teams.

Now living in Red Bank, New Jersey, remarried and raising a second family, Roger meets his thirty-hour days by using his own Lear Jet 35A (with NRP500 on its tail) as well as a Bell Jet Ranger.

Even though Roger Penske is not inclined to look back on his past achievements or grow nostalgic about the good old days, he does admit to some rather special feelings about the old Trans-Am.

Penske said, "We began racing in the Trans-Am in 1967, and then went fulltime in 1968 through 1971.

"It was great racing in its day. Certainly the most competitive series at that time due to the great interest with the factories in Detroit. Of course the teams that the factories aligned themselves with included many of the top racers of the day. The series stimulated very keen competition and strategy because of the high stakes. Coupled with the rules the way they were written no one clearly had an upper hand.

"We were 2½ years with Chevrolet Camaros and 2½ years with AMC Javelins.

"Chevrolet had great technical capability and enormous resources, such as a skid pad, and we worked very closely with them. Mark Donohue was our chief engineer who worked constantly there.

"AMC left everything up to us to do. Penske Racing built the cars from scratch.

"Both Chevrolet and AMC were very enthusiastic and loyal to us.

"I think the single incident I remember most vividly was our first win with the Javelin at Bridgehampton in 1970. We had developed the Javelins ourselves—Mark Donohue, Don Cox and Earl MacMullen, and Traco with the motor. It was a major accomplishment.

"I liked it all."

By East Coast standards, the distance you travel getting from point A to point B in the Los Angeles area is amazing. Getting lost didn't help either. However, as Deke Houlgate's busy office was just beginning to wind down, being late may have been an advantage.

Not surprisingly, as they had been close, the first person we talked about was Jerry Titus. Few people knew Jerry Titus as well as Deke Houlgate. A Los Angeles area public relations man whose professional background includes handling Carroll Shelby's Cobras, writing a syndicated motorsports newspaper column and running Riverside Raceway's press, and whose current accounts include the Pennzoil/ Rick Mears business, Deke is as expert on automobile racing as his famed sportswriter father was on football.

"Jerry was a very complex person. Not many people were aware of all the forces that were working on him. We began working together in 1964 when he ran those BMC Genies for Kjell Qvale. All of Jerry's cars in those days were, just let's say, experimental. The Cheetahs, a two-liter Webster and his Elva-Porsche took a lot of work.

"But that didn't stop Jerry from winning the national D modified championship at Riverside in the 1964 runoffs.

"Jerry was very serious about his driving. But he was a pixie. That business of the 1967

Dan Gurney, left, chats with Stirling Moss, center, and Graham Hill prior to the 1957 Sebring.

Team Terlingua Mustang, which was supposed to publicize a boys' vocational school in Texas, was pure invention. But we began getting mail and I think that *Comp Press* ran four or five stories on it before they caught on.

"Jerry was doing okay at Petersen as editor of *Sports Car Graphic*. You probably knew he was a musician too. But did you know that he had taken classical trumpet lessons at the Juilliard back in New York?

"Then came the 1966 Riverside and nothing was ever the same.

"Ford found that they had a good shot at the championship. So they had Shelby prepare a car, and Carroll got Jerry to drive it. Do you remember how he won that race in spite of that freak accident that cut his oil line?

Deke continued, "Somebody hit one of those concrete-filled tires they used as course markers and sent it spinning smack into the Mustang. It just sheared-off the oil line like a knife. But Jerry managed to crawl back to the pits with smoke pouring from his car. Somehow they got it fixed.

"The Trans-Ams were long races then and the accident happened around the middle of the race. Anyway, Jerry somehow managed to make up all that time and win the race and give Ford their first Trans-Am championship."

Deke then recalled how Jerry had reacted to signing with Carroll Shelby, an incident that Lew Spencer also had recounted.

"After Riverside, Carroll asked us to look into getting Jerry to race full time. We knew we would have to make it worthwhile for Jerry to leave the magazine. Still, we realized that racing was what Jerry really wanted to do. 'Bring him in here,' Carroll told us. 'And let's see if we can work out a deal.'"

Both Lew Spencer and Deke mentioned how absolutely deadpan Jerry had remained during his meeting with Carroll. When Carroll offered Jerry $1,000 a race plus fifty percent of all prize money, they said that all Jerry said was, "I guess that's okay."

But, as soon as he left Carroll's office and closed the door, Deke said Jerry "threw up

Dan Gurney is about to be tossed out before he could photograph this LeMans start, as his co-driver has taken the first shift. Photographer Jesse Alexander, with arms crossed, watches with amusement.

Dan Gurney (left) and Carroll Shelby in the dark at Sebring.

his hands and yelled and jumped around like a kid."

Deke didn't believe that going to the Pontiacs was the result of Jerry being unhappy with Ford. "I think that he saw a chance to run his own show. The Canadian guy was supposed to have a lot of money and Jerry had no way of knowing that Pontiac would run into so much trouble letting them have engines.

"You have to remember," Deke went on, "that Jerry was doing a lot of other racing too. He qualified for Indy in 1968, the year that it rained so much. But on Tuesday before the race, he got bumped."

Jerry's fellow racing writers make an annual award in his memory—one way that Jerry Titus is remembered.

Even though I knew that Dan Gurney was in Japan, I still stuck my borrowed hot Saab on the new freeway between Newport Beach and Santa Ana and went to visit All American Racers. Dan's future looked bright. Tom Sneva and Texaco would be with AAR in 1985, and others were talking. From designers to engines, to chassis men, AAR buzzed with activity. I'd never seen a busier or more cheerful shop.

He was one of a handful of young Yanks whom I'd watched become a part of Europe's top racing establishment. My memories of Dan are a kaleidoscopic blur.

In 1958, when driving partners wrecked his first two races in France, Le Mans and the Reims 12-Hours, where he'd booted Andrea Pilette's Ferrari coupe into the lead. At Reims one year later for Ferrari in the French GP, where he told me, "It's so much faster over here."

At Rouen, when he won his first, and Porsche's only, GP, and left the world press to get on my open line to say hello to his friends back in the States.

The pleasant dinner with his parents in London at the Steering Wheel, when it still was on Brick Street. Of parking his Lotus Ford high on the banks at Daytona, waiting

An irresistible prankster, Dan often comes up with such rigs in his Costa Mesa shop. Ford Motor Company

The senior Gurney grins as son Dan goes into a crouch to settle who was the taller. Note Goodyear jacket and Dunlop pants.

to crank over the finish line. Of taking those years-ahead-of-their-time, twitchy, rear-engined Buicks to Indy. And of changing racing history by laying the groundwork for Colin Chapman at Ford.

Above it all was June 1967, when he won Le Mans and, in his own car, the Belgium GP. Then, too, there were our differences, as Dan and I did not always see eye to eye on our Castrol deals. Humor, however, usually saved the day.

Thanks to Dan and his secretary, we learn something of how Dan Gurney viewed the Trans-Am from the letter reproduced on page 187.

It was the day before the 1960 500 and Chris Economaki, Frank Blunk (of *The New York Times)*, Bob Myer (a close friend of Economaki's who owned a flying service), John Sinclair (one of Myer's pilots), John Cooper and I were on our way to Funk's Winchester Speedway.

This shot presented this photographer with a classic dilemma, how to avoid the hand-held mike and still include the Castrol patch.

Chris still was doing a good deal of track announcing and on the way to Winchester he told us to "keep an eye on The Fike Plumbing Special. It's driven by a new hot shoe from California, Parnelli Jones." Chris said that Jones had been cleaning-up on the coast and that he figured Parnelli would soon join USAC.

John Cooper, who had worked for USAC and then was with Chrysler, had the big wagon. I recall observing that anyone who could get wheels from his company over the Indy weekend would go far. When John became president of the Indianapolis Motor Speedway after Tony Hulman died, my prophecy was fulfilled.

I'd not seen the Championship cars until the 1958 Race of Two Worlds at Monza, when ten Indy roadsters squared-off, and won, over the Ecurie Ecosse Jaguars, a mixed bag of tired Grand Prix cars and Stirling Moss in his oversized Maserati Eldorado Ice Cream Special.

Before it became obligatory to stay at the Speedway Motel, Chris Economaki had taken a small suite at the Sheraton-Lincoln in downtown Indianapolis. I don't recall that Chris tried to sleep there. But about twenty or more of his friends did.

People dropped in at odd hours. We made do with cots, chairs, pillows in odd corners and the bathtubs. There were quiet all-night bull sessions but everyone was well mannered and careful not to step squarely on your face while making their way to one of the bathrooms.

Funk's was my first look at the legendary high banks of the midwest. The racing was scary, but the plant and people had a wonderful kind of "State Fair" look. Freshly painted, bright-green grandstands, a red and gold uniformed band, family picnics on well-tended infield grass, all side by side with the wildest tail-out racing I'd ever seen.

Parnelli's number 51 won. After climbing the rickety stairs to the announcer's booth, he kissed the cute race queen, paused a moment while I took his picture, and waved to the crowd. As Chris predicted, Parnelli joined USAC the next day.

Housed in its own large, modern building in Torrence, Parnelli Jones Enterprises

All AMERICAN RACERS, INC.

2334 SOUTH BROADWAY   P.O. BOX 2186
SANTA ANA, CA. 92707   (714) 540-1771
     (213) 860-1321
TELEX: 65-5373   ANS. BK: AAR SNA

October 31, 1984

Mr. Albert Bochroch
P.O. Box 90
Solesbury, PA 18963

Dear Al,

    Sorry to have missed you on your recent visit. My secretary tells me
you are writing another book? This one about the Trans Am Series... She said
you wanted a few comments from me about "How I felt about the series" and
"My most vivid memories of the series"... Here goes...

I had great hopes for the series, but unfortunately Detroit "Chickened Out."
It would have been good for the breed. The "bean counters" prevailed along
with Ralph Nader and insurance companies, etc. In the end, they set the U.S.
Industry back verses the rest of the world, but it appears to be turning around
now. However, any successful concept in racing such as the Trans Am requires
excellent leadership in order to compete with other special interest groups
whether they be in racing (NASCAR, CART, IMSA, etc.) or in other sports (baseball,
football, golf, tennis, etc.) Don't forget that a racing series is also competing
for the same corporate dollars that would otherwise go to the big ad agencies.

Anyway, it was a great series with alot of potential.

    I remember that my team mate on the Cougar team was Parnelli and we had
some terrific races together. Later on with the Plymouth and Dodge effort, it
was ineptly administered and that was regretable... but, another lesson in life.

    Racing will soon expose weaknesses as there is really no place to hide
as the green flag drops.

    Good luck with your book Al! Evi and I look forward to reading it.

All the best,

Dnaiel S. Gurney
President

presents a dignified, solid look. While Parnelli raced for fewer years than Shelby, Gurney or Follmer, he seems to have at least as many awards; case after trophy-filled case lines the reception area as well as Parnelli's own office.

Staying loyal to Firestone may have given Parnelli some bad moments, but it must have helped him acquire thirty-five Firestone dealerships, become Firestone's major American race tire distributor and, with his friend Vel Miletich, own a Ford agency. Parnelli also owns considerable Orange County real estate. For 1984, he believes it added up to about a forty-million-dollar business.

"But," I asked Parnelli, "wasn't there a period in the Trans-Am when you might have done better on Goodyears?"

"That's absolutely true," Jones replied. "We had the best car in 1969. But I was under contract to Firestone. They had budget problems that year that resulted in their being slow in getting out a new tire. George Follmer was under contract to Firestone too. But he switched. I stuck to my commitment."

I told Parnelli that I was reluctant to introduce another controversial subject. But, so much had been made of the 1969 Mark Donohue bumping incident at Riverside (I had brought copies of Mark's account of the incident from his book), that I wanted to hear Parnelli's side of the story.

After I'd read Parnelli some of what Mark had written, Parnelli, even-tempered and direct as always, replied, "That's his version. I have a completely different viewpoint. I was leading when a tire went. And I lost a

Gurney in AAR Eagle at Silverstone. Even though Dan may be going about 140 mph, the sponsor's name, Castrol, is fairly sharp.

full lap. When I caught up with Mark in turn six, he slammed on his brakes.

"It was a cold shot. It had to be deliberate. I just couldn't believe it happened. I think that Mark may have thought it was George. Jamming on his brakes in the middle of a slow, 50-55 mile-an-hour turn; I couldn't imagine that it had happened. My front end was down anyway. So I just mashed in the entire front.

"When I started road racing," Parnelli continued, "I was surprised because it came so easy. It was as if road racing was more natural for me. I'd won the Riverside Grand Prix and a CanAm at Laguna Seca. And before I ran the Trans-Am I'd done pretty well in sedans on road courses.

"I learned about road racing from oval-track racing. And I learned about oval-track racing from road racing. I've never thought of myself as a natural driver. You may not have thought so from the number of races I used to run, but racing was very hard for me to learn. But I stuck with it . . . it didn't come easy. But it's my nature that once I learn something, I learn it well."

We talked about the ovals and the high banks with the Fike Plumbing Special. "I won a lot of races on those ovals, but I never liked them. They had that one guardrail fixed in such a way that a lot of cars would just touch the rail and get flipped out of the track. The ovals got better when they added a second guardrail. But I still wasn't comfortable on them."

"My favorite driver has always been Dan Gurney," Parnelli said. "He's so smooth." Nodding toward a large blowup of Parnelli's and Vel's Indy-winning Johnny Lightning Special, he added, "And I've always liked Al Unser as a driver too."

After asking Parnelli if his ears had been burning, I mentioned that Fran Hernandez, as well as many of the Trans-Am drivers I'd

Riverside: Delayed starter's flag resulted in number 18, as well as Parnelli Jones, the driver, boiling over. Walt Hansgen, number 17, is Par- *nelli's teammate in John Mecom's second Zerex Special.*

talked to, had rated Parnelli as tops among the drivers.

"I think that's true." Parnelli replied. "One credit I always gave myself is that I made Mark Donohue a good race driver. I'd seen Mark drive before. But he never had to really hang it out. He never had to race as hard as he did in the Trans-Am.

"I'd say that the Trans-Am I remember with the most satisfaction was the 1970 Riverside. I was in the lead and was starting to go through turn nine. It was just before where the barriers start, when somebody hit me broadside and knocked me clean off the track. I went off into the sand, but I still managed to stay upright.

"But," Parnelli related, "my door was caved-in and the front end was pushing so hard that I couldn't steer. I struggled for a while, but I had to come in and get it fixed. It wasn't as fast after they fixed it. But I man-

aged to get back in the lead. I finished first and Ford won the championship."

By coincidence, the following Dan Gurney quote is from an article on Parnelli that appeared in *Autoweek* around the time of my meetings with Parnelli.

"One thing about Parnelli," wrote Dan Gurney, "when you're racing him you don't find yourself in love with the sonofabitch. But you know you're in for a damn good contest. If any of the top ten or fifteen drivers over the last couple of decades were going to list the guys they felt were up there, Parnelli would be on that list."

"That's absolutely true," said George Follmer. "When we raced with Parnelli, all of us, Mark, Revvie and everybody else, had to give 110 percent of themselves. Unquestionably, we became better drivers for having been in the Trans-Am with Parnelli Jones.

"There was an excellence in having Parnelli Jones as a teammate. Not only did he teach me a lot, just having him there raised my level of performance."

We were in George's handsome new Porsche-Audi-Subaru dealership. And I had just told George something of Parnelli's comments regarding Mark. Located in Montclair, not far from the old Riverside Raceway, driving from Redondo Beach, where I was housed, had been a six-freeway exercise that back home may have taken me through several states. Here, however, I'm still in Greater Los Angeles!

Bright, outspoken, at times in days past almost too acerbic, I found that George had mellowed. Smiling, George said, "I suppose that running a business of this size has made a difference."

The glass cases in the reception area and throughout the dealership displayed countless trophies and racing pictures. Filling the wall behind George's desk was a large black-and-white photo mural of the Lotus Porsche that brought Follmer the 1967 US Road Racing Championship. The car carries the number 16 (as do all of George's race cars) which celebrates the date of his son's birth.

Follmer's career began with a Porsche Speedster in 1959. Racing a 300SL at River-

A pensive Parnelli awaits the start. Road America 1970. Gordon Means/Road America

side followed, and George remarked that he would bet he had put in the greatest number of miles at Riverside, his home course. Then national SCCA honors led to Porsche works rides at Le Mans and other internationals. At Phoenix, George became the first driver to win an Indy car race with a stock block engine. Having been both a CanAm and Trans-Am champion, Follmer also ran F/5000 and he had a good shot at Formula One.

"Until very recently," George said, "I had run the most Trans-Ams and still was the leading money winner. But someone, I think it was Greg Pickett, passed me.

"American drivers," George went on, "always thought of Formula One as the pinnacle of road racing. I've a feeling that's not true anymore. Now I think it's CART [Championship Auto Racing Teams]. They are using most of the road courses. The dollars are good. And, you don't have to buy your ride like you do in Formula One. Although I guess that it helps in CART too."

I told George that his having raced Camaros, Mustangs and Javelins for the leading Trans-Am teams made me eager to hear his views on their differences.

"That's interesting," George commented, "because when you compare the different operations, you find that they achieved the same results in totally different ways.

"Let's see . . . I ran the Camaro for Roger in '67. Then I drove for Caplan and Jim Jeffords when they had the Javelins in '68. But they really weren't ready for them. Bud Moore's Mustangs were in '69 and '70. And '70 and '71 were part Ford and part Roy Woods' Javelins. Then I drove again for Roy when he had the factory Javelins in 1972.

"Penske's operation was very small, very compact and very efficient. Ford used more of a shotgun approach. It wasn't only that they were larger, they were totally committed to the program. When it came to finances, they were a money machine.

"Of course, Roy Woods' team had factory support too. But it didn't have the same

Blurred background indicates that Parnelli is doing what he did best, driving flat out. Road America 1970. Gordon Means/Road America

Wheel marks on Mustang's door and ample use of silver tape support George Follmer's ability to keep running. Ford Motor Company

total commitment we had at Ford. All the teams had different personalities. But I would have to say that Bud Moore's was the best."

Sorting out his thoughts and speaking with care, George went on to say, "Parnelli, Dan and I were the cutting edge of the sword for Ford. With Plymouth, Dan brought in his own people and did most of the work on the cars. Then he'd re-engineer them at the racetrack.

"There was nothing like the old Trans-Am. You ran so hard, and you had to run just as hard all the way. You couldn't even give away a half-second in the pits. Of course there were some rough times. I found the 1970 Mid-Ohio very hard to accept when I was ahead and wasn't allowed to go on and win.

"Ford's backing of Bud Moore went way up the corporate ladder, well beyond Passino.

We saw a lot of young Edsel Ford too. He was still in college then and came to a lot of Trans-Ams. Everyone treated him just like one of the boys. He was a nice kid."

Reaching into his desk, George showed me a batch of color prints of his 1970 Boss 302 that a fan recently had restored. It carried number 16 and it still looked like a winner.

"Once in awhile I still run the Trans-Am in my Corvette. I won the '76 Championship in Vasek Polak's 934. But from 1980 on, the SCCA just dropped the rule book. What's running now is nothing like the old Trans-Am. We used to use the roll cages to tie the old cars together. But everything goes now. The rule book has just been thrown away. Today's Trans-Ams are more true race cars. And they are very expensive to maintain.

"When will I stop? I don't know. I plan to keep on racing as long as it's fun."

Although he drove the Trans-Am for all the major teams, including Bud Moore, Roger Penske and Roy Woods, and as an independent, George Follmer retained his enthusiasm for the series. Only recently has George's total of 13 Trans-Am victories been surpassed. Road & Track *photo*

Stirling Moss with friends at Laguna Seca.

Appendix

TRANS-AM RULES HISTORY

The Trans-Am Championship is currently in its sixth major rules format. The latest format began in 1980 and continues without major revisions today. Below are brief descriptions of the major rules formats:

1966 through 1969: The series was born in 1966 with a two-class structure – Over-and-Under-Two-Liters. The O-2 class for American-built sedans – "pony cars" – while European sports sedans were in the U-2 class. O-2 cars had maximum wheelbase of 116 inches, a minimum weight of 2,800 pounds and a maximum wheel width of eight inches. Both classes were based on FIA Groups 1 and 2 and the U-2 cars drew their specifications from the FIA "homologation" forms.

1970 through 1972: The series had its first "single class" format during these years. The small European sedans were split into their own series in 1970 (which became known as the 2.5 Challenge for 1971) leaving the American-built pony cars in a single class. The five-liter maximum displacement was retained while a 3,200 pound full-of-fuel (or 3,050 dry) minimum weight was in effect.

1973 and 1974: The series hit its low-water mark. A total of nine races were run these two years. Euro-pean Group 4 cars formed the backbone of the series while American-built cars employed liberal Group 4 bodywork and engine displacement, up to 454 cu. in. An Under 2-Liter class was recognized in the three-race 1974 season.

1975: The series was totally reconstructed into a single class series, using SCCA Club Racing cars of the A-, B- and C-Production and A-Sedan classes. Both foreign and domestic cars were eligi-ble, though US cars won six of seven races.

1976 through 1979: The series went into its dual class Category I/Category II years with the addition of Group 4 and 5 and "U.S.G.T." machines to the 1975 format cars.

1980 through 1985: The ailing Category II was dropped for 1980. Using Category I cars as a basis, the series became made up of US and imported production cars with performance handicapped by a weight/displacement table. The cornerstone for the formula is five-liter machines at 2,600 pounds and all cars had a maximum ten-inch wheel width and 110-inch wheelbase.

1986: The weight/displacement formula continued unchanged, but the wheel width was adjusted to a twelve-inch maximum.

TRANS AM RECORDS AT A GLANCE

Most Races:
Career: 65, George Follmer

Victories:
Career: 29, Mark Donohue
Season: 10, Mark Donohue (1968)

Consecutive Victories:
Career: 10, Bob Tullius (1978-79)
Season: 8, Mark Donohue (1968)

Closest Margin of Victory:
3 feet – Dan Gurney over Parnelli Jones, Green
Valley, 1967

Most Money Won:
Career: $255,233, Tom Gloy (1982-1985)
Season: $132,933, Willy T. Ribbs (1985)

Most Championships:
Driver: 3*, Mark Donogue (1968, 1969, 1971)
2, George Follmer (1972, 1976)
2, Bob Tullius (1977, 1978)
2, Peter Gregg (1973, 1974)

Manufacturer: 9, Chevrolet
5, Porsche

*Driver champions were not recognized in the
formative year, although Donohue is credited
with three season victories.

Fastest Qualifying Speed (since 1980):
113.152 mph, Bob Lobenberg, Riverside, 1984

Fastest Race Lap Speed
109.946 mph, Willy T. Ribbs, Brainerd, 1985

Fastest Race Speed:
99 Miles or Less:
105.990 mph, Willy T. Ribbs, Brainerd, 1984
100 Miles or More:
108.898 mph, Mark Donohue, Watkins Glen,
1969

Most Career Races (Top-20):

George Follmer	65	Peter Revson	44	Elliott Forbes-Robinson	40
Bob Tullius	60	Michael Oleyar	44	Willy T. Ribbs	39
Tom Gloy	57	Jerry Titus	43	Les Lindley	39
Greg Pickett	56	Ludwig Heimrath, Sr.	42	Rob McFarlin	38
Mark Donohue	54	Roy Woods	41	John Bauer	37
John Brandt, Jr.	51	Jim Derhaag	41	Bob Zulkowski	37
Paul Miller	49	Peter Gregg	40		

Career Wins (Top-20):

Mark Donohue	**29	Elliott Forbes-Robinson	7	John Greenwood	5
Bob Tullius (15-I)	*****†21	Parnelli Jones	7	Tom Gloy	5
Willy T. Ribbs	16	Jerry Titus	*7	Jerry Hansen	5
George Follmer	13	Ludwig Heimrath, Sr.	6	Monte Shelton	*5
Peter Gregg	**11	John Paul, Sr.	6	Hurley Haywood	***4
Greg Pickett	11	Gene Bothello (5-I)	5	David Hobbs	4
John Bauer (4-I)	**8	Wally Dallenbach, Jr.	5		

† – In 1966, Tullius/Adamowicz and Jennings won Over 2-Liter class victories but finished second overall and are
included in total.
(-I) – Indicates number of Category I wins included in total.
* – Indicates number of wins as a co-driver. On the list are overall victories plus 1976-1979 Category I wins.

Season Wins:

Mark Donohue, 1968	10	Willy T. Ribbs, 1983	5	Elliott Forbes-Robinson,	
Willy T. Ribbs, 1985	7	Bob Tullius, 1977	5	1982	4
Bob Tullius, 1978	7	Peter Gregg, 1977	5	John Bauer, 1980	4
Mark Donohue, 1971	7	Parnelli Jones, 1970	5	Gene Bothello, 1979	4
John Paul, Sr., 1979	6	Greg Pickett, 1984	4	Greg Pickett, 1978	4
Mark Donohue, 1969	6	Willy T. Ribbs, 1984	4	George Follmer, 1972	4
Wally Dallenbach, Jr., 1985	5	David Hobbs, 1983	4	Jerry Titus, 1967	4

Career Earnings (Top-20)

Tom Gloy	$255,233	Eppie Wietzes	$ 89,950
Willy T. Ribbs	$252,233	Peter Gregg	$ 84,835
Greg Pickett	$178,082	Ludwig Heimrath, Sr.	$ 81,589
Wally Dallenbach, Jr.	$169,023	John Bauer	$ 73,810
Elliott Forbes-Robinson	$166,415	Jim Miller	$ 73,703
George Follmer	$127,466	Roy Woods	$ 66,351
Bob Tullius	$120,448	Darin Brassfield	$ 65,775
Mark Donohue	$103,375	Paul Newman	$ 65,325
Paul Miller	$ 97,858	Monte Shelton	$ 61,255
David Hobbs	$ 95,183	Phil Currin	$ 56,620

Season Earnings (Top-10)

Willy T. Ribbs, 1985	$132,933	Willy T. Ribbs, 1984	$ 62,750
Wally Dallenbach, Jr., 1985	$123,583	John Paul, Sr., 1979	$ 60,700
Tom Gloy, 1984	$ 87,800	David Hobbs, 1983	$ 59,350
Elliott Forbes-Robinson, 1985	$ 85,483	Willy T. Ribbs, 1983	$ 56,550
Greg Pickett, 1984	$ 74,050	Elliott Forbes-Robinson, 1982	$ 52,700

TRANS-AM MANUFACTURERS' CHAMPIONS

(Points awarded on a 9-6-4-3-2-1 basis to highest finishing entry on each make in the top six.)

	PTS	WINS
1966		
1. Ford	46	4
2. Chrysler/Plymouth	39	1
3. Dodge	33	2
4. Chevrolet	3	
1967		
1. Ford	64	4
2. Mercury	62	4
3. Chevrolet	57	3
4. Dodge	11	1
1968		
1. Chevrolet	90	10
2. Ford	59	3
3. American Motors	51	
4. Pontiac	22	
1969		
1. Chevrolet	78	8
2. Ford	64	4
3. Pontiac	32	
4. American Motors	13	
1970		
1. Ford	72	6
2. American Motors	59	3
3. Chevrolet	40	2
4. Dodge	18	
5. Plymouth	15	
1971		
1. American Motors	72	8
2. Ford	61	2
3. Chevrolet	17	
4. Pontiac	7	
1972		
1. American Motors	48	4
2. Ford	34	2
3. Pontiac	28	1
4. Chevrolet	24	
1973		
1. Chevrolet	42	4
2. Porsche	37	2
3. Ford (Escort)	3	

	PTS	WINS
1974		
1. Porsche	36	3
2. Chevrolet	14	
3. BMW	3	
4. American Motors	1	
1975		
1. Chevrolet	69	6
2. Datsun	24	1
3. Porsche	9	
4. American Motors	6	
5. Triumph	4	
1976		
1. Porsche	132	5
2. Chevrolet	97	2
3. American Motors	41	
4. Datsun	41	
5. Volkswagen	36	
6. BMW	18	
1977 (Category I)		
1. Porsche	76	3
2. Jaguar	74	5
3. Chevrolet	69	3
4. Ford	2	
1977 (Category II)		
1. Porsche	117	11
2. Chevrolet	33	
1978 (Category I)		
1. Jaguar	73	7
2. Chevrolet	69	3
3. Datsun	3	
1978 (Category II)		
1. Chevrolet	74	6
2. Porsche	65	4
3. Pontiac	10	
1979 (Category I)		
1. Chevrolet	72	6
2. Triumph	27	3
3. Porsche	7	
4. Ford	3	

	PTS	WINS
1979 (Category II)		
1. Porsche	81	9
2. Chevrolet	44	
3. BMW	2	
1980		
1. Chevrolet	64	4
2. Porsche	53	5
3. Datsun	8	
4. Ford	2	
1981		
1. Chevrolet	64	4
2. Porsche	36	1
3. Jaguar	35	3
4. Ford	13	1
1982		
1. Pontiac	65	4
2. Chevrolet	42	2
3. Porsche AG	37	2
4. Ford	22	1
5. Datsun (Nissan)	16	1
6. Mercedes Benz	1	
1983		
1. Chevrolet	97	10
2. Pontiac	59	2
3. Ford	43	
4. Porsche	13	
5. Nissan	8	
1984		
1. Lincoln Mercury	119	11
2. Chevrolet	66	3
3. Pontiac	55	1
4. Porsche AG	18	1
5. Nissan	8	
1985		
1. Lincoln Mercury	124	12
2. Buick	46	2
3. Pontiac	24	0
4. Porsche	16	1
5. Nissan	15	0
6. Chevrolet	8	0

YEAR-BY-YEAR TRANS-AM CHAMPIONS

YEAR	DRIVER	CAR	EARNINGS	POINTS	NUMBER OF WINS
1966	#Horst Kwech*	Alfa GTA	$ 1,675	68	0
	#Gaston Andrey*	Alfa GTA	$ 1,675	68	0
1967	#Jerry Titus	Mustang	$ 6,850	122	4
1968	#Mark Donohue	Camaro	$19,725	222	10
1969	#Mark Donohue	Camaro	$23,200	156	6
1970	#Parnelli Jones	Mustang	$26,600	142	5
1971	Mark Donohue	Javelin	$38,800	155	7
1972	George Follmer	Javelin	$26,800	95	4
1973	Peter Gregg	Porsche Carrera	$18,800	71	1
1974	Peter Gregg	Porsche Carrera	$ 8,750	60	2
1975	John Greenwood	Corvette	$ 7,725	116	3
1976 I	George Follmer	Porsche 934	$12,550	110	2
1976 II	Jocko Maggiacomo	Javelin	$12,050	90	2
1977 I	Bob Tullius	Jaguar XJS	$14,410	170	5
1977 II	Ludwig Heimrath, Sr.	Porsche 934	$15,985	173	3
1978 I	Bob Tullius	Jaguar XJS	$38,797	189	7
1978 II	Greg Pickett	Corvette	$36,597	132.5	4
1979 I	Gene Bothello	Corvette	$37,357	115	4
1979 II	John Paul, Sr.	Porsche 935	$60,700	169	6
1980	John Bauer	Porsche 911SC	$35,700	127	4
1981	Eppie Wietzes	Corvette	$38,300	179	2
1982	Elliott Forbes-Robinson	Trans-Am	$52,700	147	4
1983	David Hobbs	Camaro	$59,350	158	4
1984	Tom Gloy	Capri	$87,800	225	3

\# - A Driver's Championship was not officially instated until the 1971 season.
* - Co-drivers.

ALL-TIME TRANS-AM CHAMPIONSHIP STANDINGS

1966

	Driver	Car	Pts.	Sebring	Mid-America	Bryar	Virginia	Marlboro	Green Valley	Riverside
							Finishing Positions			
1.	Horst Kwech	Alfa GTA	68	5	2	3	3	—	2	6
2.	Gaston Andrey	Alfa GTA	68	5	2	3	3	—	2	6
3.	Bob Johnson	Barracuda	67	—	1	4	1	9	3	8
4.	Bob Tullius	Dart	60	2	15	7	33	1	6	2
5.	Tony Adamowicz	Dart	54	2	15	—	33	1	6	2
6.	Tom Yeager	Mustang	52	—	1	4	1	9	—	—
7.	Bruce Jennings	Barracuda	40	7	8	2	6	3	13	25
8.	Charlie Rainville	Barracuda	37	7	8	23	34	2	3	8
9.	John McComb	Mustang	32	—	7	—	—	1	1	4
9.	Brad Brooker	Mustang	32	—	—	—	—	—	1	4

1967

	Driver	Car	Pts.	Daytona	Sebring	Green Valley	Lime Rock	Mid-Ohio	Bryar	Marlboro	CDR	Crow's Landing	Riverside	Stardust	Seattle
									Finishing Positions						
1.	Jerry Titus	Mustang	122	4	1	5	3	1	28	3	1	1	32	3	21
2.	Mark Donohue	Camaro	115	31	2	4	2	—	24	1	8	3	—	1	1
3.	Peter Revson	Cougar	55	—	—	—	1	—	1	11	18	2	—	19	—
4.	Ed Leslie	Cougar	52	—	5	—	5	—	—	11	2	6	2	—	—
5.	Dick Thompson	Mustang	44	25	3	3	—	—	3	13	4	—	—	—	—
6.	Craig Fisher	Camaro	41	2	34	—	20	6	16	1	—	—	—	—	4
7.	Parnelli Jones	Cougar	37	3	42	2	—	—	—	—	—	—	—	4	22
8.	Horst Kwech	Alfa GTA	37	34	31	—	4	4	18	—	5	16	15	5	16
9.	David Pearson	Cougar	35	—	—	—	—	2	—	—	—	1	—	—	—
10.	Bob Tullius	Dart	30	1	8	25	21	27	—	5	19	—	23	—	—

1968

Driver	Car	Pts.	Daytona	Sebring	War Bonnet	Lime Rock	Mid-Ohio	Bridgehampton	Meadowdale	Mt. Tremblant	Bryar	Watkins Glen	Castle Rock	Riverside	Kent
1. Mark Donohue	Camaro	222	4	1	1	1	1	1	1	1	1	3	1	24	1
2. George Follmer	Javelin	97	17	—	2	—	—	2	—	2	2	8	10	29	7
3. Jerry Titus	Firebird/Mustang	83	1	3	16	2	2	18	11	14	10	1	12	31	18
4. Craig Fisher	Firebire/Camaro	82	—	2	—	18	—	—	4	4	16	21	2	3	2
5. Peter Revson	Mustang/Javelin	82	—	5	4	3	3	15	2	18	20	4	DSQ	2	19
6. Tony Adamowicz	Porsche 911	60	20	—	—	6	4	7	5	5	5	3	13	23	—
7. Sam Posey	Camaro/Mustang	53	11	21	9	—	—	—	3	3	3	6	2	—	—
8. Ronnie Bucknum	Mustang	47	1	3	—	—	—	—	—	—	—	—	—	8	3
9. Bob Johnson	Camaro	35	4	2	—	—	—	4	—	—	—	—	—	—	—
10. Horst Kwech	Mustang/Alfa GTA	30	17	15	—	5	12	19	—	8	16	18	—	1	22

1969

Driver	Car	Pts.	Michigan	Lime Rock	Mid-Ohio	Bridgehampton	Donnybrooke	Bryar	Mt. Tremblant	Watkins Glen	Laguna Seca	Kent	Sears Point	Riverside
1. Mark Donohue	Camaro	156	2	—	7	2	9	1	1	1	1	—	1	1
2. Parnelli Jones	Mustang	130	1	—	2	18	1	17	34	2	27	2	2	26
3. Jerry Titus	Firebird	91	3	25	19	3	4	5	2	31	24	3	4	3
4. Peter Revson	Mustang	72	29	—	4	5	3	3	28	19	4	4	34	4
5. Rusty Jowett	Camaro	68	7	6	6	4	—	21	5	3	25	6	6	5
6. Ronnie Bucknum	Camaro	63	40	—	1	—	—	—	—	—	—	1	5	2
7. George Follmer	Mustang	57	34	—	3	1	16	4	27	26	23	20	3	24
8. Ed Leslie	Camaro	54	—	27	—	—	2	2	3	18	2	—	—	—
9. Ron Grable	Javelin	25	35	20	5	26	14	—	30	5	13	—	8	6
10. Milt Minter	Firebird	24	30	5	15	16	—	—	—	29	5	7	7	—

1970

Driver	Car	Pts.	Laguna Seca	Lime Rock	Bryar	Mid-Ohio	Bridgehampton	Donnybrooke	Road America	Mt. Tremblant	Watkins Glen	Kent	Riverside
1. Parnelli Jones	Mustang	142	1	1	13	1	3	13	5	3	4	1	1
2. Mark Donohue	Javelin	141	2	13	3	3	1	19	1	1	2	2	3
3. George Follmer	Mustang	129	3	—	1	2	2	2	35	2	3	4	2
4. Sam Posey	Challenger	60	6	3	23	5	20	20	3	4	29	3	31
5. Swede Savage	Barracuda	49	4	19	18	21	22	5	2	29	6	18	4
6. Jim Hall	Camaro	44	21	4	5	18	4	—	4	—	—	—	—
7. Milt Minter	Camaro	41	5	—	—	—	—	1	6	35	10	9	7
8. Peter Revson	Javelin	35	18	18	2	*	—	—	33	5	5	7	28
9. Mo Carter	Camaro	30	—	—	19	4	5	6	13	6	8	8	—
10. Vic Elford	Camaro	28	—	—	—	—	—	—	—	26	1	5	22

1971

Driver	Car	Pts.	Awards	Lime Rock	Bryar	Mid-Ohio	Edmonton	Donnybrooke	Road America	St. Jovite	Watkins Glen	Michigan	Riverside
1. Mark Donohue	Javelin	155	$38,800	1	*	2	1	1	1	1	1	1	—
2. George Follmer	Mustang/Javelin	136	31,350	—	1	1	2	—	2	2	2	2	1
3. Peter Gregg	Mustang	71	16,350	4	2	3	*	—	4	3	3	*	—
4. Peter Revson	Javelin	51	11,400	*	3	*	—	2	—	4	9	3	*
5. Tony DeLorenzo	Mustang	45	10,500	2	*	4	—	3	5	—	*	—	*
6. Jerry Thompson	Mustang	44	11,400	18	*	*	—	4	3	6	6	13	4
7. J. Marshall Robbins	Camaro	41	12,200	5	6	7	—	8	—	7	7	7	5
8. Warren Agor	Camaro	36	10,700	3	5	9	—	5	9	10	*	8	—
9. Bob Tullius	Tempest	26	6,550	*	4	5	—	*	—	—	15	5	—
10. Vic Elford	Javelin	25	5,300	—	—	—	—	—	25	—	4	—	2

1972

Driver	Car	Pts.	Awards	Lime Rock	Bryar	Mid-Ohio	Watkins Glen	Donnybrooke	Road America	Sanair
							Finishing Positions			
1. George Follmer	Javelin	95	$26,800	1	1	2	1	1	•	—
2. Milt Minter	Firebird	60	16,150	—	2	1	•	4	2	•
3. Warren Tope	Mustang	56	16,900	5	7	7	•	•	1	1
4. Warren Agor	Camaro	51	14,100	2	3	3	•	6	•	6
5. Bill Collins	Javelin	45	12,000	7	—	4	•	7	3	2
6. Paul Nichter	Camaro	44	10,500	6	4	—	4	20	6	3
7. Roy Woods	Javelin	42	10,500	4	—	5	3	3	11	—
8. Jerry Thompson	Mustang	30	7,350	—	—	—	2	2	•	•
9. Carl Shafer	Camaro	17	5,500	—	—	11	—	8	7	4
10. Dick Brown	Camaro	14	3,800	—	—	—	6	—	5	•

1973

Driver	Car	Pts.	Awards	Rd. Atlanta, April 15	Lime Rock, May 5	Watkins Glen, June 16	Sanair Int'l, July 15	Rd. America, July 28	Edmonton, Aug. 19
						Finishing Positions			
1. Peter Gregg	Porsche Carrera	71	$18,800	1	2	2	6	•	2
2. Al Holbert	Porsche Carrera	59	15,150	2	3	8	4	3	4
3. J. Marshall Robbins	Corvette	54	8,975	3	5	4	3	•	3
4. John Greenwood	Corvette	52	13,425	—	•	3	—	1	1
5. Jerry Thompson	Corvette	46	7,325	7	5	4	3	•	3+
6. Warren Agor	Camaro	39	13,650	•	7	•	1	2	•
7. Milt Minter	Porsche RS	38	10,700	13	1	•	•	5	4•
8. Maurice Carter	Camaro	26	7,500	•	6	1	17	•	•
9. Paul Nichter	Camaro	21	7,900	—	•	6	2	•	•
10. John Buffum	Ford Escort	18	4,150	5	—	•	7	6	—

1974

Driver	Car	Pts.	Awards	Lime Rock	Watkins Glen	Road America
					Finishes	
1. Peter Gregg	Porsche Carrera	60	$8,750	•	1	1
2. Ludwig Heimrath	Porsche Carrera	53	7,650	2	2	5
3. Hurley Haywood	Porsche Carrera	50	4,700	0	1	4
4. Al Holbert	Porsche Carrera	32	8,600	1	—	3
5. Jim Cook	Porsche Carrera	30	1,700	—	2	—
6. Tony DeLorenzo	Camaro	27	2,350	—	3	8
7. Maurice Carter	Camaro	24	1,200	—	3	•
8. Jacques Bienvenue	Porsche Carrera	22	1,850	—	4	9
9. Marc Dancose	Porsche Carrera	20	850	—	4	—
10. Sam Posey	Porsche Carrera	20	2,333	5	6	—

1975

Driver	Car	Pts.	Awards	Pocono	Seattle	Portland	Nelson Ledges	Watkins Glen	Rd. America	Brainerd
							Finishing Positions			
1. John Greenwood	Corvette	116	$7,725	1	—	1	1	7•	—	—
2. Babe Headley	Corvette	88	2,500	3	—	—	16	1	•	—
3. Jerry Hansen	Corvette	72	5,000	—	—	—	—	—	1	1
4. Paul Misuriello	Corvette	72	1,300	—	—	—	—	1	—	—
5. Bob Sharp	Datsun 280Z	72	3,125	—	—	—	2	3•	3	—
6. Walt Maas	Datsun 280Z	64	4,400	—	1	•	3	—	4	—
7. Bill Jobe	Corvette	56	1,150	•	—	—	5	2	—	—
8. Rick Stark	Corvette	53	3,600	—	3	2	—	—	6	5
9. John Orr	Corvette	52	1,250	7	—	—	—	2	—	—
10. John Bauer	Porsche Carrera	39	2,650	—	4	8	—	—	—	2

1976

Ps. I	Ps. II	Driver	Car	Pts.	Awards	Pocono	Nelson	Portland	Glen	Rd. America	Brainerd	Mosport	Trois-Rivieres
						Finish +							
1.	1	George Follmer	Porsche 934	110	$12,550	3	1	6	6	2	2	3	1
2.	2	Hurley Haywood	Porsche/BMW	101	9,400	1	2	6	1	—	4	—	10
3.	1	Jocko Maggiacomo	Javelin	90	12,050	1	1	—	—	2	4	2	4
4.	2	John Bauer	Porsche 911SC	89	9,150	10	5	*	1	*	3	5	1
5.	3	Babe Headley	Corvette	84	7,650	2	2	—	2	16	*	3	3
6.	4	Joe Chamberlain	Camaro	76	9,650	6	3	2	3	6	2	6	8
7.	3	John Graves	Porsche Carrera	64	5,234	*	5	—	2	6	2	6	*
8.	4	Ludwig Heimrath	Porsche Carrera	60	5,900	5	—	—	3	5	—	1	*
9.	5	Al Holbert	Porsche 934	59	6,550	2	9	—	10	4	—	2	2
10.	6	Carl Shafer	Camaro	52	6,600	—	—	—	7	1	1	4	9

1977 CATEGORY I

Driver	Car	Pts.	Awards	Seattle	Westwood	Portland	Nelson Ledges	Watkins Glen	Hallett	Brainerd	Mosport Park	Road America	Road America	St. Jovite
				Finishing Positions										
1. Bob Tullius	Jaguar XJS	170	$14,410	1	1	*	8	4	1	2	1	31	1	3
2. John Bauer	Porsche 911SC	162	12,110	4	2	1	1	2	2	11	2	3	18	4
3. Tom Spalding	Porsche 911SC	125	7,600	18	3	6	2	2	9	4	1	4	4	—
4. John Wood	Porsche 911SC	80	4,000	—	5	*	5	1	—	—	5	*	*	5
5. Brian Fuerstenau	Jaguar XJS	60	1,800	—	—	—	—	4	—	—	1	—	—	—
6. Michael Oleyar	Corvette	60	2,660	23	*	16	4	5	4	*	3	—	—	—
7. Bob Lazier	Porsche 911	55	3,350	10	4	7	*	1	—	—	—	—	—	—
8. John Brandt Jr.	Corvette	53	3,010	7	11	*	—	5	7	*	3	9	*	8
9. Nick Engels	Corvette	45	4,050	—	—	—	*	8	3	—	6	*	27	2
10. John Huber	Corvette	34	2,300	—	—	—	*	9*	—	—	—	2	2	—

1977 CATEGORY II

Driver	Car	Pts.	Awards	Seattle	Westwood	Portland	Nelson Ledges	Watkins Glen	Hallett	Brainerd	Mosport Park	Road America	Road America	St. Jovite
				Finishing Positions										
1. Ludwig Heimrath	Porsche 934	173	$15,985	1	6	4	2	6	2	2	1	1	7	2
2. Peter Gregg	Porsche 934	145	10,085	—	1	—	4	4	1	1	#	2	1	1
3. Monte Shelton	Porsche 934	101	8,060	3	3	2	—	5	3	3	7	4	—	—
4. Hal Shaw, Jr.	Porsche Carrera	71	4,810	6	7*	7	3	—	—	5	4	8	6	7
5. Greg Pickett	Monza	65	5,960	—	2	*	9*	*	5	4	—	5	4	3
6. Bob Hagestad	Porsche 934	60	5,125	—	—	—	1	1	—	—	—	—	—	—
7. Paul Miller	Porsche 934	52	2,475	—	—	—	—	1	—	—	2	—	—	—
8. Hurley Haywood	Porsche 934	40	2,625	—	—	—	—	1	—	—	—	—	—	—
Peter Overing	Porsche Carrera	40	2,517	—	—	—	7	—	6	—	5	—	—	6
Klaus Bytzek	Porsche Carrera	40	2,384	—	—	—	—	—	—	—	3	—	—	4

1978 CATEGORY I

Driver	Car	Pts.	Awards	Sears Point	Westwood	Portland	St. Jovite	Watkins Glen	Brainerd	Mosport	Road America	Laguna Seca	Mexico City
				Finishing Positions									
1. Bob Tullius	Jaguar XJS	189	$38,797	9	2	3	1	1	1	1	1	1	1
2. Babe Headley	Corvette	98½	16,532	3	3	5	14	3	4	6	2	9	5
3. Frank Joyce	Corvette	72	15,052	11	13	6	3	4	3	3	8	14	3
4. Brain Fuerstenau	Jaguar XJS	45	8,472	—	—	—	—	1	—	—	—	3	8
5. John Huber	Corvette	44½	7,767	—	—	—	4	3	6	5	—	—	10
6. Nick Engels	Corvette	43½	11,137	—	1	14	6	13	20	4	17	25	12
7. Gene Bothello	Corvette	43	8,470	1	12	—	—	4	5	—	2	21	—
8. Bill Adam	Corvette	30	5,220	—	—	—	2	—	—	2	—	23	—
9. John J. Brandt, Jr.	Corvette	28	4,782	—	—	16	—	8	16	—	6	7	4
10. Rick Stark	Corvette	26	3,980	—	4	2	—	—	—	—	—	10	—
11. Gary Carlen	Corvette	26	3,270	2	15	17	—	—	—	—	—	5	—

1978 CATEGORY II

Driver	Car	Pts.	Awards	Sears Point	Westwood	Portland	St. Jovite	Watkins Glen	Brainerd	Mosport	Road America	Laguna Seca	Mexico City
								Finishing Positions					
1. Greg Pickett	Corvette	132½	$36,597	1	3	9	9	12	4	1	1	1	2
2. Tuck Thomas	Monza	114½	26,597	4	8	1	3	20	2	3	2	5	3
3. Ludwig Heimrath	Porsche 935	102	23,547	10	1	2	2	9	14	2	16	3	1
4. Hal Shaw, Jr.	Porsche 935	73	14,657	3	2	—	—	1	16	6	4	13	11
5. Monte Shelton	Porsche 935	71	17,120	—	—	7	1	1	3	4	15	12	—
6. Bruce Leven	Porsche 934	49	8,152	—	4	4	—	14	6	10	7	6	7
7. Tom Frank	Monza	47	8,350	2	7	5	4	14	12	5	11	—	—
8. Rich Sloma	Corvette	42	7,297	9	—	8	—	—	5	—	5	4	5
9. Janet Guthrie	Porsche 935	30	3,832	—	—	—	—	4	—	—	—	—	4
10. Roger Schramm	Porsche Carrera	25	3,850	—	—	—	—	5	7	9	6	—	—

1979 CATEGORY I

Driver	Car	Pts.	Awards	Mexico City	Westwood	Portland	Watkins Glen	Road America	Watkins Glen	Mosport	Trois-Rivieres	Laguna Seca
							Finishing Positions					
1. Gene Bothello	Corvette	115	$37,357	6	2	1	—	1	—	1	1#	3
2. Bob Tullius	Triumph TR-8	76	20,550	—	—	—	1#	—	1#	—	—	1#
3. Frank Joyce	Corvette	60	13,550	—	10#	4#	3	9	20	4#	*	2
4. Gary Carlen	Corvette	57	12,850	—	1	2	—	3	13	*	13	4
5. Miguel Muniz	Camaro	47½	12,750	1#	4	*	5	22	17	14	—	—
6. Paul Canary	Corvette	46	8,350	—	—	—	2	4	12	2		6
7. Michael Oleyar	Corvette	40	7,000	—	5	8	2	20	19	11	5	14
8. Brian Fuersteneau	TR-8	30	4,650	—	—	—	1	—	—	—	—	—
9. Jim Sanborn	Corvette	27	4,100	—	—	—	—	17	3	2	16	—
10. Doug Rippie	Corvette	23	5,807	2	14	5	—	—	—	—	—	—

1979 CATEGORY II

Driver	Car	Pts.	Awards	Mexico City	Westwood	Portland	Watkins Glen	Road America	Watkins Glen	Mosport	Trois-Rivieres	Laguna Seca
							Finishing Positions					
1. John Paul	Porsche 935	169	$60,700	1#	1#	1#	2	4#	1#	1#	1#	14
2. Tuck Thomas	Monza/Porsche	71	21,007	2	3	7	8	7	5	6	2	9
3. Ludwig Heimrath	Porsche 935	57	17,207	6	2	9	10	2	4	8	—	—
4. Bruce Leven	Porsche 935	46	11,607	3	4	4	14	5	—	—	—	6
5. Peter Gregg	Porsche 935	44	17,000	—	—	—	14	1	—	—	—	1#
6. Mo Carter	Camaro	43	11,650	—	—	—	11	10	2	2	3	—
7. Rich Sloma	Corvette	33	8,907	4	5	2	—	12	—	—	—	11
8. Roy Woods	Porsche 935	29	5,950	—	—	—	1	—	—	—	—	8
9. Bob Akin	Porsche 935	26	5,950	—	—	—	1	—	—	—	—	—
10. Al Holbert	Porsche 935	25	3,600	—	—	—	2	—	—	—	—	—

1980

Driver	Car	Pts.	Awards	Hallett	Portland	Watkins Glen	Road America	Brainerd	Trois-Rivieres	Westwood	Laguna Seca	Riverside
							Finishing Positions					
1. John Bauer	Porsche 911SC	127	$35,700	1	2	1	4	1	*	1	21	5
2. Greg Pickett	Corvette	76	24,100	—	—	—	36	2	2	—	1	1
3. Monte Shelton	Porsche 911SC	72½	18,225	—	3	3	1	15	—	2	*	6
4. Roy Woods	Camaro	71	18,666	32	7	5	3	14	1	18	26	2
5. Mark Pielsticker	Monza	62	16,150	6	1	16	2	25	—	17	3	3
6. John Brandt	Corvette	42	9,441	3	24	16	—	4	3	—	5	27
7. Bob Raub	Camaro	31	8,225	2	18	5	27	—	20	—	—	—
8. Larry Green	Porsche 911SC	30	5,950	—	—	1	—	—	—	—	—	—
9. Andy Porterfield	Corvette	24	6,775	25	29	—	15	3	—	3	—	—
10. Herb Forest	Corvette	21½	5,006	6	—	6	7	23	—	9	9	28

1981

Driver	Car	Pts.	Awards	Charlotte	Portland	Lime Rock	Road America	Brainerd	Trois-Rivieres	Mosport	Laguna	Sears Point
							Finishing Positions					
1. Eppie Wietzes	Corvette	179	$38,300	1	2	7	2	2	1	34	3	3
2. Bob Tullius	Jaguar XJS	126	29,450	2	1	18	21	1	21	1	5	28
3. Phil Currin	Corvette	91	14,600	10	31	4	5	6	6	4	8	4
4. John Bauer	Porsche 911SC	79	14,200	—	3	5	3	4	26#	5	40	—
5. Roy Woods	Camaro/Corvette	78	13,975	34	17	11	6	3	2	11	4	25
6. George Follmer	Camaro	66	13,750	4	9	—	—	—	—	—	1#	5
7. Doc Bundy	Porsche 924 Carrera Turbo	62	12,850	3	22	3	39	—	27	2	—	—
8. Greg Pickett	Corvette	61	14,800	15#	40#	1	44	17#	—	—	—	2
9. Tom Gloy	Mustang	57	12,050	—	—	—	46	12	3	27#	25	1#
10. Monte Shelton	Porsche 911SC/930	49	9,900	6	47	9	1#	27	—	—	43	—

1982

Driver	Car	Pts.	Awards	Road Atlanta	Sears Point	Portland	Laguna Seca	Seattle	Mid-Ohio	Road America	Brainerd	3-Rivieres	Sears Point
								Finishing Positions					
1. Elliott Forbes-Robinson	Trans-Am	147	$52,700	—	2	2	1#	1#	1	42	5#	1#	3#
2. Doc Bundy	Porsche Carrera Turbo	92	31,250	32	1	1	16	3	5	5	28	18	2
3. Phil Currin	Corvette	92	26,100	3#	—	—	2	6	3	3	4	6	—
4. Tom Gloy	Mustang	72	24,650	11	13	4	3	20	*#	35#	2#	—	1
5. Darin Brassfield	Trans-Am	49	13,825	4	5#	10	29	23	*	39	17	4	11
6. Rob McFarlin	Mustang	44	11,025	9	9	17	8	—	—	41	6	12	8
7. Tony Brassfield	Trans-Am/Corvette	43	12,200	—	29	7	9	3	—	14	40	7	27
8. Jerry Hansen	Corvette	42	17,100	1	—	—	—	—	—	1#	36	—	—
9. Paul Miller	Porsche Carrera Turbo	41	9,800	—	—	—	—	—	—	7	8	3	6
10. Tim Evans	Trans-Am	34	9,300	10	—	—	—	—	—	4	—	3	14
11. Rick Stark	Corvette	34	8,025	—	—	12	20	4	14	4	12	—	19
12. Frank Leary	Datsun 280ZX Turbo	34	6,900	—	23	5	5	—	—	—	—	—	4

1983

Driver	Car	Pts.	$ Prize	Moroso May 1	Summit Point May 15	Sears Point June 5	Portland June 12	Seattle June 26	Mid-Ohio July 17	Road America July 31	Brainerd August 7	Trois-Rivieres Sept. 4	Sears Point Sept. 18	Riverside Sept. 25	Caesars Palace October 8
									Finishing Positions						
1. David Hobbs	Camaro	158	$59,350	2	1	1	4	25	2	1	2	—	26	1	4
2. Willy T. Ribbs	Camaro	148	56,550	5	21	7	1	23	1	52	1	12	1	2	1
3. Tom Gloy	Mercury Capri	143	44,900	26	2	3	3	3	3	3	5	5	2	26	3
4. Elliott Forbes-Robinson	Trans-Am	102	32,250	—	—	4	1	5	2	4	3	5	30	12	
5. Frank Leary	Trans-Am	79	20,150	4	#	25	6	5	22	11	7	—	3	4	10
6. Jim Derhaag	Firebird	76	17,850	13	12	11	10	9	9	16	8	8	7	6	7
7. Gene Felton	Trans-Am	59	19,500	1	27	2	5	26	23	38	6	—			
8. Dave Watson	Firebird	59	15,600	—	6	#	—	—	7	25	4	4	35	2	
9. Paul Newman	Datsun 280ZX Turbo	51	13,975	10	3	—	21	30	7	33	24	—	8	3	18
10. Lyn St. James	Mercury Capri	45	11,950	19	8	19	11	4	29	9	30	28	13	11	11

1984

DRIVER	CAR	PTS	$PRIZE	Road Atlanta May 2	Summit Point May 20	Sears Point June 3	Portland June 17	Detroit June 23	Daytona July 3	Brainerd July 8	Road America August 5	Watkins Glen August 19	Trois-Rivieres September 2	Mosport Park September 9	Seattle September 23	Sears Point September 30	Riverside October 7	Texas Challenge October 28	Caesars Palace November 11
										FINISHING POSITIONS										
1. Tom Gloy	7-Eleven Mercury Capri	225	87,800	25	3	2	2	1	2	3	2	1	4	2	5	4	12	1	
2. Greg Pickett	Roush Protofab Motorcraft Capri	189	74,050	19	5	1	1	3	11	4	7	24	2	2	1	1	6	19	4
3. Willy T. Ribbs	Roush Protofab Motorcraft Capri	155	62,750	#	-	-	-	2	1	1	36	1	8	3	17	2	3	1	21
4. Wally Dallenbach, Jr.	Colorado Connection Camaro	142	40,440	4	22	4	6	4	13	6	5	4	9	6	5	30	2	18	2
5. Bob Lobenberg	STP Son of a Gun! Huffaker Trans-Am	138	45,350	2	1	7	14	25	3	2	8	21	24	5	20	3	7	#	6
6. Darin Brassfield	DeAtley Budweiser Corvette	120	46,400	1	13	3	3	28	6	7	6	22	18	7	25	7	1	20	20
7. Jim Miller	MTI Vacations/Huffaker Trans-Am	110	30,020	17	23	8	5	17	4	5	3	6	10	3	32	30	3	26	
8. David Hobbs	DeAtley Budweiser Corvette	106	32,550	3	2	10	-	7	21	8	-	3	-	9	4	29	12	21	3
9. Paul Miller	Herman & Miller Porsche Carrera Turbo	76	26,950	6	6	21	26	16	-	-	-	26	5	1	16	4	5	15	32
10. Jim Derhaag	Derhaag Racing Trans-Am	59	14,610	18	8	6	9	26	9	19	11	25	23	11	7	8	29	23	30

Index